THE
CHRISTIAN
BURIAL CASE

THE
CHRISTIAN
BURIAL CASE

An Introduction to
Criminal and Judicial Procedure

Thomas N. McInnis

PRAEGER

Westport, Connecticut
London

Library of Congress Cataloging-in-Publication Data

McInnis, Thomas N., 1958–
  The Christian burial case : an introduction to criminal and judicial procedure /
Thomas N. McInnis.
    p.   cm.
  Includes bibliographical references and index.
    ISBN 0–275–97027–2 (alk. paper)—ISBN 0–275–97028–0 (pbk. : alk. paper)
    1. Williams, Robert Anthony—Trials, litigation, etc.   2. Trials (Murder)—United
States.   3. Criminal procedure—United States.   4. Criminal justice, Administration of—
United States.   I. Title.
KF224.W553 M38   2001
345.73'02523—dc21   00–032619

British Library Cataloguing in Publication Data is available.

Library of Congress Catalog Card Number: 00–032619
ISBN: 0–275–97027–2
      0–275–97028–0 (pbk.)

First published in 2001

Praeger Publishers, 88 Post Road West, Westport, CT 06881
An imprint of Greenwood Publishing Group, Inc.
www.praeger.com

Printed in the United States of America

The paper used in this book complies with the
Permanent Paper Standard issued by the National
Information Standards Organization (Z39.48–1984).

10 9 8 7 6 5 4

To my family, friends, and Jan—the best of both.

Contents

Preface

This book is intended to be a supplemental text, which will introduce students to the American criminal justice process and legal system. The vehicle by which this is accomplished is a case study involving the *Williams* case, that was twice appealed to the U.S. Supreme Court. The *Williams* case was selected due to its interesting factual and legal issues, which quickly capture the students' attention, making them want to read more. While the facts of the case at first seem simple, leading to what one would expect to be a quick resolution of the case, the story goes on to reveal the complexity of the law and the judicial process. The *Williams* case also nicely illustrates the weakness of some of the myths that the public has come to believe about the legal system.

The central pedagogical feature of the text is its ability to unite a discussion of the criminal justice process and the legal system with a concrete case through a narrative-based text. This enables the reader to learn about the process by which a case moves through the legal system while at the same time having a consistent storyline to follow throughout the book. For most students this will allow the information to be more accessible, and should lead to better retention. While the book is not intended to be an all-inclusive text, it should provide students with a basic understanding of the inner workings of criminal trials and the appellate process. It emphasizes the role that discretionary choices make in the judicial process. The book will also leave the student with substantial knowledge of the rights against self-incrimination, the right to counsel, and the role of the exclusionary rule in the judicial process.

The book does not assume the need for any prerequisites on the part of the student and could be assigned to any level of student. Ideally, it will be assigned to students as they are first introduced to the criminal justice process and the legal system. The book is designed to be used in courses covering a range of topics, including the judicial process, criminal justice, American courts, and civil liberties.

Acknowledgments

I am indebted to a number of people for help in completing this project. First, I would like to thank those people at the University of Central Arkansas who have made the project possible. This includes my fellow political scientists, past and present, for working my schedule so that it allows me the time necessary to undertake projects such as this. Chris Perkins and Lisa Murphy spent a great deal of time arranging for loans in the library. The University Research Council of the University of Central Arkansas aided with financial support in the development of the manuscript. Finally, thank you to the University of Central Arkansas for granting me a sabbatical leave to allow me to finish this project. Next, I would like to thank the people at Greenwood Press for taking an interest in the project and making the process pleasurable. Thank you to the anonymous reviewers for reminding me that less can be more. Thank you to all of my teachers and students. Finally, thanks to my friends for allowing me to get away from my working world with no questions asked.

Chapter 1

The Crime and the Problem

A novelist could hardly have come up with a more wrenching scenario [than the Williams case] for a dispute over fundamental legal issues and basic social values.
                                              —Silas Wasserstrom and Williams J. Mertens[1]

Judicial decisions have been rendered more acceptable because of the belief that the Justices merely pronounce the law, deciding nothing.
                                              —Alpheus Thomas Mason[2]

THE CRIME

December 24, 1968, was not unlike many previous Christmas Eves. Throughout the country people were involved in last-minute shopping, visiting relatives, going to church services, and waiting to open presents. In the theaters, moviegoers could see the Beatles's *Yellow Submarine*, Barbra Streisand in *Funny Girl*, Rock Hudson in *Ice Station Zebra*, and Walt Disney's *The Horse in the Gray Flannel Suit*. What made it distinguishable from other Christmas Eves was the "Merry Christmas" from the Apollo 8 astronauts on a lunar trip in space. However, this message of happiness and the spirit of the season were lost on the Merlin Powers family of Urbandale, Iowa, due to the events that had taken place that day.

On December 24, 1968, the Powers family—consisting of Mr. and Mrs. Merlin Powers, their fifteen-year-old daughter Vickie, their fourteen-year-old son Mark and their ten-year-old daughter Pamela—went to a wrestling tournament on the second floor of the Y.M.C.A. building at 101 Locust Street in Des Moines, Iowa. The family was there to cheer on Mark, who was participating in the tournament in the 103-pound division. In one of the few happy moments for the Powers family on that day, Mark ended up winning the tournament in his weight class.

Before noon, Mr. Powers and Vickie left the Y.M.C.A. to exchange a Christmas gift at a local shopping center. When they returned, Pamela, who was in the fourth grade, was not sitting with the rest of the family. When Mr. Powers asked his wife where Pamela was, she told him that Pamela had gone downstairs to wash her hands. Pamela had gotten a candy bar and remembered that she had been playing with some puppies, so she asked her mom if she could go wash her hands before eating. Her mom then gave her permission to wash her hands. Although she had only been gone five minutes, Mr. and Mrs. Powers decided to find Pamela and make sure that she was okay. When Pamela could not be found in the washroom, the search was continued. According to Mr. Powers they "started looking everywhere, knocking on doors, yelling her name."[3] The family continued its search for about twenty minutes, looking in the basement of the Y.M.C.A., various rooms, and in storage places. Failing to find Pamela, Mr. Powers instructed his wife to go to the front desk and have someone phone the police.

Shortly before 1:30 P.M., as Mr. and Mrs. Powers intensified their search for Pamela, John Knapp, a security officer who worked for the Y.M.C.A., saw a man who lived in the building walk into the lobby carrying a bundle in his arms. The bundle appeared to be something wrapped in a blanket. Knapp didn't know that Pamela Powers was missing and thought that the man was trying to leave the Y.M.C.A. without paying rent that might be due. Knapp yelled at the man as he headed out the front door and asked him what he was carrying. The man answered that he was carrying a mannequin. By that time Knapp had gotten the attention of Don Hanna, the physical education director at the Y.M.C.A. The two men then ran out after the man with the bundle. Knapp and Hanna failed to catch up with the man because Kevin Sanders, a 14-year-old boy, opened the door to let the man leave the Y.M.C.A. Sanders then helped the man by also opening the door to a car that was waiting at the curb. Sanders later told police that when the man set the bundle in the car the blanket was pulled back and it exposed "skinny white legs."[4]

By the time that Knapp and Hanna got outside, the man was sitting in his parked car at the front curb on Locust Street. The car, a green 1959 Buick, had the doors locked. Knapp kept asking the man what he had in the bundle. The man answered "I've got to go away for a minute—I'll be back and show it to you."[5] Hanna told the driver of the car that he was going to break the car windows if the man didn't open the car door. As the car took off, traveling east on Locust, Hanna ran alongside it, holding onto the door handle for a short distance. In the meantime, Knapp went inside to call the police.

Shortly after the two calls were placed to the Des Moines Police Department from the Y.M.C.A., the police realized that they might be related. When police learned of the disappearance of Pamela Powers, she was described as being 4-feet-9 inches tall, weighing 63 pounds, with blonde hair, and blue eyes. She had been wearing an orange, striped blouse and orange slacks. Her coat and hat were left where she had been sitting with her mother. The police department sent Detective Forrest Speck to investigate. Under his direction, another search for Pamela was conducted inside the Y.M.C.A.

Due to John Knapp's information, suspicion soon focused on Robert Anthony, who was identified to police by Knapp as the man who had carried the bundle out of the building and had driven off. Police later learned that Robert Anthony was one of many aliases that was used by Robert Anthony Williams. Knapp informed the police that Williams had driven off in a 1959 light green Buick with a 1968 Iowa license plate, number 63–2904. According to state records, the car was registered to Robert Anthony Williams. Knapp said Williams had been living at the Y.M.C.A. since October 26, 1968, renting a single room for $16.83 a week. Knapp informed the police that he had known Williams for a month and a half and had talked to him on occasion. Williams was described by Knapp as a light-skinned Negro with short hair, about 5-feet-7 or -8 inches tall, and 175 pounds.

The case was assigned to Captain Cleatus Leaming. Leaming was a 19-year veteran of the Des Moines Police Department and was the chief of detectives. Leaming instructed the police to search the entire Y.M.C.A. for Pamela and to give special attention to the room of Robert Williams, the primary suspect. The police were unsuccessful in their attempt to locate Pamela Powers in the Y.M.C.A. Although the police declined to reveal what types of evidence were found in Williams's room, room 724, one of the detectives involved in the search said that there was no indication that a struggle had taken place. Officials at the Y.M.C.A. reported that police had removed Williams's clothes and personal property. A spokesperson for the Y.M.C.A. also stated that there was no blood in the room. Detective Leaming reported that it could not be determined whether Pamela Powers had been taken to Williams's room.

Based on the accounts given by witnesses, the police issued an arrest warrant for Robert Williams on December 24, 1968, on the charge of child stealing. Detective Leaming told reporters that the charge of child stealing was selected for two reasons. First, it carried a stiffer possible sentence (up to ten years) than kidnaping, which only carried a possible sentence of five years. A second reason for the child stealing charge was that there had been no ransom note to indicate that financial gain was the motive behind the crime.

After the search of the Y.M.C.A. for Pamela proved unsuccessful, the police enlarged the area of the search to the entire city of Des Moines. Overnight and into Christmas morning, 20 patrolmen from the Des Moines Police Department drove down every street in the city looking for Robert Williams's 1959 Buick. The Federal Bureau of Investigation also entered the investigation on Christmas Day. Meanwhile, Pamela's family had not opened their Christmas presents. As they silently waited for news at home they began to expect the worst. Mr. Powers told reporters, "I'm sure if Pam had been conscious, she would have struggled or yelled or screamed. She would never even talk to strangers. I don't think there's much hope. . . . I'm afraid it may be too late now. All we can do is wait and pray."[6]

On Christmas Day the investigation began to bear some fruit. Williams's car was found in Davenport, Iowa, parked at Ninth and Ripley streets. Davenport is 160 miles east of Des Moines on Interstate 80. The car was found by Patrolman Charles Rubley at 10:42 A.M. Due to this discovery, Detective Leaming traveled to Davenport to help coordinate the investigation between the two police departments. A search warrant was obtained to enter the car and its trunk. Several things were confiscated, including two brooms, a block of wood, some clothes, floor mats, and tire irons. That night, at around 7:00 P.M., a nearby apartment building on Gaines Street was entered by officers under a search warrant. Although the apartments were searched, neither Williams nor Pamela Powers was found. It was later learned that Williams had spent Christmas in Davenport two blocks from the apartments that the police searched.

On Christmas Day a maintenance man found a pair of orange stretch slacks, a white bobby sock, a man's shirt, a pair of men's trousers with the name "Anthony" sewed on the inside, a handkerchief, and a Y.M.C.A. blanket in a garbage can at a rest stop on Interstate 80 near Grinnell, about 40 miles east of Des Moines. Late Christmas Day the stretch pants and sock were identified by Pamela's father as the ones she was wearing when she was abducted. The Iowa Highway Patrol then intensified its search efforts along Interstate 80. Its search along the interstate included all the rest stops, culverts, overpasses, bridges, and ditches. The search of the interstate was hindered by adverse weather conditions, which included falling snow, blowing snow, and near-zero temperatures. One highway patrol sergeant confirmed, "We're looking for the girl's body."[7]

As the police continued their search for Pamela Powers and Robert Williams, they started to receive disturbing information regarding Williams's background. Police learned that Williams was from Kansas City, Missouri, and had at least 14 different arrests under a half-dozen aliases. Williams, who was 24 years old, had a police record going back six years. That record included auto theft, writing bogus checks, molestation, attempted rape, and statutory rape involving several underage girls.

Police further discovered that Williams was an escapee from the Fulton

State Hospital in Fulton, Missouri. Williams had been committed to that facility as a result of being found guilty by reason of insanity in the rape of two Kansas City, Missouri, girls who were ages eight and six. A spokesperson for the Fulton State Hospital said Williams had been a patient from the time of his commitment on June 24, 1965, until his escape on the night of July 4, 1968. While there, he had originally been placed in a maximum security ward. He stayed there until October of 1966, when due to his improved condition, he was transferred to a closed rehabilitation ward. In February of 1967 he was moved to an open ward with access to the yard. On July 4, 1968, he simply walked away from the hospital. Local police officials were informed of the escape and told that Williams was not considered dangerous. Superintendent Donald Peterson stated that while at Fulton Hospital, "He gave us very little trouble and seemed to be improving."[8]

While the investigation continued, Des Moines police also familiarized themselves with the friends and associates Williams had made since he had escaped from the Fulton State Hospital and had taken up residence in Des Moines. One of the most surprising aspects about Williams's personal life was that he was a licensed minister at the Maple Street Baptist Church. The Reverend G. H. Parrish, who was the ordained minister at the church, stated that Williams had joined the church in late July. Rev. Parrish then licensed Williams as a preacher in August. As a licensed preacher, Williams aided the ordained minister during church services. He could deliver sermons during services, but could not administer the sacraments or perform baptisms or marriages. Rev. Parrish explained that Williams did whatever was necessary around the church. In that capacity, he played the piano and organ for the junior and senior choirs, read devotions during services, shoveled snow, and preached three or four times. He did not, however, teach Sunday School classes. Rev. Parrish described Williams as "an exceptional musician, a good vocalist, a likeable, lively fellow, the type that most people like to be around."[9]

At the time of the abduction, Williams was employed by Blue Cross. He had started working there on December 16 as a unit clerk involved in billings. He had last worked on December 23 since the business was closed on December 24. A Blue Cross spokesperson stated that Williams was a good worker who typed 75 words per minute. They noted that when they hired Williams he appeared to be intelligent and they found no problems in their contacts with past employers or with the members of the Maple Street Baptist Church, who all gave him good recommendations.

When Williams arrived in Davenport on Christmas Eve, he went to the home of Mrs. Sadie Wakefield Cade at 1134 Gaines Street. Mrs. Cade, who had known Williams for about five years and did not know about the manhunt, was told by Williams that he had been traveling to Chicago with a friend but instead decided to be dropped off in Davenport. That night Williams and Mrs. Cade crossed over to Rock Island, Illinois, and went to the Clover Club. While at the Clover Club, Williams, who normally didn't

drink, drank three shots of scotch and 7-Up. This was more alcohol than
Mrs. Cade had ever seen him consume. They stayed at the Clover Club until
3 A.M. and then returned to Mrs. Cade's residence, where they celebrated
Christmas the next day. At 10 P.M. on Christmas night, they again went to
the Clover Club with another couple, but when they arrived Williams refused to go into the tavern. Mrs. Cade came out of the tavern at 11:30 P.M.
to check on Williams, who had been waiting in the car, but he was gone.
When Mrs. Cade and the other couple were ready to leave, Williams had
not returned to the car, so they returned to Davenport.[10]

On the morning of December 26, around 8 A.M., Williams, who was still
in Rock Island, Illinois, called Henry McKnight, a Des Moines attorney.
According to McKnight, who knew Williams from church-related activities,
Williams identified himself. McKnight told Williams that everyone was upset
about what had happened. Williams then asked McKnight for help and
McKnight replied that he would help if Williams gave himself up. McKnight
made one other condition that had to be met in order for him to take the
case. He told Williams, "You must give me the facts about the girl when
you get here."[11] Williams replied that he would. McKnight advised Williams
to return to the state of Iowa and give himself up, thereby resolving any
extradition problems. After the initial conversation between McKnight and
Williams, McKnight called the Davenport Police Department to inform the
officers of Williams's intention to surrender. Almost immediately after
McKnight finished that conversation, Williams called back, worried that the
police might jump him when he surrendered. He also wanted to reassure
himself that McKnight was going to represent him.

After McKnight reassured him, Williams took a cab from the Arsenal
Courts federal housing project in Rock Island, Illinois, back to Davenport.
Williams's first stop in Davenport was the home of Mrs. Cade; he tried to
convince her to accompany him to the police station. When she told him
that he needed to explain why she needed to go to the police station with
him, he silently walked out of the house and got back in the taxi. Williams
then arrived at the Davenport police station about 9 A.M., December 26,
1968. Williams walked in and identified himself. He owed the cabbie $3.60
and only had $2.64, so the police supplied the extra dollar. Lt. John Ack-
erman, who was the booking officer, said Williams was "very calm and cool,
very polite and well-dressed and clean. And he [was] a gentleman, to us
anyway."[12]

While Williams was traveling in the cab, McKnight had gone to the Des
Moines Police Department to discuss Williams's transportation back to Des
Moines. When McKnight arrived there, he received a phone call from Williams, who by then was in custody. In the presence of Chief of Police Wendell Nichols and Detective Cleatus Leaming, McKnight told Williams that
he would be picked up in Davenport by the Des Moines police and transported to Des Moines. McKnight also stated that during the trip Williams

would not be mistreated or grilled and that he should make no statement until he reached Des Moines and they had a chance to consult. At this point, there was a factual disagreement between Detective Leaming and McKnight. McKnight argued at the trial that there had been an agreement not to question Williams until he was returned to Des Moines and had the chance to consult with McKnight. Detective Leaming argued that no deal had been made.

After his conversation with McKnight, Williams was booked and given his *Miranda* warnings, which explained that he had a right to remain silent and a right to an attorney. At 11 A.M., Williams had his initial appearance before a state court judge who notified him of the charges against him and again gave him his *Miranda* warnings. Before leaving the courtroom Williams conferred with Thomas Kelly, a Davenport attorney, who advised him not to make any statements until he had a chance to consult with McKnight upon his return to Des Moines.

After the discussion between McKnight and the Des Moines police, Detective Leaming and Detective Arthur Nelson, a 15-year veteran who was then serving on the homicide squad, drove to Davenport to pick up Williams. Leaming and Nelson arrived in Davenport at noon and upon finding that Williams was eating lunch, went to lunch themselves. When they returned from lunch around 1 P.M. they had a conversation with Thomas Kelly and Williams. At this time Detective Leaming again gave Williams his *Miranda* warnings and explained that the two of them would be "visiting" on the way back to Des Moines.

After this interaction between Leaming and Williams, Kelly, acting as Williams's attorney, conferred privately with Williams. Kelly and Leaming then had a discussion, the results of which were some points of disagreement at the trial. The first point of disagreement was that Kelly believed that he had made it clear and gotten assurances from Leaming that Williams was not to be questioned until after he was returned to Des Moines and had a chance to consult with McKnight. Leaming did not believe that such an arrangement had been made. Kelly also claimed, with Leaming disagreeing, that he was denied permission to ride along with Williams and the detectives in the police car to Des Moines in order to protect Williams's rights.

The two detectives handcuffed Williams's hands behind his back, placed him in the back seat of the car and then left on the 160-mile trip to Des Moines. At no time did Williams express a willingness to be interrogated during the trip. In fact, he told Detective Leaming that he would talk after they returned to Des Moines and he consulted with McKnight.

Based on the background check that was done on Williams, Leaming knew that Williams was mentally unbalanced and had deep religious convictions. On the way back, Leaming engaged Williams in a number of conversations concerning, among other topics, religion, Williams's reputation, his minister, and police procedures. Leaming informed Williams that he himself had religious training as a child and was more likely to pray for Williams than abuse him or strike him. Then, according to Leaming's own testimony, in an effort to obtain statements from Williams concerning the missing girl, Leaming addressed Williams as "Reverend" and went into what has become known as the Christian burial speech. The speech goes as follows:

I want to give you something to think about while we're traveling down the road. . . . Number one, I want you to observe the weather conditions, it's raining, it's sleeting, it's freezing, driving is very treacherous, visibility is poor, it's going to be dark early this evening. They are predicting several inches of snow for you tonight, and I feel that you yourself are the only person that knows where this little girl's body is, that you yourself have only been there once, and if you get a snow on top of it you yourself may be unable to find it. And, since we will be going right past the area on the way into Des Moines, I feel that we could stop and locate the body, that the parents of this little girl should be entitled to a Christian burial for the little girl who was snatched away from them on Christmas [E]ve and murdered. And I feel we should stop and locate it on the way in rather than waiting until morning and trying to come back out after a snow storm and possibly not being able to find it at all.[13]

Williams then asked Detective Leaming why he believed that they were going to go past the body. In an attempt to induce Williams to divulge the location of the body, Leaming told him that he knew it was somewhere near Mitchellville, despite the fact that he had no such information.

At the same time that Williams was being arrested, making his initial appearance, and readied for transport, the police had begun a more intensive search for the body of Pamela Powers. The search was initiated based on the discovery of Williams's car in Davenport and several items of clothing belonging to Williams and the victim found at the rest stop on Interstate 80 near Grinnell between Des Moines and Davenport on December 25. This caused the police to conclude that the body of Pamela Powers would probably be found between Des Moines and Grinnell, most likely near the interstate.

The search was placed under the control of Thomas Ruxlow of the Iowa Bureau of Criminal Investigation. The search was conducted by about 250 people. This included police, sheriff's officers, highway patrolmen, state agents, Boy Scouts, and assorted volunteers. The first step of the search involved obtaining maps of Jasper and Poweshiek counties, the two counties east of Polk County in which Des Moines is located. Interstate 80 divides these two counties in half so the decision was made to search an area from roughly seven miles north of the interstate to seven miles south of the interstate. The search began at the eastern border of Poweshiek County and moved west. The section to be searched was divided into grids, with responsibility for each grid placed on teams containing between four and six volunteers. The searchers were instructed to check all roads and ditches from the roadbed. When the searchers came upon culverts, they were told to get out of their vehicles and check the insides. Searchers were also instructed to examine abandoned farm buildings and any other places where a small child could be hidden.[14] The searchers attempted to use airplanes, but bad weather conditions made flying impossible.

While the search was being conducted, Williams was being transported to Des Moines by Detectives Leaming and Nelson. As they neared Grinnell, Iowa, Williams asked if the police had found the victim's shoes. Without reminding Williams of his rights, Detective Leaming discussed with Williams what evidence had been found. Williams then stated that he would show the detectives the Skelly gas station where he had hidden the shoes. Upon stopping at the gas station, no shoes could be located. Next, after further discussion, Williams offered to lead the detectives to a blanket at a rest stop, but when they stopped, they found out that it had already been discovered.

As they continued down the interstate toward Des Moines, there were further discussions about people, religion, intelligence, and what people thought about Williams. While they were still some distance east of Mitchellville, Williams told the detectives that he would show them where the body was located. Due to the cooperation of Williams, the search for Pamela Powers was called off at 3 P.M. on December 26, when the officers coordinating the search were told to meet Detective Leaming at a truck stop near Grinnell. During the period in which the search was ongoing, it had covered all of Poweshiek and Jasper counties, and had made it to the Jasper–Polk County line. The search was never resumed because, at about 5:45 P.M., Williams led the police to the body, which was located two miles south of Interstate 80 on a gravel road in Polk County, 2½ miles west of the Jasper County line. As is typical of many of Iowa's country roads, there were cornfields on both sides of the road and no buildings in the immediate area. Although it took officers five minutes to discover the body, they did find it. The victim was dressed in an orange-and-white, striped blouse, which is what first attracted the attention of the officers conducting the search. Bare from the waist down, the body was partially covered with snow, with the left leg frozen in midair and the back resting against a cement culvert. One officer who was on the scene said that due to the recent snow, it would have taken a long time to find the body without Williams's cooperation.[15]

Williams was then transported the rest of the way back to Des Moines, arriving at about 7:30 P.M. When Detective Leaming brought Williams into the Des Moines Police Department, McKnight was angry with him. This was because he believed that there had been an agreement that there would be no interrogation of Williams during the trip and that all questioning would take place with counsel present. McKnight stated that the Des Moines police "really double-crossed me. They violated all the gentlemen's agreements we had."[16] McKnight also said that, according to Williams, the officers kept questioning him on the trip back as to the location of the body until he cooperated. Police Chief Nichols, however, stood up for his officers, stating that "The two officers who brought Williams back from Davenport deliberately refrained from asking him for details of the abduction and slaying."[17]

Williams was then given a second initial appearance, this time before Municipal Judge Howard Brooks on an open charge of murder. During the proceedings, Williams only identified himself, told the judge that he was indigent, and asked that Henry McKnight be appointed as his attorney. Judge Brooks then appointed McKnight as Williams's attorney, ordered Williams held without bail, and set the preliminary hearing for January 10, 1969, at 1:30 P.M.

The reason why Williams was arraigned on an open charge of murder was that in Iowa an "open" charge of murder included first degree, or premeditated murder; second degree, unpremeditated murder; and manslaughter, death by negligent behavior or careless use of a potentially dangerous instrument. This open charge of murder would allow the prosecuting attorney to later bring whatever formal charges against Williams the facts warranted. The charges of child stealing, for which the original arrest warrant had been issued, were dropped.

Public outrage over the abduction and killing of Pamela Powers quickly mounted after Williams's arrest. Even though a complete autopsy could not be performed until the body had thawed out, public outrage was only exacerbated when the *Des Moines Register* reported on December 29, 1968, that the preliminary autopsy report showed that Pamela had probably been sexually assaulted. This fact was confirmed when the official autopsy report was filed. The autopsy also showed that Pamela died of suffocation, probably prior to being taken from the Y.M.C.A. By this time, Mr. Powers was frustrated with the way the police had handled the case. He told reporters "I don't know of anybody I've met so far who is satisfied with police action on the case."[18] Despite freezing temperatures and snow, a group of mothers reacting to Williams's criminal record picketed outside the Des Moines police headquarters on December 28 calling for stricter punishment for people who sexually abused children. The women said that their picketing would create an interest in passing laws with tougher penalties for people like Williams.

Shortly after Williams's incarceration, Des Moines police received threats concerning his safety from people both within and outside of Iowa. For this reason, Williams was transferred from the Des Moines City Jail to the Polk County Jail. This allowed Williams to be isolated from other prisoners who were thought to be a possible source of danger to his safety.

While Williams was being held without bail for further judicial hearings, the Powers family had a funeral to arrange. Services for Pamela were conducted at St. Andrew's Episcopal Church in Urbandale, Iowa, on December

30, 1968. About 300 people attended the service, which was taken from the church's Book of Common Prayer. The St. Andrew's Junior Choir, which Pamela had belonged to, sang "Fairest Lord Jesus." Pamela was then buried at Chapel Hill Cemetery.

THE PROBLEM

Ignorance and Myth

Given the factual scenario of the *Williams* case, it seemed like an open and shut case that should have been easy to prosecute and bring to a conclusion. Few would have expected that it would take fifteen years for the case to move through the legal system to a final resolution. Most members of the public do not understand that the two values that form the cornerstones of our legal system do not complement each other; in fact, they add to the system's inefficiency. The first value that serves as a foundation of America's legal system is a desire for the government to obey the law and interfere in the lives of its citizens as little as possible. The second core value is a desire to ensure that the government can efficiently catch and punish criminals. Even though these two values are often at odds with each other, the public believes that justice should be quick and sure. The lack of knowledge that most Americans have about the legal system adds to the expectation of quick and sure justice.[19] This lack of knowledge has led to the acceptance of a number of myths about how the legal system should operate.

One of the most prominent myths is that judges make decisions based solely on the rule of law, thus removing judicial decisions from the political world. This myth emphasizes the neutrality of the law in legal decisions. Judges have long sought to reinforce this myth.[20] As long ago as 1824, Chief Justice John Marshall illustrated this point, writing, "Judicial power is never exercised for the purpose of giving effect to the will of the Judge; always for the purpose of giving effect to the will of the . . . law."[21] Statements such as this are meant to promote public acceptance of the idea that we are governed by laws rather than men. This myth helps to preserve public support for the legal system and to advance the goal of maintaining judicial legitimacy.[22]

The belief that we are governed by laws rather than the individual decisions of judges coincides with the public's view of how the legal system operates. The general public's conceptualization of how the judicial process operates reflects a view that scholars refer to as *mechanical jurisprudence*.[23] Actors within the legal system are guilty of helping to sustain the myth of mechanical jurisprudence.[24] According to the school of mechanical jurisprudence, the legal system works like this: A court first recognizes an existing law, such as Iowa's first-degree murder law, applies the law to the facts of a case as they become apparent at trial, and then, *mechanically*, arrives at the only logical decision that could be made. In other words, Law × Facts = Verdict. The simplicity of this process is attractive to citizens who desire quick and sure justice.

According to mechanical jurisprudence, it is believed that a judge's or jury's decision is a preordained event that is commanded by the clearness of the law as applied to the facts. The reason the decision is thought to be so clear is due to the role of the law. Because the law has already been set down by the legislature, it is assumed that the law gives judges and juries clear guidance on how to apply itself to the case at hand. Plus, once a rule of law has been applied in one case, it then becomes a precedent for future cases. According to the principle of *stare decisis*, once a precedent is established, that rule of law should be used to decide future cases with similar factual situations. Therefore, legal decisions should be predictable: When a judge recognizes facts in a current case that resemble those in an earlier case, the rule of law that applied in the earlier case should be used to settle the current case. This constant application of the law is meant to bring consistency to the legal system.

The Role of Facts and Law

Even though the concept of mechanical jurisprudence oversimplifies the judicial process, facts and the law do play a central role in resolving legal cases. Normally, in mechanical jurisprudence's formula of Law × Facts = Verdict, the determination of the facts is thought to be simple to ascertain. Scholars, however, have understood for at least the last fifty years that determining the facts can be one of the most difficult jobs of a trial court.[25] The difficulty in fact finding is trying to settle what actually happened, since facts do not walk into court and make themselves known. Instead, the facts have to be reconstructed based on the evidence and memories of the individuals involved in the sequence of events under consideration. The testimonies of witnesses are subject to memory loss and embellishment over time. Jerome Frank stated that as a result of this faulty process of reconstructing the facts, courts must guess as to what actually are the facts. Therefore, the facts that influence a judicial verdict are in reality the judge's or jury's reaction to the testimony. The facts accepted by the judge or jury may or may not coincide with the actual events that brought the case into court.[26]

This realization caused Frank to distinguish between what he termed real or objective facts and subjective facts. Real or objective facts can never be known at trial. Subjective facts are the facts determined to exist at trial.[27] In noting this distinction, it is important to realize that objective facts and subjective facts are not the same things. The outcome of a trial turns on subjective facts because they are the facts that the judge or jury accept as true.

It is also important to know that the facts may be disputed at trial. At trial, the determination of the subjective facts between the two competing versions presented by the parties to a case is often the only point of contention when the law is clear. The *Williams* case demonstrates that judges and juries are confronted with choices when they are called on to decide what are the subjective facts of a case. The dispute that existed between Detective Leaming and Henry McKnight as to whether there had been an agreement not to interrogate Williams on the trip between Davenport and Des Moines serves as an example.

Beyond the difference that exists between the unknowable objective facts and the subjective facts accepted by the judge or jury, there are still more problems that weaken the explanatory power of mechanical jurisprudence. One of the difficulties that causes delay in the application of justice is that not all subjective facts carry the same legal weight. This is because at trial there are two types of subjective facts—admissible and inadmissible. The admissibility of facts turns not only on a resolution of what the court believes the subjective facts to be, but also on a determination of whether the procedural law allows those facts to be entered as evidence in court. For example, Williams claimed that his statements leading to the discovery of the body were gained in violation of the right against self-incrimination and should not be admissible at trial.

According to mechanical jurisprudence, next to the facts of a case, the law is the other factor on which the verdict is based. Law is a body of rules that can be enforced by the coercive power of the state. Laws are grouped into separate families based on the differing types of behavior that are regulated. The families of law the *Williams* case involved were criminal law and constitutional law. Criminal law is a substantive family of law that defines certain actions as crimes against the public and establishes appropriate punishments for violations of the law. The goal of criminal law is to prevent and control criminal behavior.

In the *Williams* case, because Iowa's law regarding murder was stable, mechanical jurisprudence would assume that the real challenge of the trial court was to determine the facts. If, however, this was the only task required of the state trial court, then there would have been little delay in the resolution of this and most other cases. What has been overlooked by mechanical jurisprudence's simplification of the judicial process is an awareness that there is more than one type of law that has to be considered prior to a verdict being reached in a case. Along with the criminal law, the courts also have to apply *procedural laws*. Procedural laws comprise a set of laws that must be followed to ensure that suspects' legal rights are protected. As they did in the *Williams* case, procedural laws often involve constitutional law. Derived from the U.S. Constitution, constitutional law is the supreme law of the land and takes precedence over other forms of law.

Most procedural laws deal with due process of law. Due process of law, which is a provision of both the Fifth and the Fourteenth Amendments, refers to the procedural requirements that the national and state governments must observe when they act in a manner that can deprive a person of life, liberty, or property. The due process safeguards are meant to place checks on the ability of governments to harass citizens by flagrantly using their powers to arbitrarily interfere with the lives of citizens and subject them to prosecution and possible conviction. The procedural laws relating to due process are used to determine when facts are admissible at trial. Because of the due process safeguards and our adversarial system of justice, the atmosphere in which American courts conduct their work is a highly charged one. The U.S. judicial system operates on the premise that justice is best served when both sides to a dispute have the ability to enter evidence and challenge the evidence of the other party. This allows for a sharper development of the facts of the dispute. Hopefully, the subjective facts that come out in court will then be closer to the objective facts than if just one side were capable of framing the facts.

The Constitution does not specify the exact procedures that must be followed to accord a person due process. The vagueness of procedural law plays a crucial role in the judicial process, one that is often glossed over by the myths the public has accepted about the American legal system.

Discretion and Judicial Decision Making

The myths accepted by the public about the legal system are based on a superficial image of how courts operate. Superficial images do not, however, necessarily match reality. By concentrating on the role of law and facts and the limiting effect these have on judicial choice, one very important factor, which helps to explain how decisions are reached within the legal system, has been ignored. That factor is the role of *discretion*. Discretion is such a prominent reality in the judicial decision-making process that scholars often look beyond an examination of the law to discretionary factors, such as personal or policy preferences, to explain how judges actually make their decisions.[28]

Discretion plays an important role throughout the judicial decision-making process. Discretion not only has an impact on the determination of the subjective facts, it also plays a large role as judges decide the procedural law applicable to a case. Despite a long-running interest by scholars in judicial discretion, the role that it plays in the judicial process remains a mystery.[29] Judicial discretion refers to the authority of a judge to select between two or more legal courses of action. Defined as such, judicial discretion does not give to judges arbitrary freedom of choice. Instead, it only allows judges to select between alternative legal options when the law itself is unclear. According to Wolfgang Friedman, "Freedom means choice, responsible choice."[30] Responsible choice should mean exercising discretion only within the limitations allowed by the legal system. James Gibson has described how judges use their ability to exercise legal options by stating that "judges' decisions are a function of what they prefer to do, tempered by what they think they ought to do, but constrained by what they perceive is feasible to do.[31] This means that when a case involves a variety of legal options, a number of judges would not mechanically decide the case in the same manner.

The constitutional requirements of due process of law have come to be defined through the discretionary choices expressed in the opinions of judges and especially the justices of the Supreme Court. The ability to control the evolution of the law through written opinions has allowed members of the judiciary to reinforce the myth of the neutrality of the law. By incorporating prior opinions into new decisions, judges have the capacity to render rulings supported by the history of the law and prior precedent. Indeed, this often is the case. It is not, however, necessarily true. At times, new directions in the law are masked because judges rely on the language of old cases and precedents, despite the fact that they are changing the direction of the law. This is often accomplished by taking the old cases out of context. Thus, even though there may be a significant change in the direction of the law, reliance on old cases makes it seem as if the continuity of the law remains.

Judicial discretion makes the legal system more complex and the resolution of legal cases more difficult than the process of mechanical jurisprudence would lead us to believe. That is because judges have the discretion to accept one of several competing versions of the facts and procedural laws. In exercising this discretion, judges and juries can differ dramatically in the decisions that they make and in the verdicts they reach. While judicial discretion makes it difficult to be able to predict the direction of decisions in advance, it also benefits the legal system by giving judges flexibility of action to make what is perceived to be a just decision based on the facts of the case.

Due to the realities of the legal system, the *Williams* case was not as simple a case as mechanical jurisprudence would suggest or the public would have believed. Instead, the *Williams* case was riddled with perplexing factual, procedural, and legal issues. In resolving the case, the delays that became a part of the record can be traced to two primary sources both resulting from judicial discretion. These discretionary choices centered on what the subjective facts of the case were, and how the procedural laws should be applied. Therefore, an examination of the *Williams* case allows us to reconsider common myths about the legal system by introducing the reader to the realities of how the American legal system operates.

NOTES

1. Silas Wasserstrom and William J. Mertens, "The Exclusionary Rule on the Scaffold: But Was it a Fair Trial?" *American Criminal Law Review* 22 (1984): 130.

2. Alpheus Thomas Mason, "Myth and Reality in Supreme Court Decisions," *Virginia Law Review* 48 (1962): 1404.

3. *Des Moines Register*, 25 December 1968.

4. *Des Moines Register*, 1 May 1969.

5. *Des Moines Register*, 25 December 1968.

6. Ibid.

7. *Des Moines Register*, 26 December 1968.

8. *Des Moines Register*, 29 December 1968.

9. *Des Moines Register*, 27 December 1968.

10. Ibid.

11. Ibid.

12. Ibid.

13. *Brewer v. Williams*, 430 U.S. 387, 392–93 (1977).

14. *Nix v. Williams*, 467 U.S. 431, 448 (1984).

15. *Des Moines Register*, 27 December 1968.

16. *Des Moines Register*, 28 December 1968.

17. Ibid.

18. *Des Moines Register*, 29 December 1968.

19. Lawrence Baum, *American Courts* (Boston: Houghton Mifflin Co., 1994), p. 1.

20. For an extended discussion of this effort see Mason, "Myth and Reality"; and Christopher E. Smith, *Courts, Politics, and the Judicial Process* (Chicago: Nelson-Hall Publishers, 1993), pp. 3–6.

21. *Osborn v. Bank of the United States*, 22 U.S. (9 Wheat.) 738 (1824).

22. Joel Grossman and Richard Wells, *Constitutional Law and Judicial Policy-making*, 3rd ed. (New York: Longman, 1988), p. 11.

23. On the general public's acceptance of mechanical jurisprudence see Mason, "Myth and Reality," and Richard Engstrom and Michael Giles, "Expectations and Images: A Note on Diffuse Support for Legal Institutions," *Law and Society Review* 6 (1972): 631–636.

24. Wesley Skogan, "Judicial Myth and Judicial Reality," *Washington University Law Quarterly* (1971): 309–334.

25. Jerome Frank, *Courts on Trial* (Princeton, N.J.: Princeton University Press, 1950), p. 74.

26. Frank, *Courts on Trial*, p. 15.

27. Ibid., p. 24.

28. For examples, see Jeffrey A. Segal and Harold J. Spaeth, *The Supreme Court and the Attitudinal Model* (New York: Cambridge University Press, 1993); and Lee Epstein and Jack Knight, *The Choices Justices Make* (Washington, D.C.: Congressional Quarterly Press, 1998).

29. Aaharon Barak, *Judicial Discretion* (New Haven: Yale University Press, 1989), p. 3.

30. Wolfgang Friedman, "Judicial Philosophy and Judicial Lawmaking," *Columbia Law Review* 61 (1961): 830.

31. James L. Gibson, "From Simplicity to Complexity: The Development of Theory in the Study of Judicial Behavior," *Political Behavior* 5 (1983): 9.

_____

Chapter 2

The Criminal Justice Process

Facts as such, never settle anything. They are working tools only. It is the implications that can be drawn from facts that count.

—Clarence Beldon Randall[1]

DUE PROCESS AND THE CRIMINAL JUSTICE PROCESS

The *Williams* case would have never come before the courts and entered the criminal justice system if there had not been an accusation that Robert Williams had violated the criminal law. Criminal acts are public wrongs that are prosecuted and, if conviction follows, punished by the state. After a legislative body has criminalized a certain act, the wheels of the criminal justice process begin to turn with the commission of a crime. Throughout the criminal justice process, one of the most basic assumptions is that all suspects are considered innocent until proven guilty. This assumption limits the ability of the government to incarcerate its political enemies or members of unpopular groups without evidence and proof of guilt presented at trial. It also gives rise to an adversarial system of justice in which the government has the burden of proving the guilt of individuals suspected of criminal activity. The adversarial process is praised for creating an environment in which the evidence put forth at trial can be thoroughly challenged and tested for truthfulness. This is seen as a necessity because fact finding is subject to a number of weaknesses that can create inaccuracies. Therefore, because the stakes involved in criminal sentencing are so high, punishment should only be imposed after all evidence and testimony has been subjected to scrutiny by the opposing attorney.

The American criminal justice system also places a heavy emphasis on the due process rights of the criminally accused. Due process of law is a concept that can be traced back to English common law and the signing of the Magna Carta in 1215. The purpose of due process is to restrain the ability of the state to unfairly deprive a person of life, liberty, or property. Due process recognizes the inherent inequalities between the power of the state and the individual. It is hoped that by establishing specific procedural guidelines, which must be followed prior to a finding of criminal guilt, a fair system of justice will result. The procedural requirements that must be followed in the prosecution of the criminally accused may be found in the U.S. Constitution, state constitutions, federal and state statutes, court decisions, and local customs. Even in seemingly open and shut cases where there is a strong likelihood of guilt—as there seemed to be in the case of Robert Williams—due procedural requirements must be followed.

The criminal justice process can be divided into a number of steps. Due to differences in state and federal law, however, there are variations in the specific requirements that each jurisdiction must follow. The criminal justice process is further complicated by the fact that the various stages do not always proceed in the same order. For example, in most cases arrest comes before the accused retains an attorney, but in the *Williams* case Williams arranged for an attorney prior to his arrest. Finally, in some jurisdictions not all the steps are necessary and/or a defendant can waive some preliminary procedures.

Arrest

From the point of arrest through the rest of the criminal justice process, discretion plays a large role in the decision-making process. The arrest is the initial contact between the accuser (the government) and the accused. Most crimes, however, do not end in an arrest.[2] The reasons for this are numerous. Most often, crimes do not take place in the presence of police officers, so police must rely on private citizens to report criminal activity. The more serious the crime, the more likely it is to be reported. In other instances, even when knowledge of the crime does exist, suspects cannot be identified or apprehended. At other times, the prosecutor will make a conscious decision not to pursue a case.

The law governing arrests is regulated through the Fourth Amendment, which prohibits unreasonable searches and seizures. Arrests can be made through the use of a warrant. Warrants may be issued after a person swears out a formal complaint, which claims facts charging another person with a crime. The facts in the complaint are then reviewed by an independent magistrate to determine if there is probable cause to believe that the accused did indeed commit the action. Despite the warrant provision of the Fourth Amendment, 95 percent of all arrests are made without a warrant.[3] The most common form of arrest is a summary arrest in which officers independently make the decision to arrest a suspect based on information they discovered or on information given by another person such as the victim of the crime.[4] Even in summary arrests, due process requires that the standard for arrest must be *probable cause* that the accused did indeed commit the crime.

Oftentimes, even when police officers are aware of a crime and can identify a suspect, they will still not make an arrest. Each police officer has the discretion to make such decisions. There are four main categories of cases that scholars have identified in which officers are often hesitant to make an arrest: (1) minor offenses, where the officer may believe alternatives to an arrest will create a better deterrent to future violations; (2) cases where the victim will not press charges; (3) situations in which victims were also involved in misconduct and thereby helped to bring on their own misfortunes; and (4) when the criminal behavior is thought to be consistent with that community's mores.[5]

Even though there was an outstanding arrest warrant charging Williams with child stealing, the arrest of Robert Williams occurred as a result of his surrender in Davenport, Iowa, on December 26, 1968. Williams first considered surrendering when he was in Rock Island, Illinois, and contacted Henry McKnight in Des Moines by phone to see if McKnight would act as his attorney. Williams knew McKnight through work that they had done for their respective churches in Des Moines. Through his acquaintance with McKnight, Williams believed that McKnight could be trusted. McKnight suggested that it would be better if Williams crossed back into Iowa before he surrendered. This would allow Williams to bypass the extradition process and expedite the legal process that would follow once Williams was in custody. After a second call to McKnight to assure himself that he would not be mistreated by the police, Williams returned to Davenport, Iowa, and turned himself in to the police. Lieutenant John Ackerman was the police officer who formally arrested Williams. After the arrest, except in the case of minor offenses, the suspect is normally booked at a police station. Lieutenant Ackerman was responsible for booking Robert Williams. He started by advising Williams of his rights. Booking also involved the taking of fingerprints and mug shots and allowing the suspect to make at least one phone call. Shortly after his arrest, Williams was allowed to talk to McKnight in Des Moines over the phone. At the time of that conversation, McKnight was sitting in the office of Cleatus Leaming, the officer in charge of the investigation in Des Moines. Police Chief Wendell Nichols was also in the office and both police officers overheard the conversation in which McKnight told Williams that some members of the Des Moines Police Department would pick him up and transport him back to Des Moines.

McKnight told Williams that he would not be abused or questioned during the trip, but that when he got back they would have to talk about the missing girl.

After the arrest of Williams, the formal criminal justice process began. For any arrest to be legitimate it must meet the proper procedural standard of probable cause. The arrest warrant for the charge of child stealing helped to ensure that this requirement was met in the *Williams* case. After his call to McKnight, Williams was placed in jail until he was taken before a judge for his initial court appearance.

Initial Appearance

The initial appearance is the first time that a criminal suspect enters the court system. In some jurisdictions, such as Iowa, the initial appearance is referred to as an *arraignment*. The initial appearance is supposed to be held without delay. Historically, in most states, that has meant within twenty-four hours of arrest. In 1991, however, the Supreme Court ruled that police may hold a person up to forty-eight hours prior to the initial appearance and judicial review of the arrest.[6]

At the initial appearance, if the person was arrested without a warrant, the police must convince the judge or magistrate that there was probable cause for the arrest. In all cases, suspects are brought before a judge or magistrate and informed of the charges against them. Suspects are also informed of their constitutional rights and guarantees. Even if they have already been informed of their right to remain silent and their right to an attorney, the judge will again remind them. If the accused is indigent and wishes to have an attorney appointed by the court, counsel may be appointed at this time.

The judge will also determine if the accused may be released on bail and, if so, what the amount of bail will be. The purpose of bail is to ensure that the defendant will show up for all court appearances rather than fleeing the jurisdiction. Bail is a guarantee in either money or property that the defendant will make all court appearances. If the defendant makes all appearances, bail is returned. If not, it is forfeited. Judges have wide discretion in the setting of bail. In deciding what amount to set as bail, two factors weigh the most heavily: the seriousness of the crime and the prior record of the defendant. A more serious charge usually results in a higher bail being set, as does a more serious prior record.[7] When judges believe that a person will not show up at future judicial proceedings, they will often set such a high bail that the defendant will not be able to raise enough money for a bond. If bail cannot be raised, or is denied, then the defendant will have to await trial in jail. Bail is not a constitutional right in state prosecutions and may be denied altogether, as it was in Robert Williams's case.

Robert Williams's initial appearance was on the morning of December 26,

1969, in Davenport Municipal Court. Judge Bertram Metcalf presided over the initial appearance. Judge Metcalf advised Williams of the charge of child stealing for which the warrant against him had been issued. He also again advised Williams of his rights. Bail was denied to Williams. Williams was given a second initial appearance in Des Moines after he led police to the body of Pamela Powers. This appearance took place before Judge Howard Brooks. At the second appearance, Williams was again informed of his rights, but the charge against him was changed to an open charge of murder with the charge of child stealing being dropped. During the appearance, Williams's only words were to state his name to the judge, inform him that he had no money, and to ask that Henry McKnight be appointed as his attorney—a request that was granted.

Decision to Prosecute

After the initial appearance, the prosecutor controls whether there will be further court appearances by deciding whether to file formal charges and prosecute. The decision to charge is a discretionary one that is left up to the prosecutor in the jurisdiction in which the crime was committed. George D. Cole's research has found that prosecutors are likely to base their decision on three criteria: evidential, pragmatic, and organizational.[8]

The evidential criteria rank high in the charging decision. When considering evidential criteria prosecutors are likely to ask themselves whether a prosecution will result in a conviction. The higher the chances for conviction, the more likely a prosecution. In cases where the evidence is flimsy and leaves a good chance of acquittal, prosecutors will be wary of charging the individual. Acquittals weaken people's confidence in the prosecutor and the prosecutor's office. Acquittals also weaken the position of the prosecutor in plea-bargaining arrangements. The weight of the damaging evidence against Robert Williams was one of the primary reasons for bringing charges. Among the evidence against him was eyewitness testimony that Williams left the Y.M.C.A. with a bundle, plus his leading police to the body.

The pragmatic criteria that a prosecutor considers in the decision to charge are often founded on a concern that justice be individualized in each case. To this end, prosecutors will often try to determine whether the individual involved deserves the full severity of the law or to be given some degree of mercy. In making this decision, prosecutors can decide not to file any charges. A prosecutor may look at the personal characteristics of the offender and decide that justice would be better served by filing a misdemeanor charge that would be less stigmatizing than a felony charge, which may harden the individual involved. Based on Williams's criminal record, there was a deep desire to prosecute and remove the threat of future incidents.

In considering organizational criteria, prosecutors focus on the needs of their own office before making the decision to charge an individual with a crime. One of the main concerns of the organizational criteria is to ensure that the prosecutor's office maintains good working relationships with the police and judges. Prosecutors may be hesitant to bring charges in cases where a particular judge has shown, through sentencing decisions, that he or she does not consider a particular type of criminal activity to be serious. Prosecutors also look at their own workloads when considering organizational criteria in the charging decision. To advance a good working relationship, prosecutors may bring charges in cases that have weak evidence to ensure future cooperation with the police. In a similar manner, prosecutors may refuse to bring charges in some cases to prompt police to do a better job of criminal investigation. In the *Williams* case, there were real concerns about whether the police had violated Williams's Fifth and Sixth Amendment rights on the trip between Davenport and Des Moines. This was, however, too big of a case and the stakes were too high for the prosecution to try to use it as a teaching tool for police.

Preliminary Hearing

If the prosecutor does file charges, then in most states the next step in the criminal justice process is the *preliminary hearing*. Not all states use preliminary hearings. The purpose of the preliminary hearing is to protect defendants from unwarranted prosecution and prolonged incarceration. The preliminary hearing is the first point in the criminal justice process in which our adversarial system of justice is put to the test. At the preliminary hearing, the prosecution must convince a neutral judge through the submission of evidence—which can be challenged by the defense—that there is probable cause to believe that the defendant did indeed commit the crime and should be held over for trial. Probable cause can be shown by proving that there was a crime that was committed and that the defendant was likely to be the perpetrator. If the judge does not believe that probable cause has been shown connecting the defendant to the crime, the defendant will be released and the charges will be dropped. The reality of the situation is that in few felony cases are charges dismissed or reduced to a misdemeanor for lack of probable cause after the preliminary hearing. Despite the low percentage of cases where defendants have charges dropped as a result of preliminary hearings, these hearings can be beneficial to defendants by informing them about the prosecution's evidence.

The preliminary hearing for Robert Williams was held in the Des Moines Municipal Court before Judge Luther Glanton on Friday, January 10, 1969. Security was a real concern since, according to Polk County Sheriff Wilbur Hildreth, there had been threats made against Williams. Despite the fact that the hearing didn't get started until 1:40 P.M., spectators began to arrive at 10 A.M. All spectators, except for news reporters, were searched prior to admission. The men were searched in the hallway and the women were searched in a rest room by a matron. The searches yielded a total of three pocket knifes that were returned to the individuals after the hearing. The crowd was so large that the courtroom, which regularly sat 70 people, was enlarged to seat 100 by placing extra chairs in the back and aisles of the courtroom.

Williams was brought into the courtroom and placed at the defendant's table with his attorney Henry McKnight and his co-counsel Louis Lavorato. The hearing started with a warning from Judge Glanton to the spectators to refrain from any outbursts because "The defendant, like all other defendants, is entitled to a fair and impartial trial, and this court is going to do everything possible to assure just such a trial."[9] He then threatened to have anyone who created a disturbance removed.

Assistant Polk County Attorney Michael Hanson had the duty of proving that there was probable cause to hold Williams over for trial on an open charge of murder. To accomplish this goal Hanson called a variety of witnesses. The first group of witnesses were all present at the Y.M.C.A. at the time of Pamela Powers's disappearance. This group included Pamela's mother, who explained the circumstances concerning what happened just prior to the time that Pamela was noticed as missing. Don Hanna, the physical education director at the Y.M.C.A., was also called. He testified that he saw Williams leave the Y.M.C.A. carrying something wrapped in a blanket, which Williams then placed in a car before driving off.

Hanson next called Captain Cleatus Leaming, chief of detectives of the Des Moines Police Department. Leaming's testimony led to a series of objections by McKnight who accused Leaming of double-crossing him on an agreement that had been struck not to interrogate Williams while he was being transported between Davenport and Des Moines. Leaming denied that any agreement had existed between him and McKnight and stated that he had informed Williams of his constitutional rights. He also testified that, after he got back to the Des Moines police station and McKnight found out that Williams had led him to the body, McKnight threatened to hit him in the mouth.

McKnight stated that he would object to any use as evidence of information that was obtained during Williams's transport since it was gained through a violation of his constitutional rights as specified in *Miranda, Escobedo*, and other comparable cases by the Supreme Court. Judge Glanton then met briefly with the attorneys in chambers to determine if evidence regarding Williams's incriminating statements could be used to help prove that there was probable cause to hold Williams over for trial. After the conference, Judge Glanton overruled the objection of McKnight, stating, "I think in the trial of the case you'll have something there, but for the purpose of this hearing the court will permit this officer to state what he did."[10] Captain Leaming went on and testified that Williams had indeed led him to the body of Pamela Powers.

Lieutenant John Ackerman of the Davenport Police Department testified that Williams had been advised of his rights by himself and at his initial appearance. He also testified that in Davenport, Williams was allowed to consult with Thomas Kelly, a Davenport attorney, at least twice. The last witness called was Dr. Leo Luka, the Polk County medical examiner, who testified that Pamela had been smothered to death. He also told the judge that she was dead prior to being placed in the ditch in which she was found.

After all the testimony, McKnight made a motion for the judge to dismiss the murder charge against Williams since the state had failed to prove premeditation and Williams's constitutional rights had been violated. Judge Glanton denied the motion and ordered Williams to be held over on the charge with no bail. Judge Glanton then ordered everyone to stay seated until Williams had been removed from the courtroom.

GRAND JURY

In federal criminal prosecutions all cases must be presented to the grand jury for investigation according to the Fifth Amendment. The Supreme Court has ruled that the Fifth Amendment grand jury requirement is not mandatory in state criminal prosecutions.[11] As a result, and because it is repetitious of the work of the preliminary hearing, only about half of the states use grand juries as a means of criminal indictment. Grand juries are designed to stop individuals from harassing prosecutions when there is no legal basis for the charges that are filed. They are also meant to ensure that there is sufficient evidence for the charges that are filed against an individual accused of a crime. This is because grand juries are made up of citizens who must be convinced that there is probable cause that a suspect committed a crime before the government is allowed to indict.

Grand juries are led by the prosecutor in that jurisdiction. They secretly investigate criminal activity that is brought to their attention for the term of their impanelment. Grand juries can consider evidence that legally would not be admissible at trial. Typically, neither suspects nor their attorneys are allowed to observe the proceedings of the grand jury. Suspects are not allowed to contest the evidence presented by the prosecutor, or to present their own evidence. After examining the evidence, the grand jury takes a vote to determine whether probable cause exists to indict a suspect on the charges presented to it by the prosecutor. If a majority of the jurors vote for indictment, called a *true bill*, an indictment will be issued listing the formal charges brought against the defendant and if an arrest has not previously been made, one will be made. In reality, it is rare that a *no true bill* is returned by grand juries, since their investigations are under the firm guidance and control of the prosecutor. After the preliminary hearing, Williams's case was sent to a grand jury for the State of Iowa. The grand jury deliberated and returned a true bill indicting Robert Williams on an open charge of murder.

If a grand jury is used and a true bill returned, the indictment serves as the formal charging instrument. In states that do not use grand juries, the prosecutor files a bill of information explaining to the court that probable cause has been found to hold over the defendant on the precise charges against him or her. Whichever system of charging is used, the charging document must include the name of the defendant, a brief description of the crime and the circumstances surrounding its commission, and a listing of the specific statutes that were allegedly violated. The Sixth Amendment requires that defendants be informed of the charges against them, so a copy will be given to the defendants. This is normally done at the arraignment.

ARRAIGNMENT

The arraignment happens after either the preliminary hearing or the grand jury indictment. It takes place before the judge in the court where the trial will be held. The arraignment has several functions. The first is to inform defendants of the specific charges of which they are accused. A second is to ensure that defendants are apprised of their rights and have an attorney. A third function of the arraignment is to allow defendants to enter a plea. There are a number of pleas that can be entered, all with differing results. Both a plea of guilty and *nolo contendere*, no contest, will result in no trial being held; the criminal justice process then moves on to the sentencing phase. The *nolo contendere* plea has the same effect as a guilty plea, but cannot be used as evidence of a criminal conviction should the defendant later be sued in a civil trial. Defendants who plead not guilty or not guilty by reason of insanity will go to trial so the issues of the case may be resolved. The judge will then set a trial date and, if the case is serious, inform defendants of their right to a jury trial if so desired.

The indictment in the *Williams* case confronted the suspect with an open charge of murder to which he pleaded not guilty. Chapter 690 of the *Code of Iowa* defined murder in the following manner:

690.1 Murder. Whoever kills any human being with malice aforethought, either express or implied, is guilty of murder.

690.2 First degree murder. All murder which is perpetrated by means of poison, or lying in wait, or any other kind of willful, deliberate, and premeditated killing, or which is committed in the perpetration or attempt to perpetrate any arson, rape, robbery, mayhem, or burglary, is murder in the first degree, and shall be punished by imprisonment for life at hard labor in the penitentiary and the court shall enter judgement and pass sentence accordingly.

690.3 Second degree murder. Whoever commits murder otherwise than as set forth in section 690.2 is guilty of murder in the second degree, and shall be punished by imprisonment in the penitentiary for life, or for a term of not less than ten years.

690.4 Degree determined. Upon the trial of an indictment for murder, the jury, if it finds the defendant guilty, must inquire, and by its verdict ascertain and determine the degree; but if the defendant is convicted upon a plea of guilty, the court must determine the degree, and in either case must enter judgment and pass sentence accordingly.[12]

Before Williams could be convicted, the prosecutor would have to be able to produce evidence of the *corpus delecti* or the "body of the crime." The *corpus delecti* is made up of two elements that must both be proven in order to sustain a criminal charge. The first is the *actus reus* which means "guilty act." Prior to proving who killed Pamela Powers, the prosecutor would have to prove that Pamela had indeed been killed. Furthermore, if the prosecutor wanted to be able to convict Williams of first-degree murder he would also have to prove either that Williams had planned the killing prior to it happening or that the killing took place during an arson, rape, robbery, mayhem, or burglary. The second element of the *corpus delecti* that would have to be proven was the *mens rea* or the existence of a "guilty mind." To establish the *mens rea*, the prosecution would have to show that Williams intended to commit the crime for which he was charged or that the crime resulted from a wrongful purpose that Williams willingly undertook. Given Williams's mental history, the prosecutor had to be concerned with being able to prove the *mens rea*, since this element may be absent if a person can be proved to have diminished mental capacity.

While awaiting trial, Robert Williams was denied bail, and during his confinement at the Polk County Jail, he proved to be less than a perfect prisoner. On February 27, 1969, a jailer, Darrell Kinney, intercepted two notes discussing an escape plan. One of the notes was in a book and the other was found in a candy bar. The notes came from cell block 7 where Robert Williams; Michael Niccum, another murder suspect; and Lawrence T. Holmes were all being held. Holmes had previously escaped from the Polk County Jail and was charged with jailbreak and armed robbery. The notes were being sent to cell blocks 5 and 6, the other felony cell blocks.

The jailer had been on heightened alert since earlier in the week when it was reported that sawing noises could be heard in the cell blocks at night. Some prisoners had even complained that their sleep was being interrupted by the noise at night. The jailers had been unable to determine the source of the noise because each time they went to investigate, the noises stopped. The intercepted note stated that Lawrence Holmes would break out of his cell between midnight and 1 A.M. on March 1, 1969. He would then overpower the guard, take the keys, and free the other prisoners in cell block 7 and anyone who wanted to be freed in cell blocks 5 and 6. Upon finding the note, a shakedown of cell block 7 was conducted. In the search it was discovered that one bar in Holmes's cell was completely sawed free and held in place by soap. A second bar was almost sawed through. Two hacksaw blades were also discovered in the cell.

As a result of the attempted jailbreak, all three prisoners in cell block 7, including Williams, had their privileges revoked and were placed in solitary confinement. This meant that they would no longer be able to freely walk through the entire length of their cell block. Instead, each would be confined to their individual cells. It was in solitary confinement in the Polk County Jail that Williams then awaited trial.

NOTES

1. Cited in John O. Songsten, Roger Haydock, and James J. Boyd, *The Trialbook* (St. Paul, Minn.: West Publishing Company, 1984), p. 318.

2. Kathleen Maguire and Ann L. Patore, eds., *Sourcebook of Criminal Justice Statistics 1995* (Washington, D.C.: U.S. Government Printing Office, 1996), pp. 425–426.

3. Robert A. Carp, and Ronald Stidham, *Judicial Process in America* (Washington, D.C.: Congressional Quarterly Inc., 1993), p. 157.

4. Howard Abadinsky, *Law and Justice: An Introduction to the American Legal System*, 2nd ed. (Chicago: Nelson-Hall Publishers, 1991), pp. 226–227.

5. Carp and Stidham, *Judicial Process*, p. 157–161.

6. *County of Riverside v. McLaughlin*, 500 U.S. 44 (1991).

7. David W. Neubauer, *Judicial Process: Law, Courts, & Politics in the United States* (Pacific Grove, Calif.: Brooks/Cole Publishing Company, 1991), p. 199.

8. George D. Cole, "The Decision to Prosecute," *Law and Society Review* 4 (1970): 331–343.

9. *Des Moines Register*, 11 January 1969.

10. Joint Appendix, p. 35, *Brewer v. Williams*, 430 U.S. 387 (1977).

11. *Hurtado v. California*, 110 U.S. 516 (1884).

12. *Code of Iowa*, vol. II (State of Iowa, 1966), p. 2791.

Chapter 3

The First Trial

> The Supreme Court's resolution of *Brewer* revolved upon two factual issues. The first was whether an interrogation of the accused occurred; the second was whether Williams waived his right to counsel. . . . The majority's resolution of the former two issues can be disputed indefinitely, depending upon one's view of facts in the record.
>
> —Edward F. Pohern[1]

After Robert Williams was formally charged and entered a plea of not guilty at the arraignment, the process moved forward toward trial. Judge James Denato would preside over the trial while Vincent Hanrahan would be the lead prosecutor and Henry McKnight would be the lead defense counsel. Criminal trials create a forum in which the subjective facts of a case can be determined, the law can be applied to those facts, and a conclusion about guilt or innocence can then be reached. The conclusion that is reached in a trial may depend on the set of facts that are accepted, the law that is applied, or a combination of facts and law. The facts of a case are central to the outcome and play a prominent role in the adversarial process. Prosecuting and defense attorneys do their best to make the most essential facts necessary to winning their case come out at trial and to make other facts seem less important and credible. Attorneys also try to influence judges in their decisions regarding which laws are applicable to the case.

THE PRETRIAL PROCESS

As the case proceeded toward trial it contained disputes about both the facts and law. The central factual dispute was, of course, the question of whether Robert Williams had indeed killed Pamela Powers. Beyond that factual question others remained. For example, did the police promise not to interrogate Williams on the trip from Davenport to Des Moines? Was the Christian burial speech a form of interrogation? Did Williams properly waive his rights? The answer to some of these questions would depend, in part, on the judge's interpretation of the law. The law involved in the case included not only the Iowa state law prohibiting murder, it also included the application of procedural laws of due process meant to protect several legal rights found in the United States Constitution. These included the Fifth Amendment right against self-incrimination, the Sixth Amendment right to counsel, and the Fourteenth Amendment's Due Process Clause which makes the prior two rights applicable to the states.

Despite the importance of trials as a method of sorting out the facts and law, trials are not the norm within our criminal justice system. Most cases are settled through plea bargains. That makes those cases which do go to trial different than those which do not. Usually, trial cases involve more serious crimes. They also often have a larger impact on later cases by providing legal precedents. Of the cases which do go to trial, most are not prolonged events. In Philadelphia, for example, nonjury felony trials average less than an hour in length.[2]

Once the judicial process starts, its ability to function is dependent on a number of players other than the attorneys and judges. Bailiffs are responsible for maintaining order and decorum within the courtroom. They also provide security and guard prisoners who are on trial or appear as witnesses. A court clerk is responsible for keeping the record of the trial, which includes a transcript of all court proceedings made by the court reporter using a stenographic device. Along with the transcript of the trial, other components of the record include all motions, memoranda, exhibits, discovery documents, jury instructions, and notices of appeal. The accuracy of the record is essential in the appeals process when it will be relied upon to provide a record of both the facts that came out at trial and the legal rulings.

Rules of Evidence

The purpose of the extensive preparation an attorney makes for trial is to get as much helpful and credible evidence before the factfinder, the judge or jury, to help them reach a favorable outcome. Evidence refers to all the information presented at trial in an attempt to establish the facts of the case. Judges are in control of the decision of how much evidence can actually be presented at trial. They are guided by rules which have been developed to regulate the submission of evidence at trial.

The largest consideration in whether a piece of evidence will be admitted is its relevance.[3] All relevant evidence is admissible unless prohibited by the Constitution, statute, or judicial rule. Irrelevant evidence is not admissible. To be relevant a piece of evidence must be related to an issue at trial. An attorney hoping to submit a piece of evidence must show that the evidence speaks to one of the elements of the crime, or who was responsible for the crime. Thus, in Williams's trial, evidence about the motive of attempted rape was relevant and admissible. Evidence about his past criminal record was irrelevant to the critical trial issues and therefore inadmissible. Another basic criteria necessary for admissibility is trustworthiness.[4] The desire to admit only trustworthy evidence at trial limits testimony from individuals who may not be competent to testify, such as the mentally incompetent. It is also the basis for the *best evidence rule*. This rule requires the submission of original documents at trial rather than copies, which may more easily be altered.

The rules of evidence divide evidence into different types and forms. There are two fundamental types of evidence—direct and indirect.[5] Both are admissible and both may lead to conviction. *Direct evidence* is evidence that proves a fact without having to rely on any other evidence. Because direct evidence has the ability to demonstrate a fact on its own, the fact finder does not have to draw conclusions in order to reach a fact. The only question before the fact finder when direct evidence is presented is whether it is credible. *Indirect evidence* is also known as *circumstantial evidence*. Indirect evidence does not prove a fact directly. Instead, it requires a con-clusion to be reached by the fact finder. The difference between these two types of evidence can be seen in the following example. Testimony by John Knapp that Williams was seen leaving the Y.M.C.A. with a bundle only provides indirect proof that he carried out the body of Pamela Powers. However, Kevin Sanders's testimony that he saw two white skinny legs when Williams set the bundle down provides direct evidence that there was a body in the bundle. To accept indirect evidence, the fact finder has to draw a conclusion; this is unnecessary with direct evidence.

Direct and indirect evidence can come in three different forms.[6] The first is *testimonial evidence*, which normally comes into a trial by way of a witness testifying orally under oath. Less often, testimonial evidence is presented in the form of a written deposition that was taken under oath prior to trial because the witness was unable to attend the trial. As a general rule, wit-nesses cannot give *hearsay testimony* as evidence. Hearsay is defined as sec-ondhand evidence. Hearsay evidence is testimony repeated by an individual at least once removed from the source. In other words, when a witness testifies that a friend told her that the defendant told the friend something, this constitutes hearsay. The reason why hearsay evidence is normally frowned upon is that its trustworthiness cannot be challenged through the adversarial process of cross-examination. Furthermore, the individual who originally made the statement had not taken an oath to speak the truth. There are, however, a number of exceptions to the strict application of the hearsay rule. The most familiar exception is the acceptance of the dying declaration of an individual who names his or her killer.

The rules concerning testimonial evidence generally forbid lay persons from presenting opinions as part of their testimony. Such witnesses are expected to keep their testimony strictly focused on the facts of the case. Due to this rule, witnesses are also prohibited from drawing legal conclusions in their testimony. Expert witnesses do not have this limitation placed on their testimony. Because of their specialized training, expert witnesses can give opinions that reach conclusions based on their awareness of the facts. Such opinions, which often deal with highly technical areas of medicine, engineering, forensics, psychology, and the like, serve to assist fact finders in sorting out the credibility of the facts presented at trial. In Williams's trial, for example, Dr. Leo Luka, the Polk County medical examiner, could give his opinion that based on his examination of the body, there had been an attempt at rape shortly before or after the death of Pamela Powers.

Another form of evidence is *tangible evidence*. This is nontestimonial evidence that is presented in the form of physical exhibits. Tangible evidence is normally divided into two categories—real evidence and demonstrative evidence. *Real evidence* includes physical objects that played an actual role in the crime that was committed. The clothes found at the rest stop on Interstate 80 in the *Williams* case exemplify real evidence. In order for real evidence to be admitted at trial, an attorney must be able to demonstrate that it is authentic. The need to verify the authenticity of evidence at trial has led to the development of the *chain of custody rule*. The purpose of the chain of custody rule is to require an attorney to account for where a piece of evidence has been and who has handled it since it was originally gathered. This helps to ensure that the evidence is indeed what it is claimed to be and that it has not been subject to tampering. Only after the chain of custody has been demonstrated can a piece of evidence be introduced into the trial and to the fact finder.

Demonstrative evidence, another type of tangible evidence, serves as a visual or audiovisual aid so the fact finder can better picture events involved in the crime or understand the testimony of a witness. A picture of the location where the body was located is an example of demonstrative evidence. Other examples of demonstrative evidence include diagrams of the crime scene, maps, charts, models, and x-rays.

A third form of evidence is *judicial notice*. At trial it is unnecessary to prove widely established facts, such as dates and days on the calender, when they are generally known within the community. Instead of requiring proof, the judge will instruct the jurors to accept these matters as proven.

Objections

The rules of evidence that exclude certain types of evidence and questions require that an attorney pay close attention to the opposing attorney's questions and strategies. Since most evidence comes out in the form of testimony, it is crucial for attorneys to attempt to keep inappropriate evidence from the fact finder's ears by objecting to improper questions and testimony. Objections are the procedure by which attorneys oppose the introduction of evidence, testimony, argument, or a procedure that they believe to be improper at trial. The primary reason for bringing an objection is to stop the introduction of some form of evidence that will harm an attorney's ability to win the case. An important secondary reason for objecting is to preserve the issue in the trial record for re-argument at the appellate level. For this reason, any time during the judicial proceedings against Williams when Detective Leaming testified about Williams leading police to the body, McKnight objected.

When attorneys raise an objection, they should always give the legal grounds for the objection so that it can be preserved for appeal. An attorney can object to the opposing counsel's questions on a wide variety of grounds. There are over twenty-six legal grounds for objections. These are as varied as relevance, competence, leading questions, speculation, nonresponsive volunteered answers, assuming facts not in evidence, and credibility.[7] If an objection is made, the judge must rule on the law of evidence and procedure to determine if the question is appropriate. When the judge sustains an objection, the question or evidence will be disallowed. The attorney who is denied the ability to ask a question may make an offer of proof. The offer of proof informs the judge about what the attorney hopes to accomplish with the question, in an effort to reverse the ruling. If an attorney is unhappy with the judge's ruling, the attorney may make an exception. The making of an exception preserves the issue for appeal. In effect, the exception is a claim that the judge has, in the opinion of the attorney, made an error and been notified of the possible error.[8]

Normally, objections must be timely. This means that the objection must be made prior to evidence being entered into the record.[9] Simply put, objections should be made when an inappropriate question is asked, not after the answer has been given and the damage has been done. At times it is impossible to make a timely objection; that is, a question may be appropriate but the answer may violate the law of evidence. If an objection is not made until after the jury has heard the evidence and the objection is upheld, the jury will be told to disregard the evidence. When inadmissible evidence is so prejudicial that the defendant may no longer be able to get a fair trial, then the judge may declare a mistrial.

The question as to when an attorney should object does not have a standard answer. Many opportunities to object are not exercised by seasoned attorneys. They often realize that the attorney who objects often may wear out the patience of the jurors, who may draw the conclusion that an attorney is interfering with the truth-finding process. For this reason, attorneys will often allow questions that are improperly framed to be answered, even though an objection could legitimately be raised. Experienced attorneys will also rarely raise an objection to the introduction of evidence or testimony that does not harm their case. Attorneys also take into consideration the likelihood of being successful before objecting, since objections often heighten the perceptions of jurors as to the importance of a piece of evidence.

Pretrial Motions

Prior to trial, there are several steps that hasten the processing of issues once the case comes to trial. One step is the use of pretrial motions. Pretrial motions constitute a request on the part of the prosecutor or the defense team for the judge to make legal rulings about aspects of the coming trial. The party that desires a clarification of the law will make a formal written motion—termed a pleading—arguing its position to the judge. The other party to the case will also be allowed to respond in pleadings prior to the decision. Knowing that objections and rulings on objections may be perceived in a negative way by the jury, attorneys often seek to keep evidence out of trial through the use of pretrial motions rather than waiting for the trial to start. If successful, objecting to the use of evidence in pretrial motions also has the advantage of never allowing the jury any knowledge of a damaging line of evidence. Furthermore, when a pretrial motion is unsuccessful, the issue is preserved for appeal, since a full record of the decision is made.

There are a number of different types of motions that can be filed prior to trial. Among the commonly used ones are a motion to dismiss, a motion to disqualify the judge, a motion to request a psychological examination, a motion for a change of venue, a motion for discovery, and a motion to suppress evidence.

A motion to dismiss involves a routine request by the defense for the judge to quash the indictment because it contains insufficient evidence to bind the case over for trial. Motions to dismiss are rarely successful. A motion to disqualify the judge can be made when it is believed by either party to the case that the judge will not be neutral in his or her rulings.

A motion to request a psychological examination may be made if the sanity of the defendant is at issue. This motion can be made to give both parties to the case an opportunity to have their own psychological tests done. In the trial of Robert Williams, a psychological examination was ordered by Judge James Denato after Henry McKnight filed an insanity plea with the court on April 25, 1969. Williams was examined at the Iowa Mental Health Institute to determine whether he was competent to stand trial. In the interview, the doctor told Williams that anything they discussed would not be confidential; the doctor could report anything that was said to the court. During the course of the interview, Williams told the doctor two different versions of what had happened. In his first story, Williams denied killing Pamela Powers. To elicit the second version, the doctor explained to Williams that his attorney had told the doctor that Williams had confessed to luring a young girl into his room, molesting her, killing her, and carrying her out of the Y.M.C.A. When confronted with this information, Williams told the doctor that he had given McKnight that story because that was the story that McKnight wanted to hear. After the examination, the doctor reported that Williams did not trust his attorney. He also found that Williams was sane and competent to stand trial.

Motions for a *change of venue* are made when the defense believes that a fair trial cannot be obtained in the community in which the crime took place due to pretrial publicity. The defense can request that the trial be moved to a different location. If the judge agrees, then the trial is moved to a different venue.

Motions for *discovery* are made to help the defense in preparation for trial. The discovery process helps trials to move along more quickly by heading off surprises that might lead to legal disputes and cause delays at trial. Discovery allows the defense to examine the evidence gathered by the prosecutor. This may include a list of the witnesses that the prosecution plans to call. Discovery may also require the prosecution to give the defense access to all material evidence and the opportunity to subject it to independent testing. Normally, if the defense takes advantage of discovery, the prosecutor may also examine the defense evidence. If the defense case rests on the defendant's mental capacity to support the *mens rea*, then any mental examinations done on the defendant may also be subject to discovery. This explains the doctor's notification to Williams that their discussions would not be confidential. The extent of discovery varies depending on the jurisdiction of the court. At the time of the first trial, Iowa had limited rules of discovery that only required the prosecution to give to the defense evidence that was actually going to be used in court.

A *motion to suppress* is filed when the defense believes that evidence was gathered illegally. If the judge agrees that there was indeed a violation of the law in the evidence-gathering process, then, normally, the evidence will be excluded from trial. Most cases do not involve motions to suppress evidence and they are successful in even fewer cases.[10] In the trial of Robert Williams, however, the most important pretrial motion to impact the trial and appeals process was a motion to suppress evidence. Prior to Williams being placed on trial, his attorney filed a motion on March 25, 1969, to suppress evidence. The motion asked Judge Denato to "suppress the State's evidence offered by all witnesses as to admissions against interest, statements, demonstrations and confessions made by him [Williams] while in police custody on an automobile trip from Davenport to Des Moines, Iowa, on December 26, 1968."[11] The motion also requested that all the state's evidence linked to these violations be suppressed. This evidence would include the body and any physical evidence found at the site where the body was located. The motion argued that the aforementioned evidence should be suppressed because it was gathered in violation of the Fifth Amendment right against self-incrimination and the Sixth Amendment right to counsel, applicable to the states under the Fourteenth Amendment's Due Process Clause. In effect, the defense was arguing that the State had failed to meet the burden of proving that Williams had voluntarily relinquished his rights when he cooperated with the police and led them to Pamela Power's body on the ride from Davenport to Des Moines.

Prior to a legal ruling on this motion, Judge Denato held a hearing on April 2, 1969, to help him make a determination of the facts of the case. At the hearing, the defendant and his attorneys were present, as was the prosecutor, Vincent Hanrahan. In making his decision, there were several areas where Judge Denato had the discretion to decide between two versions of the facts. The first area was whether there had been agreement not to question Williams on the trip from Davenport back to Des Moines between McKnight, who argued that there was, and Detective Leaming, who argued that there wasn't. The second factual dispute arose between Williams's contention that Detective Leaming had intermittently questioned him about the location of the body on the trip back to Des Moines and Detective Leaming's position that, although there had been conversations between him and Williams during their trip, it did not involve questioning Williams about the case. A third factual variation existed as well: Thomas Kelly and Detective Leaming disagreed over whether Leaming had denied Kelly permission to ride with Williams to Des Moines.

To clarify the defense's view of the facts, McKnight first requested and was granted a *stipulation* that if Thomas Kelly had been able to testify he would have told the court that Leaming refused to allow him to ride with Williams while he was being transported by the police. Stipulations are agreements about the facts of the case that do not have to be proven at trial, thus saving time. McKnight then called Police Chief Wendell Nichols of the Des Moines Police Department. Chief Nichols testified that McKnight, Leaming, and he were all in the same office when McKnight received a call from Williams, who had surrendered in Davenport. He went on to state that, during the phone conversation, McKnight had told Williams that officers from Des Moines were going to transport him back to

Des Moines. Furthermore, McKnight had said that the officers "would be nice to him, that they were nice people, that they weren't going to grill him or beat him around, and to come back to Des Moines with the officers and that we would talk it over in Des Moines."[12] Chief Nichols then stated that it was his understanding that Williams would be brought straight back to Des Moines. On cross-examination Prosecutor Vincent Hanrahan asked and received a negative answer as to whether there had been a specific agreement that there would be no conversation between Williams and the police on the trip back to Des Moines.

The next witness called by McKnight was John Ackerman of the Davenport Police Department. Officer Ackerman testified that he had processed Williams when he surrendered. He explained that after the arrest Williams was told his constitutional rights and indicated that he didn't wish to say anything until he talked to his attorney in Des Moines. Officer Ackerman then testified that, after his arraignment in Davenport, Williams consulted with Thomas Kelly, a Davenport attorney. He also said that it was his understanding that Detective Leaming was going to take Williams straight back to Des Moines.

Robert Williams was the next witness called by McKnight. Williams testified that in his phone conversation with McKnight after his surrender he was told not to answer any questions until he was back in Des Moines and in the presence of his attorney. He also stated that Thomas Kelly told Detective Leaming that Williams wouldn't answer any questions until he got back to Des Moines. Despite these indications that he would not cooperate with the police, Williams testified that Detective Leaming periodically questioned him about the location of the body. Twice during the trip, Williams said that Detective Leaming had told him that the police knew the body was somewhere near Mitchellville. He also testified that Detective Leaming told him that McKnight wasn't feeling well and that his heart was bothering him. He went on to state that Detective Leaming had said, "that I was supposed to show them where the body was, and there would be a waste of time to go all the way to Des Moines to get you [McKnight] and come back, and that's what we would have to do, probably be on the road all hours of the night, and this would be bad for your [McKnight's] health."[13]

To prove the State's version of the facts, Vincent Hanrahan called Cleatus Leaming of the Des Moines Police Department. Detective Leaming testified that he had overheard the phone conversation between McKnight and Williams, but stated that he had made no agreement not to interrogate or have conversations with Williams on the trip back to Des Moines from Davenport. He went on to tell the court that, upon taking custody of Williams, he advised the defendant of his rights and informed him that he knew he was represented by McKnight and Kelly. He also told Williams that they would be visiting on the trip back to Des Moines. When asked, he told the court that at no time did Thomas Kelly ask to accompany Williams back to

Des Moines and that Williams also made no such request. During the trip, Detective Leaming indicated that, while not interrogating Williams, he did have conversations with him about a variety of subjects such as religion, what acquaintances of Williams thought about him, youth groups, and music. He also explained that Williams had initiated the conversations about the case. When asked if Williams had ever indicated that he did not want to talk, Detective Leaming answered *no*. Detective Leaming did say that Williams had not specifically stated that he wanted an attorney present. Instead, he had indicated that he would tell the whole story when he saw McKnight in Des Moines. Detective Leaming then explained how Williams voluntarily led them to two locations—the Grinnell rest stop and a Skelly gas station in Grinnell—where Williams indicated evidence had been hidden.

Upon cross-examination Detective Leaming told the court that despite Williams's remark concerning future cooperation once in contact with McKnight, Leaming continued to attempt to elicit whatever information he could out of Williams during the trip. Despite being in the same room, Detective Leaming claimed not to have overheard the content of the phone conversation between Williams and McKnight. He denied any agreement not to question Williams on the trip. He disputed Williams's claim that he had told Williams that McKnight was having health problems. He also denied the claim that Thomas Kelly had told him that Williams should not be questioned until he contacted his attorney in Des Moines. Detective Leaming told the court that he had not asked Williams about the case. Instead, he testified that he had told Williams things. When asked what type of things, Detective Leaming replied:

I said to Mr. Williams, I said, "Reverend, I'm going to tell you something. I don't want you to answer me, but I want you to think about it when we're driving down the road." I said, "I want you to observe the weather. It's raining and it's sleeting and it's freezing. Visibility is very poor. They are predicting snow for tonight. I think that we're going right past where that body is, and if we should stop and find out where it is on the way in, her parents are going to be able to have a good Christian burial for their little daughter. If we don't and it does snow and if you're the only person that knows where this is and if you have only been there once, it's very possible that with snow on the ground you might not be able to find it. Now I just want you to think about that when we're driving down the road." That's all I said.[14]

Detective Leaming went on to say that this statement was said close to Davenport and that as they approached Mitchellville Williams volunteered to take them to the body.

The purpose behind the hearing was to allow Judge Denato to determine what subjective facts he accepted and to apply the proper procedural law to them. By doing so, he could make a ruling on whether there were any inadmissible facts that had to be suppressed during the trial. Judge Denato stated that the facts showed that there was an agreement between McKnight and the Des Moines police that Williams would not talk to the police until after he had consulted with McKnight. He went on to state that the facts also show that judicial proceedings had begun against Williams prior to the trip between Davenport and Des Moines. This combination of facts meant that the trip had to be considered a critical stage in the proceedings against Williams.

Judge Denato then ruled that, regardless of any agreement to limit the ability of the police to question Williams during the trip, no evidence resulting from the trip would be suppressed. This was because Judge Denato accepted as a fact that Williams voluntarily gave information to the police after waiving his right to have an attorney present. Judge Denato also found that Williams had adequately been informed of his rights and understood them. In the words of Judge Denato: "The time element involved on the trip, the general circumstances of it, and more importantly the absence on the Defendant's part of any assertion of his right to desire not to give information absent the presence of his attorney, are the main foundations for the Court's conclusion that he voluntarily waived such right."[15]

Judge Denato's finding that Williams had waived his rights so closely intertwined the facts and the procedural law that it made the actual facts irrelevant with regard to the two other factual disputes. This was because, regardless of whether Leaming had questioned Williams about the case and/ or denied to Kelly the chance to accompany Williams on the ride back to Des Moines, Williams could still voluntarily waive his rights. While not settling with finality either of the two remaining factual questions, Judge Denato did shed some light on what he believed to be an accurate reflection of one of the issues by stating that "the Court is not entirely convinced that Chief of Detectives Leaming testified with complete candor at this hearing, regarding the 'agreement' with Defendant's attorney." Judge Denato added that all of his findings were made "beyond a reasonable doubt."[16] Judge Denato's ruling, then, allowed all the evidence in question to be admitted.

Prior to trial there also may be a *pretrial conference* between both attorneys and the judge. The purpose of pretrial conferences is to clarify issues and procedures in order to promote a fair trial without delays.[17] At this conference, the judge may set the date of the trial and try to establish the approximate length of the trial, based on the attorneys' assessment of how much evidence they will be presenting. The judge may also explain the procedures that should be followed for marking documents and exhibits in order to limit confusion over what is being placed on record. At the pretrial conference any stipulations made by either attorney will also be recognized. In the *Williams* trial, both attorneys accepted as fact that Robert Williams was an escapee from the Fulton State Mental Hospital at the time the crime took place.

Plea Bargains

After pretrial motions, the trial date is set. In 80–90 percent of felony cases—the percentage is even higher in misdemeanor cases—there is no trial due to a *plea bargain*.[18] Plea bargains create a huge funneling effect on the number of criminal cases that actually go to trial.

Plea bargains can be made at any stage of the process, but most often they are struck shortly before trial after both sides have a full understanding of what evidence will and will not be admissible at trial. The prevalence of plea bargaining may be explained by the benefits that all the sides derive from the practice. Plea bargains are attractive because they give each player involved, including the defendant, an acceptable resolution of the case. For defendants, plea bargains almost always guarantee a less severe penalty than they would receive if they were convicted at trial. For prosecutors, plea bargains ensure that even when their evidence may have been weak, punishment will follow with no chance of an appeal. One additional advantage that all the attorneys and the judge receive from plea bargains is the quick disposition of cases. If there is no agreement on a plea bargain, as in the *Williams* case, the case will move on to trial.

Burden of Proof

In criminal cases, the State, which prosecutes, has to meet the *burden of proof*. The standard of proof that must be met for a guilty verdict in a criminal case is a finding of guilty beyond a reasonable doubt. While this standard eludes precise definition, there is agreement that defendants do not have to prove their innocence to be found not guilty. It is enough for defendants to raise doubts about their guilt. For the fact finder, this burden of proof does not require a 100 percent belief that the defendant committed the crime before a guilty verdict can be returned; if there are any reasonable doubts, however, the fact finder should not return a guilty verdict.

Trial Strategy

Because the burden of proof rests on the State, the State faces a different set of expectations in criminal trials than defense attorneys do. It is incumbent on the prosecutor to present a set of facts that establishes that a crime did indeed happen and that the defendant was responsible for that crime. Defense attorneys, on the other hand, can draw on several strategies to attempt to win the case. One of these is to claim that the prosecution has not met its burden of proof. Using this strategy, the defense attorney does not have to present any evidence or witnesses. The defense may be able to win the case by picking apart the evidence presented by the prosecutor or by challenging the credibility of the State's witnesses. If the prosecution successfully shows that a crime was indeed committed, the defense can also deny that the defendant was involved in the crime. While asserting that the defendant is innocent, the defense does not have to offer any alternative theories about who committed the crime. Defendants don't even have to take the stand to assert their innocence.

Justice in a criminal trial depends on the ability of the adversarial system to develop all the evidence that is legally relevant to the resolution of the case. Through the evidence presented at trial, the subjective facts that will be accepted by the fact finder are developed. It is incredibly important for the attorneys to enter all relevant evidence into the record of the trial since this is the record that will be used throughout the appeals process. Judges help to protect against the admittance of irrelevant evidence through their application of the rules of evidence. It is also important to fully develop the facts of a case at trial because appellate judges are normally hesitant to over-rule trial judges and juries on questions of fact, since they have not had the benefit of hearing the witnesses and seeing their demeanor as they testified. The bottom line for attorneys planning their trial strategy is that if they believe a fact will be helpful to their case, they should enter it into the record.

Because of the importance of bringing out all the facts that may help win a case, attorneys normally put considerable time and effort into planning the presentation of their case. Getting ready for trial includes identifying and interviewing witnesses. To avoid surprises, a good attorney will also explore the possibility that potential witnesses may be biased or prejudiced against one of the parties to the case. If attorneys don't want to present all possible witnesses, they must determine which witnesses will seem most credible and subpoena those who will present the strongest case for their side. Attorneys also have to decide in what order to present the evidence to build the strongest possible case.

Attorneys do prepare witnesses to testify. This begins with an explanation of the role of the witnesses at trial and an overview of trial procedures. The preparation of witnesses has two separate goals.[19] The first is to help wit-nesses to testify in as much detail as possible. This does not mean that attorneys tell witnesses what to say, but they need to know what the answers will be to the questions they ask of their own witnesses. To that end, wit-nesses should be told what questions they will be asked at trial so that there are no surprises. It may also be beneficial to explain to witnesses the theory of the case and the purpose of their testimony. Witnesses should be told that as the case evolves there may be a need to change the precise questions they are asked to bring out any information that is important to the trial strategy. When witnesses are going to be testifying about exhibits that will be entered into the record, they need to have access to them prior to trial so they will be comfortable using them. Attorneys may also prepare their witnesses by role-playing a mock cross-examination by the opposing attorney. Attorneys should explain their role in protecting the witness from the opposing attorney. All this preparatory work should be done prior to the trial, so that if a witness needs to alter his testimony, he will have adequate time to incorporate the attorney's suggestions.

A second goal in witness preparation is to help the witness to appear credible. This can be accomplished in a number of ways. One of the simplest is telling the witness what clothes to wear while testifying. It may also be beneficial to tell witnesses the importance of making eye contact with the judge, jury, and attorney during the examination. Witnesses should also be forewarned about the need to appear honest and sincere, not to stretch the truth, not to speculate in their testimony, not to answer questions if they don't know the answer, and not to lose control of their temper.

THE TRIAL PROCESS

Despite the relative rarity of criminal trials, the American public is more familiar with trials than any other step in the criminal justice process. Even though criminal trials are a rarity in the legal system, jury trials in criminal cases are even rarer. Only 5 percent of all felony cases are settled by jury trials nationwide and in Des Moines, Iowa, where Robert Williams was put on trial, only 8 percent of felony cases are resolved by use of jury trials.[20] The actual process of a trial will vary, depending on the jurisdiction in which it takes place, but the general steps are as follows:

1. The defendant must choose between a judge or a jury trial.

2. If a jury trial is selected, the jury must be picked.

3. The prosecutor gives the State's opening statement.

4. The defense counsel gives an opening statement.

5. The prosecutor presents the State's case.

6. The defense counsel presents the defense's case.

7. Both sides are allowed to present rebuttal evidence.

8. The prosecutor makes a closing statement.

9. The defense counsel makes a closing statement.

10. The prosecution makes a final closing statement in response to the defense counsel's closing statement.

11. If a jury was selected, the judge must give it instructions.

12. Deliberations are conducted by either the judge or jury.

13. The verdict is announced.

Jury Selection

The determination of whether the verdict will be decided by a judge or a jury is left up to the defendant. Robert Williams chose to have his fate decided by a jury. Iowa required a twelve-person jury and a unanimous verdict in order to convict.

The jury's role is to determine the guilt or innocence of the defendant. In reaching its decision, the jury is supposed to be guided by two primary considerations: (1) the facts of the case as developed in testimony and evidence and (2) the law of the case as explained by the judge. In making their decision, jurors have a lot of leeway in deciding the subjective facts. They are also given considerable freedom in interpreting the legal instructions given to them by the judge. This freedom is enhanced because when they reach a verdict neither the jury as a whole nor individual jurors have to explain their actions. There will be no report issued explaining which witnesses were considered unbelievable, which evidence seemed credible, or how strictly they applied the law to the facts of the case.

Because the jury is free to interpret the subjective facts and substantive law, both the prosecutor and the defense attorney will try to select jurors who may be disposed to accepting their version of the facts and law. Many attorneys believe that trials can be won or lost based on the jury that is selected.[21] While attorneys for each side try to select a jury that will be favorable to the result they seek, the trial court works to seat a "fair" jury. This entails several steps, including compiling a master list of jurors, the venire, and the voir dire.

The pool of prospective jurors is established by developing a *master list of possible jurors.* Most jurisdictions rely on voter registration lists to develop their master lists of prospective jurors. Increasingly, jurisdictions are also relying on additional sources, other than voters, such as lists from the Census rolls, driver's licenses, and taxpayers, to create a more inclusive master list, since voter registration lists tend to underrepresent the poor, the young, the less educated, and racial minorities.

The second stage in jury selection is the *venire.* The venire is made up of individuals whose names are drawn from the master list. Each member of the venire receives a summons to appear for possible jury service. Those who appear at the courthouse are divided into a number of different panels for different prospective trials. Each panel generally has three or four times as many people as needed for the actual jury. The selection process then moves on to the next stage, the *voir dire.*

The voir dire is a method of trying to determine if prospective jurors have biases or prejudices that would limit their ability to objectively consider the evidence. Voir dire is usually translated as "to speak the truth." During the voir dire, prospective jurors are subjected to a series of questions. Usually the questions are presented by the attorneys in state courts and the judge in federal courts.[22] Iowa's normal practice, however, was to have the judge ask questions during the voir dire. Prospective jurors are urged to answer honestly to help the judge and the attorneys determine whether they will show any bias in the trial based on preconceived views. Any prospective juror who shows an inability to examine the evidence with impartiality may be challenged by either of the attorneys with cause. If the judge agrees that there is cause to believe that the prospective juror will not be able to objectively examine the evidence, the individual will be dismissed. It is not uncommon for potential jurors to be removed for specific bias, such as knowing someone involved in the trial, or nonspecific bias, such as a general bias like racism that limits their ability to remain open-minded. There is no limit to how many individuals may be challenged and excused for cause.

At the end of the voir dire process, each attorney is also given a number of *peremptory challenges.* The number of these challenges varies from case to case, depending on the seriousness of the charges. In Iowa, both sides in a murder trial are given eight peremptory challenges. In exercising a peremptory challenge, attorneys do not need a reason to dismiss a prospective juror. Peremptory challenges allow both attorneys to exercise any hunches they have about individuals within the panel whom they believe may be showing leanings toward the other side.

Voir dire serves a larger purpose than just trying to determine any biases that the prospective jurors may display. Voir dire also serves an educational function by explaining the important role that a jury plays in the judicial process and the necessity of each one of them to keep an open mind and be fair. After the voir dire and peremptory challenges were completed in the *Williams* trial, the attorneys were left with a panel of seven men, five women, and three alternates.

Opening Statements

The trial of Robert Williams began on April 30, 1969. The first step at trial is the opening statements. There are several purposes for the opening statement.[23] One is to inform the jury about the case. A second is to persuade the jury about the merits of the case. A third is to try to gain sympathy from the jury. If the opening statements are clear, they will provide the jurors with a road map for the rest of the trial, making it easier for them to follow the evidence. By law, the prosecution is always the first to give an opening statement in criminal trials. The prosecution is followed by the defense counsel, but the defense counsel does not have to give an opening statement, or may postpone it until after the prosecution has rested its case.

Although most judges give wide latitude to attorneys in the presentation of opening statements, there are some basic rules concerning what can be included.[24] All facts that an attorney can prove at trial can be included in opening statements. An attorney will want to include the major facts of the case in order to provide an overview of what the jury should pay attention to throughout the trial. Although it will be the duty of the judge to explain the applicable law to the jury before it begins its deliberations, the attorneys may make short references to the law to help the jury understand their case. For example, either attorney may want to explain the burden of proof in the case or the elements that must be proven in order for the jury to convict. While attorneys are not allowed to make arguments in their opening statements, they may present theories about the case at this time. Any theory must be prefaced by remarks such as, "The evidence will show," but attorneys are not allowed to draw conclusions without placing those conclusions within the context of facts that will be developed at trial. Conclusions and arguments about what the evidence has shown are reserved for closing arguments—after all evidence has been presented.

Direct Examination

In criminal trials, the prosecution is the first to present its case. This is done primarily through the presentation of witnesses subjected to direct examination. Attendance of witnesses may be either voluntary or by command of the court. If attorneys believe that a witness may not voluntarily make an appearance at the trial, they may subpoena the individual, compelling the witness to appear. Once the subpoena is served, the witness must testify or risk being found in contempt of the court and punished for that contempt. Attorneys can also obtain a *subpoena duces tecum* in order to command that documents be brought to trial to be entered into the record.

In direct examination, an attorney calls a witness and after she swears to tell the truth, the attorney attempts through questioning to draw out the relevant facts to allow the fact finder to reach the desired verdict. Direct examination has two primary goals—to make testimony clear to the fact finder and to make it memorable.[25] When considering what to include in direct testimony, attorneys planning their strategy for trial must strike a delicate balance, presenting a full factual picture that advances a strong argument to achieve the desired result, but not dizzying the jury with so many facts that they become bored and quit paying attention. In order to balance these two concerns, attorneys must keep a sharp eye on the issue of relevance and ask whether the introduction of additional evidence is really necessary to prove their case. As noted earlier, attorneys must also decide in what order to present witnesses and evidence. The order can be crucial to making the evidence memorable. Evidence must be given to the fact finder in an order that is understandable and that makes sense.

Direct testimony is given through a series of questions presented by the attorney, followed by the answers of the witnesses. This format limits the testimony to those items that are relevant to the case. Questions can take a variety of forms, which widen or narrow the latitude given to witnesses in their answers. *Open, narrative questions,* such as "Please tell the court everything that happened leading up to Pamela's disappearance," allow witnesses a great deal of freedom to tell their own story. Narrative questions often enhance the credibility of a witness, since the fact finder sees that witnesses are telling the story in their own words. However, when asking narrative questions, the attorney must make sure that the witness stays on track and does not digress, boring the fact finder.

In contrast to narrative questions, *closed questions* are worded so as to place limits on the witness' response. The purpose of a closed question is to elicit a particular fact from the witness. An example would be, "Can you identify the man you saw leaving the Y.M.C.A.?"

Generally, the attorney who calls the witness for direct examination cannot ask *leading questions.* Leading questions typically can be answered with a simple *yes* or *no.* As an example, an attorney may ask, "And when you saw Mr. Williams leave the Y.M.C.A., is it correct that you saw him drive off in a 1959 Buick?" This form of direct examination would not be allowed, since it suggests an answer and effectively gives the attorney—rather than the witness—an opportunity to testify.

Cross-Examination

After a witness has been subjected to direct examination by the attorney who called that witness, the opposing counsel has an opportunity to cross-examine the witness. Not all witnesses are subjected to cross-examination. The decision as to whether a witness will be cross-examined is left up to each attorney. Chances are that if a witness has not damaged the opposing attorneys' case, there will be no cross-examination. If, however, the witness has harmed the opposing attorneys' case and the attorneys believe that they might be able to cast doubts on the testimony, there is incentive to cross-examine. One caveat to this general rule is that cross-examination is not helpful when harmful testimony consists of facts that can't be disputed.

Cross-examination has several purposes. The most important is to give opposing attorneys a chance to impeach witnesses by challenging the version of the facts to which they have testified and/or to question the credibility of witnesses.[26] If, during cross-examination, an attorney can raise doubts about what witnesses actually observed or their ability or desire to tell the truth, it may sway the fact finder to discount the witness' testimony. Witnesses may therefore expect that the accuracy of their memory will be challenged during cross-examination. If witnesses testify in a manner inconsistent with either earlier statements or other evidence entered into the record or they omit some facts they had earlier stated, they can expect to be cross-examined on these points.

There are a variety of methods of impeaching the credibility of a witness.[27]

One is to draw the fact finder's attention to negative character traits that may influence witnesses' willingness to tell the truth, such as exposing past criminal convictions. A second is to demonstrate that witnesses have biases, interests, motives, or prejudices that may interfere with their ability to be objective. If attorneys believe that a witness' version of the facts supports their case, that's another reason to conduct a cross-examination. In that case, they will seek to cross-examine on those points in order to bolster their arguments.

The scope of questioning allowed during cross-examination differs from that allowed during direct examination. For example, the scope of questioning in cross-examination is narrower, usually limited to issues that came out during direct examination. One exception is the attempt to attack the credibility of a witness. As with other aspects of which evidence is allowed at trial, the judge determines the latitude of the scope of questioning in cross-examination. If a judge will not allow attorneys to investigate new areas with a witness during cross-examination, that witness can later be called for direct examination by those attorneys. An attorney can also attack the credibility of a witness by calling on direct-examination character witnesses to testify against a witness' integrity.

Another difference between direct- and cross-examination is that during cross-examination an attorney can ask leading questions. Leading questions in cross-examination are preferred because it allows the attorney to control the flow of information by not allowing the witness to interject voluntary statements that may harm the attorney's strategy. Bergman points to the important role that leading questions can play in cross-examination. He states:

[I]f a leading question cannot force a witness to change testimony, it often results in a witness' agreeing to accept the attorney's characterization of testimony. The reason is that truth can be very complex. There may be various ways to describe an event, each a little different yet each truthful. As the cross examiner, you want the fact finder aware of your version. When your version is confidently and assertively put to a witness in the form of a leading question, the witness is likely to set aside the other version and agree to yours.[28]

Limiting the response of a witness on cross-examination is so important that in Irving Younger's list of the ten commandments for cross-examination he specifically states that an attorney should never ask anything but a leading question and that a witness should never be permitted to explain anything.[29] Despite strong reasons not to use them, open questions can be asked during cross-examination and are sometimes used when an attorney has nothing but suspicions and finds it necessary to go on a fishing expedition. Such questions, do, however, present dangers.

Redirect Examination

After an attorney has cross-examined an adverse witness called by the opposing attorney, the attorney who initially called the witness has an opportunity for redirect examination. The scope of the redirect examination is limited to those subjects brought out in cross-examination. The purpose of redirect examination is to clarify any discrepancies in the testimony that may have been brought up during cross-examination or to rehabilitate the credibility of the witness. In this way, any doubts created in the jury's mind about the witness or her testimony will hopefully be resolved. When redirect examination is completed, the opposing counsel has the opportunity to recross-examine the witness. Once again, the scope of this examination, if it takes place, is limited only to those subjects brought out in redirect examination. This process of narrowing the scope of examination can continue until neither side has further questions or the judge believes that it is no longer useful.

The Prosecution's Case

In making the case for the prosecution, Assistant Polk County Attorney Vincent Hanrahan sought to use his witnesses during direct examination to create a historical storyline to explain the sequence of events surrounding the disappearance of Pamela Powers. Since the defense did not dispute the prosecution's version of these events, McKnight did not cross-examine the witnesses. Vincent Hanrahan's first witness was Pamela's mother, Nelda Powers, who described the last moments that she spent with Pamela at the wrestling tournament at the Y.M.C.A. on December 24, 1968. Mrs. Powers explained that Pamela had received permission to buy some candy. When she came back with the candy, Pamela remembered that she had been playing with a puppy and asked if she could wash her hands. Mrs. Powers said she last saw Pamela when she gave her permission to wash her hands. She then explained to the court that when Pamela failed to return, the family began to search the building for her. They continued until they were told around a half-hour later that Pamela was gone.

Following Mrs. Powers, Pamela's father, Merlin Powers, provided additional testimony about Pamela's disappearance. He told the court that he had left Pamela and Mrs. Powers at the Y.M.C.A. while he ran an errand with his oldest daughter. When he came back, Pamela was not sitting with her mom, so they went to look for her. He then explained how he and others had searched the Y.M.C.A. to no avail and then called the police. When Mr. and Mrs. Powers were done testifying, they sat in the back of the courtroom and listened to the other testimony. They were comforted there by the presence of their pastor, the Reverend Robert Kem of St. Andrew's Episcopal Church. Reverend Kem also gave testimony that he was the one who identified Pamela's body after its discovery.

The next group of witnesses for the prosecution all testified about seeing Williams leave the Y.M.C.A. The first of these witnesses was Donald Hanna. Donald Hanna, the physical education director of the Y.M.C.A., was responsible for overseeing the wrestling tournament in which Mark Powers, Pamela's brother, was participating. Hanna had been informed of the disappearance of Pamela Powers and was helping to search for her when he saw Williams in the lobby. Williams was carrying a bundle as he walked through the lobby. When Williams took the bundle outside to a waiting car, Hanna asked John Knapp, an employee at the Y.M.C.A., to check what was in the bundle. When Hanna saw Williams push Knapp away so he could get into his car, Hanna went outside to see what was going on. By the time he got outside, Williams was already in his car and refused to open the door. Hanna tried to hang onto the door handle as Williams drove off, but the car was moving too fast, so he had to let go. Hanna remembered the license plate number of the car and immediately called the police.

Fred Thompson, another employee of the Y.M.C.A., was called to testify next. He testified that on December 24, 1968, he was at the Y.M.C.A. and that he saw Williams as he got off the elevator. He said that Williams was carrying a bundle and that he moved over to give Williams room to pass by.

John Knapp, who lived and worked at the Y.M.C.A. as a desk clerk and security officer, also testified about what he had witnessed. He told the court that he had known Williams prior to the events of that day. He explained that he saw Williams walk through the lobby of the Y.M.C.A. with a bundle in his arms. Knapp asked Williams where he was going and what he had in the bundle. Williams replied that he had a mannequin. Williams then had Kevin Sanders open the door to the building and the passenger door to a car waiting outside. After placing the bundle in the car, Williams went around and opened the driver's-side door. Knapp then followed Williams outside to the car, which was parked at the curb on Locust Street on the south side of the building. Knapp then said, "Let me see what you have in the car, let me see what you have got." Williams replied, "I'll show it to you later. I've got to go, I'll be back in a few minutes."[30] Then Williams shoved Knapp and got in the car. At that time, Don Hanna came out to lend assistance, but Williams drove off as they tried to open the doors. They then called the police and gave them the license plate number.

Kevin Sanders, who was 13 years old and a member of the Y.M.C.A. in December of 1968, was also called as a witness by the prosecution. Sanders testified that he opened the door of the Y.M.C.A. for Williams, who was carrying a bundle. Williams then asked Sanders if he would also open his car door and Sanders complied with the request. When Sanders opened the car door, Williams placed the bundle inside the car and Sanders saw a pair of skinny white legs that were exposed.

The next set of witnesses called by the prosecution gave testimony about Williams's actions during his flight from Des Moines. One of these witnesses was Merle C. Killinger, a highway commission employee who was a maintenance man for interstate rest stops. Mr. Killinger testified that, while he was in a men's room at a rest stop on Interstate 80 three miles east of Grinnell, he found several items of clothing, some of which were identified as Pamela's, and a blanket. Two brothers, James and Dan Cupples, both testified that Williams stopped at their filling station in Grinnell for gas at about dusk on December 24. They also told the court that they saw Williams a second time when he was being transported from Davenport to Des Moines by the police.

A final group of prosecution witnesses included several of the police officers involved in the case and Dr. Leo Luka, the Polk County medical examiner. The police officers included John Ackerman of the Davenport police, who testified about Williams's surrender, arrest, and initial appearance in Davenport. One of the major points that the prosecution made with Officer Ackerman's testimony was that Williams had been warned of his constitutional rights at the time of arrest and at the initial appearance. Officer Ackerman also testified that Williams had been given access to Thomas Kelly, the Davenport attorney. McKnight used cross-examination of Officer Ackerman to show that Williams did not want to cooperate with authorities, even when asked direct questions about the case. McKnight asked Officer Ackerman if he had asked Williams any questions regarding the case and Ackerman answered, "I told him that we worried about the safety and the health of the little girl, and if she was alive and if she was in the area, we would like to know so that we could get help to her."[31] Officer Ackerman then stated that Williams did not reply to the question except to say that his lawyer knew.

The most important witness for the State was Detective Cleatus Leaming. Detective Leaming testified about the long sequence of events involving him and Williams that took place on December 26, 1968. He said that he first met Williams in Davenport when he and Officer Arthur Nelson arrived to pick Williams up for the trip back to Des Moines. At that time Thomas Kelly introduced Williams to the officers. Detective Leaming then informed Williams of his constitutional rights. He told Williams that he knew Williams had arranged for legal representation. He also told Williams that on the trip back the two of them would be visiting. He then allowed Williams to talk to Thomas Kelly in private. After the conversation, Williams was handcuffed with his hands behind his back and then placed in the rear seat of the car for the return trip. Detective Leaming also got in the back seat, while Officer Nelson got up front to drive.

Detective Leaming then discussed the trip back to Des Moines. He said

that they stopped on the west edge of Davenport to get gas and then headed
west on Interstate 80. At this point, McKnight objected to any further testimony concerning conversations between Williams and Detective Leaming,
since he still believed that they were inadmissible due to constitutional violations. The objection was overruled and the court let stand a continuing
objection to that particular line of questioning. Detective Leaming continued to answer questions about the trip. He said that Williams had initiated
a conversation by asking if Leaming hated him and wanted to kill him.
Detective Leaming replied that he considered Williams just another prisoner.
Detective Leaming told Williams that he had religious training and was more
likely to pray for Williams than injure him in any way. The conversation
with Williams continued and covered a variety of subjects, including intelligence, whether his room at the Y.M.C.A. had been checked for fingerprints, religion, police procedures, music, and organizing youth groups.
Eventually, Detective Leaming called Williams "Reverend" and gave the
following speech:

"I want to give you something to think about while we're travelling down the road."
I said, "Number one, I want you to observe the weather conditions, it's raining, it's
sleeting, it's freezing, driving is very treacherous, visibility is poor, it's going to be
dark early this evening. They are predicting several inches of snow for tonight, and
I feel that you yourself are the only person that knows where this little girl's body
is, that you yourself have only been there once, and if you get a snow on top of it
you yourself may be unable to find it. And, since we will be going right past the area
on the way into Des Moines, I feel that we could stop and locate the body, that the
parents of this little girl should be entitled to a Christian burial for the little girl who
was snatched away from them on Christmas eve and murdered. And I feel we should
stop and locate it on the way in rather than waiting until the morning and trying to
come back out after a snow storm and possibly not being able to find it at all. . . . I
do not want you to answer me, I don't want to discuss it any further. Just think
about it as we're riding down the road."[32]

Detective Leaming went on and told the court that, as the car approached
the Grinnell exit, Williams asked if the police had found Pamela's shoes.
Detective Leaming replied that he was not sure; he only knew that some
articles of clothing had been found at the Grinnell rest area. Williams then
explained that he had not placed the shoes with the rest of the clothes.
Instead, when he stopped to buy gas, he dropped the shoes in a box behind
the station. They then drove to the gas station to which Williams had
pointed, but when they inspected the area behind the gas station the shoes
couldn't be located. Detective Leaming said that while looking for the shoes
he got coffee for all three men and they took Williams's handcuffs off. After
twenty minutes or so, the handcuffs were put back on Williams and they all
got back in the car and started driving west again. As soon as they got back
on the interstate, Williams asked if they had found the blanket. Detective

Leaming replied that he wasn't sure, but that if it was in the trash receptacle with the other items, it had been found. Williams said it was in a different place in the men's room. At that time they were just going past the rest stop, so they turned around and went back to check on the blanket, but it had already been located. They then got back in the car and headed west once again.

Detective Leaming testified that he and Williams continued to have conversations about the same topics as earlier until they were east of Mitchellville. At that point, Williams said, "I am going to show you where the body is."[33] Williams then showed Officer Nelson where to turn off the interstate at the Mitchellville exit. Williams then continued to give instructions until he guided them to the location of the body. Detective Leaming described the body as it was found, stating:

[I]t was a white female, appeared to be frozen, her legs were in a drawn up position, she was lying in a ditch beside of a cement culvert, kind of down in the ditch, weeds were kind of pulled over her. She had snow on her, she was laying with her head pretty much toward the north and her head was back in such a position that from the road you could not see her face. She was disrobed with exception of a small T-shirt.[34]

Detective Leaming next testified that when he got back into the car with Williams the following conversation took place between the two:

"What did she look like?" I told him she looked as if she was frozen and looked like she was dead. He asked me if I saw her face and I told him no, I didn't and he asked me to go back and look at her face, which I did. And I returned to the car, he asked me what I observed about her face. I asked him what he meant. He said, "Well, how did she look!" I said, "Well, there would appear to me to be blood around her mouth," and he said, "Yes. Did you notice any discoloration around her eyes?" I said yes. I did, quite a little. He said, "What does that tell you about the way she died?" I said, "Well in her frozen condition, me not being a doctor, I can't tell too much about it." He said, "Well you have had a great deal of experience in these sort of things, surely this should tell you something about the way she died." I said, "Well, it would still have to be my opinion that she was either strangled or smothered," and he nodded his head, didn't say anything.[35]

Detective Leaming then told the court that Williams explained to him that he had planned on dumping everything that he had left the Y.M.C.A. with where the body was found, but when he was doing it the body fell out of the blanket. At that time he got spooked by a car at a house that was within sight and feared that someone might come check up on him so he put the body in the ditch and then dropped everything else off down the road at the rest stop.

Henry McKnight used his cross-examination to try to accomplish two main goals. The first was to show that there had been an agreement between him and Detective Leaming not to question Williams on the trip between Davenport and Des Moines. The second was to show that an interrogation had, in fact, taken place. Detective Leaming admitted that he was in the same room as McKnight when he was talking to Williams on the phone. He said that he was about three feet from McKnight. Detective Leaming then testified that, although he had heard parts of the conversation, he had not heard McKnight tell Williams that he would make no statement until he was back in Des Moines with his attorney. Detective Leaming was then asked if he had told Williams that McKnight's health was bad and he answered *no*. Detective Leaming next denied that he interrogated Williams on the trip. After persistent questioning by McKnight, Detective Leaming finally told the court that he was hoping to get all the information he could out of Williams before they got back to McKnight.

On redirect examination, Detective Leaming showed remarkable detail in his memory of the phone conversation he overheard between McKnight and Williams in a number of areas other than the agreement that McKnight believed had been made. In answering Hanrahan's questions, Detective Leaming told the court that he heard McKnight tell Williams that he would have to tell the officers where the body was. He also said that McKnight indicated to him during the conversation that Williams was scared that he was going to be harmed on the trip. After hearing this, Detective Leaming told McKnight that he would personally go and get Williams. He testified that McKnight then told Williams "Mr. Leaming is coming after you . . . I know this man personally. He's a fine man and he won't let any harm come to you."[36]

The prosecutor also called Des Moines Police Officer Arthur Nelson, who had driven the car in which Williams was transported. He wanted to use Officer Nelson as an additional witness to testify that that Williams had known his rights before the trip began and that he had not been coerced into revealing where the body was located. The testimony of Detective Leaming was more influential than that of Detective Nelson because Nelson told the court that he could not hear most of the conversations between Leaming and Williams, since Williams spoke in such low tones. In a couple of areas, the testimony of these two officers was contradictory. One difference in their stories was that Officer Nelson testified that when they were leaving Davenport, Detective Leaming asked Williams to think about telling them where the body was, while Leaming, in his testimony, had denied asking a direct question. Detective Leaming had also testified that Williams had spontaneously offered to lead the detectives to where he had discarded Pamela's shoes after he saw the gas station where he had dumped them. Officer Nelson, on the other hand, testified that they had asked Williams if the shoes had been with the other clothes that had been left at the Grinnell rest area. When Williams responded that they weren't, he added that he had placed them behind a gas station off the Grinnell exit. According to Nelson, they then asked what filling station were the shoes hidden at and where.

In response to questions, Officer Nelson told the court that Williams had informed them that he would give them directions to the body. After a wrong turn and an initial mistake in the location, Williams led them to a second location. Once they got there, a highway patrolman who had been following them in a separate car got out and used a spotlight to look in the ditch for the body. They didn't see anything with the spotlight so they began to look along the slope of the ditch. After they searched for a while, Williams told Officer Nelson that he may have made another mistake in the location. They were getting ready to leave when one of the men conducting the search said that he had found it and flashed his light on it.

The final witness called by the State was Dr. Leo Luka, the Polk County medical examiner. Dr. Luka testified that the autopsy revealed that Pamela had been subjected to a sexual assault and that she had been smothered to death. This piece of information was crucial to the State being able to prove the elements of first-degree murder. The State then rested its case.

The Defense Case

When the prosecution finishes presenting its case, it is the defense attorney's opportunity. Prior to presenting their own case, defense attorneys will often, as a matter of form, ask for a *directed verdict* from the judge. This is a request for the judge to declare that the prosecution did not present sufficient evidence for a prima facie case to be made against the defendant. The defense attorney then asks the judge to declare that the trial cannot continue and the defendant must be declared not guilty of the charges. Judges rarely grant motions for directed verdicts, so the defense is forced to proceed with its own case. The presentation of the defense case follows the same process as that of the prosecution. It starts with the defense calling its witnesses for direct examination; the prosecution then has the opportunity for cross-examination, followed by redirect and recross until the attorneys are satisfied.

The defense attorney has one decision to make that presents special problems not confronted by the prosecution. That is whether the defense should call the defendant as a witness. Due to the Fifth Amendment right against self-incrimination, defendants cannot be forced to testify. The decision to testify is left up to the defendant in consultation with counsel. This is a difficult decision to make. On the one hand, the jury expects to hear a claim of innocence from the defendant to help in assessing the evidence. If the defendant in a criminal case doesn't testify, jurors may draw inferences about the defendant's guilt based on his unwillingness to testify, despite warnings not to from the judge. On the other hand, the defendant does court danger by testifying. The danger comes because, as with all witnesses, the defendant will be subjected to cross-examination. Not only can prosecutors question a defendant's rendition of events, they can also try to impeach the defendant's credibility by introducing evidence of his past criminal record. Faced with this quandary, Williams did not testify at trial. If Williams had testified at trial, it would have presented the jury with additional information about Williams, which would have done considerable damage to his case. For example, the prosecution would have brought out William's criminal record, which included convictions for statutory rape.

The defense presented by Henry McKnight involved the testimony of three witnesses and only lasted one hour and ten minutes. To the surprise of many observers of the case, McKnight did not pursue the insanity defense that he had filed prior to the start of the trial.

The largest problem that McKnight was confronted with in his defense of Williams was the lack of much exculpatory evidence that could be presented to create a reasonable doubt concerning Williams's guilt. The only witness called to provide testimony that conflicted with the story presented by the prosecution was Dorothy Brown, a maid at the Y.M.C.A. She testified that she saw Williams and Albert Bowers, a Y.M.C.A. janitor, get on the seventh-floor elevator at about 1:45 on the afternoon of December 24. This was a full fifteen minutes to a half-hour after the prosecution's witness had placed Williams as leaving the Y.M.C.A. She also stated that Williams was not carrying a bundle in a blanket.

Because of the lack of other exculpatory witnesses and evidence, the central focus of the defense shifted from proving Williams's innocence to illustrating the extent to which Williams's right to counsel and his right against self-incrimination had been violated on the drive between Davenport and Des Moines. To strengthen this contention, McKnight called to the stand Thomas Kelly, the attorney who had counseled Williams in Davenport. Kelly testified that he had seen Williams advised of his rights by Davenport Municipal Judge Bertram Metcalf at his initial appearance and again by Detective Leaming when he arrived to transport Williams back to Des Moines. Kelly further testified that he told Detective Leaming that it was his understanding that Williams would not be questioned until he had talked to his counsel in Des Moines, at which time he would tell the police the location of the Powers girl. When Detective Leaming disputed this statement, Kelly said he offered to ride back to Des Moines with Williams to ensure that Williams's rights were not violated, but Detective Leaming said *no*.

McKnight also called Des Moines Police Chief Wendell Nichols. Chief Nichols testified that both he and Detective Leaming were in Leaming's office with McKnight on December 26 when McKnight received a call from Williams. Chief Nichols told the court that even though McKnight had speculated that Pamela was dead before she was taken out of the Y.M.C.A., he did not tell anybody that Williams had made this admission.

After the defense presents its case, the prosecution has the option, which

Prosecutor Hanrahan did not exercise, to present rebuttal witnesses. Rebuttal witnesses may be used to try to discredit the testimony presented by defense witnesses or to try to impeach their credibility. When rebuttal testimony is completed and both sides have rested, that ends the portion of the trial in which evidence is introduced. At this point, when the jury is not present, the defense can again make a motion for a directed verdict and argue that the prosecution has not proven enough of its case to allow it to go to the jury. If the motion is successful, the process is over and the defendant is acquitted. Normally, however, the case will be decided by the jury after the closing arguments are given.

Closing Arguments

After the attorneys on both sides have had a chance to submit proposed jury instructions to the judge, the judge will determine the instructions of law that will be given to the jury. Prior to closing arguments, the judge informs the attorneys about the content of the instructions. In writing their closing arguments, attorneys must adhere to the instructions that the judge will give to the jury. This is because the elements of the law that must be proven in order for a guilty verdict to be returned will be found in the instructions. If an attorney disregards the instructions and presents an alternative description of the law, the judge will tell the jurors to disregard that interpretation. Such a situation would harm the attorney's credibility at a pivotal point in the trial, so attorneys closely read the judge's instruction prior to giving their closing arguments.

Closing arguments give attorneys for both sides a final chance to summarize their view of how the case should be resolved and why. Songsten, Haydock, and Boyd have summarized the six important functions that closing arguments perform as follows:

1. The closing argument, prepared in advance of trial, provides the focus, structure, and themes for the entire trial process including preparation. The entire case points to the final argument and should be prepared and presented to be consistent with the closing. The focus, structure, and themes of the final argument will be those used in preparation, voir dire, opening, direct, and cross-examination.

2. Final argument is the attorney's last opportunity to summarize for the fact finder what the evidence has shown the facts to be in the case.

3. Summation is the most effective occasion in the trial to explain to the jury or judge the significance of the evidence.

4. The closing is the time when the creative lawyer can draw inferences, argue conclusions, comment on credibility, refer to common sense, and explain implications which the fact finder may not perceive.

5. Final argument is the only chance the attorney will have to explain and comment on the judge's instructions of the law and to weave the facts and law together.

6. Summation is the attorney's last opportunity to urge the fact finder to take a specific course of action.[37]

The content of closing arguments is broad. Closing arguments do not constitute evidence; they are legal arguments. Attorneys will seek to explain the issues that are relevant in the case and highlight testimony that is beneficial to their side, while pointing out weaknesses in the other side's assessment of the case. In doing so, the attorneys can remind the jurors about perceived credibility problems in the witnesses who testified. The attorneys will attempt to take the evidence that was brought out in the trial and instruct the jury on the inferences that can be drawn from the evidence. The attorneys are allowed to point out to the jury the conclusions that can be drawn from the evidence and urge that a verdict be reached based on these inferences and conclusions. Attorneys will not limit their closing arguments to the evidence brought out at trial; they will also attempt, at times, to include emotional appeals to the jury. As legal arguments, attorneys are granted great leeway in the scope of their summations. Prosecutors must be wary, however, since any prejudicial comments made in closing arguments can serve as grounds for a guilty verdict to be overturned on appeal. The prosecution is allowed to first present its closing argument, followed by the defense, and then a final rebuttal by the prosecution, which is normally limited to addressing those issues discussed by the defense attorney.

In his closing argument, Vincent Hanrahan explained to the jurors that the judge was going to instruct them that there were four possible verdicts in the case—first-degree murder, second-degree murder, manslaughter, or innocent. Despite these possible verdicts, Hanrahan said "All I'm going to talk about is the first degree because I see nothing else in this case."[38] Hanrahan explained that this was the only possible verdict because it was first-degree murder when an individual was killed during the act of rape. He noted that Williams was in the act of rape when he killed Pamela Powers and that the Polk County medical examiner, Dr. Leo Luka, had testified that Pamela had been violated. Hanrahan then reviewed the sequence of events, which showed that Williams was seen carrying a body out of the Y.M.C.A. He also reminded the jury that only the murderer would have known where the body was located and that the evidence showed that Williams himself had led police to the body.

During Henry McKnight's closing argument, Williams dried his eyes with his handkerchief as he wept. McKnight told the jurors to consider in its deliberation the fact that Williams was an escapee from a mental hospital at the time the events occurred. McKnight explained that these circumstances may have caused Williams to carry Pamela's body out of the Y.M.C.A. rather than reporting the killing. He reminded the jurors that Williams's actions did not prove that he committed the murder. McKnight told the jurors that Williams had been dealt a pat hand and the deck was stacked in the case that was presented by the State. He implied that the evidence that was not presented at trial might be as important as that which was presented. In particular, some witnesses who had seen Williams the day of the crime were not called by the prosecution. These included Albert Bowers, who had been seen with Williams just before Williams left the Y.M.C.A. McKnight wondered why the police questioned Bowers and then let him leave the state without getting any address by which he could be located for the purpose of the trial. McKnight also questioned why the prosecutor had failed to mention any of the laboratory tests that were done on Pamela's clothing, and the items found at the Grinnell rest stop. He also questioned why police had not entered into evidence hairs that were taken from Williams for the purpose of comparison to "foreign" hairs that were found on Pamela's body.

In response to McKnight's criticism of the prosecution's case, Hanrahan in his final summation told the jurors that he had stipulated that Williams was an escapee from a mental hospital, but he didn't stipulate that Williams was mentally ill. While he said that he might agree that Williams did have a mental problem, that did not mean that he was mentally ill enough to excuse him from being punished for the crime of murder. He told the jurors that the easy thing to do with Williams would be to simply send him back to Missouri to the institution from which he escaped and to allow its taxpayers to house and feed him. The problem with that solution, however, was that they might let him walk away again. Hanrahan told the jurors, "These little children have a right to see that men like this will be kept away from them . . . And you as jurors have the right to see that a crime like this will not go unpunished."[39]

Hanrahan also told the jurors that the police had done a very thorough job in its investigation of this crime. He noted that it would take the entire summer to call all the witnesses and produce all the evidence gathered in the investigation of this crime. He also explained that calling extra witnesses such as hair experts would have added unnecessary expense to the trial when the prosecution had already presented enough evidence to justify a conviction.

Jury Instructions

At the conclusion of the trial, the judge gives the jury specific instructions about its duties. This is done in open court and the instructions are entered into the record. The development of jury instructions by a judge is made difficult due to two goals. The first goal is to provide technically correct instructions that will withstand judicial appeal. If a judge rejects the jury instruction submitted by the defense counsel, the defense can object, providing grounds for an appeal. In order to protect the case from being remanded because of faulty instructions, judges are careful to be technically correct in all the finer points of the law in developing their instructions. As a result, however, the instructions may be too technical and legalistic, compromising the second goal—clear instructions. This may make it difficult for the jurors to understand their instructions.

Some of the instructions are procedural, such as reminding the jury that the defendant is presumed innocent until proven guilty and that the prosecution bears the burden of proof. Other procedural instructions include explaining how the jury should select a foreperson, cautioning the jury not to discuss the case outside the jury room, and informing them of the number of jurors required for a guilty verdict to be rendered. Other aspects of the instructions inform the jurors about what constitutes evidence and how it should be assessed. Judges also use the jury instructions to educate the jurors about the law and the specific charges against the defendant. In doing so, the judge explains the elements involved in the charges and defines terms that may not be familiar to laypersons. If the indictment against the defendant has multiple counts, the judge explains the different charges and the variety of different verdict options that the jury has on each charge. In cases in which the defense has relied on a legal defense, such as insanity, the judge must also educate the jury about the appropriateness of the defense and its legal requirements.

In the instructions that Judge Denato gave to the jury, he explained that jurors could take into consideration when weighing their decision Williams's status as an escapee from a mental hospital. He then informed the jurors that there were four possible verdicts that they could consider: first-degree murder, second-degree murder, manslaughter, or innocent.

Jury Deliberation and Verdict

Throughout the trial, the jurors are silent observers who are not asked to contribute to the process until the time of deliberation. At that time, the jurors are asked to reach a verdict in the case. The primary function of the jury is to determine what it considers to be the subjective facts of a case. In this role, the jury has considerable discretion. There are a number of difficulties in determining the facts of a case with any precision. Eyewitnesses may give differing accounts of the same incident. Some witnesses may be mistaken; others may lie on purpose. The defendant may opt not to testify, thus keeping valuable information from the jury. Other valuable evidence may be ruled inadmissible based on the rules of evidence. All these problems may make the jury's duty to determine the facts of the case difficult.

A second function that also falls to the jury is application of the criminal law. The judge's instructions to the jury may leave room for discretion in this area as well. Many legal terms are open to interpretation in their application. For example, there were a couple of elements that would meet the requirements of Iowa's definition of first-degree murder, if they were demonstrated to be true. The first was premeditation and the second was if the killing occurred during the perpetration of a rape. Despite the judge's instructions, the jury was left to determine exactly what constituted premeditation and rape. Juries must decide whether premeditation requires planning, or simply the opportunity to have time to consider the effect of one's actions.

The jury's task is further frustrated because the attorneys for both sides have done their best to make their own evidence seem unquestionable while discrediting the evidence of the other. Furthermore, in their closing arguments the two attorneys have, in many cases, shown the jurors how inferences can be made that would allow any verdict to seem reasonable. All these problems make the jury's task difficult.

Jury deliberation takes place in the privacy of a jury room. No record is made of the jury deliberations. The jury room is guarded by a bailiff who ensures that the jury will remain undisturbed in its deliberations. The first order of business for most juries is the selection of a foreperson. There are no formal rules in most jurisdictions for how a jury proceeds. Each jury may set its own informal rules for how to deliberate. During deliberation the jury can, through the bailiff, request that physical evidence be brought before it. The jury can also request that the court reporter read part of the testimony out of the record. Juries can also ask the judge to provide clarification of legal points during deliberation.

If the jurors can agree on a verdict, it will be signed by the foreperson and read aloud in court. In Iowa, as in most other states, jurors in criminal trials had to be unanimous to reach a guilty verdict. If, after thorough deliberation, the jury is unable to reach a verdict because of a lack of agreement, the jury is said to be hung. When this happens, the judge will usually instruct the jury to try to break the impasse and come up with a verdict. If the jury remains hung with no possibility of agreeing on a verdict, the prosecutor has the option of retrying the case from scratch.

In the case of *Iowa v. Williams*, the verdict was announced in open court on May 6, 1969. The jury did not spend much time deliberating the case. It began its deliberation at noon. While it deliberated, the jurors elected Norbert Moreland as its foreperson, and ordered and ate lunch. It returned with a verdict at 1:40 P.M. The verdict was guilty of first-degree murder.

When a verdict is announced, there may be a request from either of the attorneys that the jury be polled, although neither did so in this case. If such a request is made, then each juror will individually be asked by the judge if he or she concurred with the verdict. Once the verdict is announced, the jury is thanked and released from its duty. The members of the jury are then free to discuss the case and the deliberation process with anyone. When the verdict is guilty, the defense counsel may make a motion to have the judge override the verdict or for a new trial on the basis of a flaw that existed in the trial. Normally, such motions are a formality intended to preserve issues for appeal and are denied by the judge.

After the trial, both McKnight and Hanrahan stated that they expected the guilty verdict. Hanrahan stated that he was surprised that the jury came back so quickly. Despite the fact that it was a good verdict, however, he knew it "wouldn't bring Pamela back."[40] McKnight told members of the press that "There was ample evidence for this type of verdict," and added that any "appeal will be up to Williams."[41]

Sentencing

If a defendant is found guilty, the next stage of the process is *sentencing*. In most cases, judges are responsible for sentencing. There is one exception: In capital cases, the jury often imposes a sentence following a sentencing hearing after the verdict has been reached.

Before judges sentence an individual, they normally receive a presentence investigation report compiled by a probation officer working for the jurisdiction in which the individual was convicted. The report contains background information on the individual. This includes any previous criminal convictions, the individual's family situation, and his or her employment record. The Supreme Court ruled in 1991 that states may, if they wish, include victim impact statements in sentencing reports without violating the Cruel and Unusual Punishment Clause of the Eighth Amendment. Generally, the report incorporates a recommendation as to whether prison or probation should be imposed. In felony cases, the defendant appears at a sentencing hearing in which both the defense and prosecuting attorneys can address the court, arguing for certain sentences. The convicted individual is also usually asked whether she wants to address the court. During the sentencing hearing, Williams told the court that Hanrahan's actions had "not only caused this child to die in vain [but] there is some little boy or girl outside walking the streets right now who is still in danger. And me, my life, all my hopes, and dreams are going."[42] Williams again asserted his innocence and told the court that he hoped the "animalistic person, whoever it is, and I daresay it's not me, [is] brought to justice."[43] The judge usually imposes sentence at the conclusion of the sentencing hearing.

Under Iowa law, Judge Denato had no discretion in the sentence that he could impose. Because Iowa had no capital punishment, Williams would be sentenced to mandatory life imprisonment with no chance for parole. Judge Denato's normal sentencing procedure was to wait at least two weeks after trial prior to sentencing, but due to a request made on behalf of Williams by his attorney, Judge Denato set the sentencing date for May 14, 1969. McKnight explained that Williams was anxious to be sentenced so that he would be moved from the Polk County Jail, where his movement had been restricted. On May 14, 1969, Judge Denato sentenced Williams to be imprisoned for life at hard labor in the Iowa State Penitentiary at Fort Madison, Iowa.

The guilty verdict and life sentence came as no surprise to any observer of the trial. Judge Denato's decision that the subjective facts showed that Williams had properly waived his rights when he took police to the location of Pamela's body sealed Robert Williams's fate. This was because it allowed Judge Denato to rule that the applicable procedural law permitted all of Williams's statements and the body to be placed into evidence. The lack of exculpatory evidence presented by the defense left the jury with little inconsistency in the facts that were accepted between the two sides and there was overwhelming unchallenged evidence pointing to Williams's guilt. Because of the evidence allowed by Judge Denato's ruling, the verdict was easy to reach and the jury had no problem convicting Williams. Things might have been very different if Judge Denato had accepted a different set of subjective facts and ruled that Williams's rights against self-incrimination and to counsel had been violated. Williams therefore had incentive to challenge Judge Denato's ruling in the appeals process.

NOTES

1. Edward F. Pohren, "Constitutional Law—Criminal Procedure—Where Suspect Has Not Waived his Right to an Attorney's Assistance, Confession Prompted by Detective's Statements When Counsel was Absent is Inadmissible—*Brewer v. Williams*, 430 U.S. 387 (1977)," *Creighton Law Review* 11 (1978): 1029–1030.

2. G. Alan Tarr, *Judicial Process and Judicial Policymaking* (St. Paul: West Publishing Co., 1994), p. 152.

3. Joseph M. Pellicciotti, *Handbook of Basic Trial Evidence: A College Introduction* (Bristol, IN: Wyndham Hall Press, 1992), p. 93.

4. David W. Neubauer, *Judicial Process: Law, Courts, & Politics in the United States* (Pacific Grove, Calif.: Brooks/Cole Publishing Company, 1991), p. 317.

5. Pellicciotti, *Handbook*, p. 79.

6. Howard Abadinsky, *Law and Justice: An Introduction to the American Legal System*, 2nd ed. (Chicago: Nelson-Hall Publishers, 1991), pp. 241–242.

7. John O. Songsten, Roger Haydock, and James J. Boyd, *The Trialbook* (St. Paul, Minn.: West Publishing Co., 1984), pp. 291–299.

8. Songsten, Haydock, and Boyd, *The Trialbook*, pp. 309–310.

9. Pellicciotti, *Handbook*, p. 289.

10. Peter Nardulli, "The Societal Cost of the Exclusionary Rule: An Empirical Assessment," *American Bar Foundation Research Journal* (1983): 585.

11. *Iowa v. Williams*, 182, N.W.2d 396, 398–99 (Iowa 1970).

12. Joint Appendix, p. 83, *Brewer v. Williams*, 430 U.S. 387 (1977).

13. Ibid., p. 48.

14. Ibid., p. 63.

15. Ibid., p. 1.

16. Ibid., p. 2.

17. Pellicciotti, *Handbook*, p. 24.

18. David W. Neubauer, *America's Courts and the Criminal Justice System*, 2nd ed. (Monterey, Calif.: Brooks/Cole Publishing Company, 1984), p. 29.

19. Paul Bergman, *Trial Advocacy* (St. Paul, Minn.: West Publishing Co., 1979), p. 378.

20. James P. Levine, *Juries and Politics* (Pacific Grove, Calif.: Brooks/Cole Publishing Co., 1992), p. 34.

21. Neubauer, *Judicial Process*, p. 312.

22. Levine, *Juries and Politics*, p. 47.

23. Bergman, *Trial Advocacy*, pp. 248–249.

24. Songsten, Haydock, and Boyd, *The Trialbook*, p. 182.

25. Bergman, *Trial Advocacy*, p. 44.

26. Pellicciotti, *Handbook*, p. 180.

27. Songsten, Haydock, and Boyd, *The Trialbook*, p. 270.

28. Bergman, *Trial Advocacy*, p. 175.

29. Songsten, Haydock, and Boyd, *The Trialbook*, p. 281.

30. Trial Transcript, p. 91, *Iowa v. Williams* (1969).

31. Ibid., p. 210.

32. Joint Appendix, p. 81, *Brewer v. Williams* 430 U.S. 387 (1977). Yale Kamisar has pointed out that this speech is different than the one given at the suppression hearing in substantial ways. For his analysis of the difference see "Foreword: A Hard Look at a Discomforting Record," *Georgetown Law Journal* 66 (1977): 209–243.

33. Joint Appendix, p. 84, *Brewer v. Williams* 430 U.S. 387 (1977).

34. Ibid., p. 85.

35. Ibid., p. 86.

36. Ibid., p. 96.

37. Songsten, Haydock, and Boyd, *The Trialbook*, pp. 318–319.

38. *Des Moines Tribune*, 6 May 1969.

39. *Des Moines Register*, 7 May 1969.

40. Ibid.

41. Ibid.

42. *Des Moines Register*, 24 March 1977.

43. *Des Moines Register*, 17 July 1977.

Chapter 4

The Historical Development of the Rights Against Self-incrimination and to Counsel

> This litigation [the *Williams* Case] is exceptional for at least three reasons. The facts are unusually tragic; it involves an unusually clear violation of constitutional rights; and it graphically illustrates the societal costs that may be incurred when police officers decide to dispense with the requirements of the law.
>
> —Justice John Paul Stevens[1]

Many Americans hold the view accepted by mechanical jurisprudence that the operations of legal system involve a court first recognizing the existing criminal law, applying the law to the facts of the case as they become apparent at trial, and, then, mechanically, rendering the only logical verdict that could be arrived at. According to this perspective, the judicial process worked perfectly in the *Williams* case. Jurors were given the opportunity to become informed about the facts of the case through the evidence and testimony presented at trial and then they applied Iowa's first-degree murder law to those facts as they were instructed to by the judge. The verdict of guilty came as no surprise; justice seemed to have been served.

The problem with mechanical jurisprudence's understanding of the process is that it rarely considers the role of procedural laws. Along with the substantive law, making certain actions illegal and subject to specified sanctions and penalties, the courts also have to apply procedural laws. Procedural laws are concerned with due process. Due process refers to the procedural requirements that governments must observe when they act in a manner that can interfere with the life, liberty, or property of a person. As in the *Williams* case, appeals are often fought over procedural law due to the ability of appellate courts to correct a lower court's errors in the application of procedural law.

In the *Williams* case, the crucial issue in the appeals process was whether Robert Williams's Fifth Amendment right against self-incrimination and Sixth Amendment right to counsel had been violated and if evidence gathered through these violations should have been admitted at trial. The pertinent provision of the Fifth Amendment reads, "No person . . . shall be compelled in any criminal case to be witness against himself." The Sixth Amendment reads, "In all criminal prosecutions, the accused shall enjoy . . . the Assistance of Counsel for his defense." Due to the principle of *stare decisis*, the judges and justices who would be reviewing Judge Denato's rulings had an extensive body of precedents and prior law to examine. The interpretation of how prior court decisions regarding the Fifth and Sixth Amendments should be applied in the *Williams* case became crucial to a resolution of the case. In order to clarify the role that prior legal decisions would play in resolving the *Williams* case, this chapter examines the precedents concerning the rights against self-incrimination and to counsel that had shaped these areas of law.

At Williams's trial for the murder of Pamela Powers, one of the most pivotal legal issues was whether his statements leading the police to Pamela's body could be used against him at trial. The importance of the incriminating statements Williams made to the police did not make the *Williams* case unusual from many other criminal cases. In all criminal cases, if the police and the prosecution have been able to take incriminating statements from a defendant and are able to use them at trial, conviction will be easier. Because William's incriminating statements were admitted, the jury heard that it was Williams who showed the police where the body had been dumped, making his conviction much easier to gain.

THE RIGHT AGAINST SELF-INCRIMINATION

There are three different types of statements that are made to police and prosecutors by criminal defendants. An admission of guilt is a *confession*. A statement in which defendants show knowledge of the crime of which they are suspected is known as an *admission*. Williams's statements were admissions, since he never confessed to the crime. The term *exculpatory statement* is given to any statement made by suspects in which they try to assert their innocence, regardless of whether it actually clears them or really amounts to an admission or a confession.[2]

The question of whether any of these types of statements can be admitted at trial not only has huge consequences for the outcome of the trial, it also may influence whether there will even be a trial. The prosecutor's strength in a plea bargaining situation is relevant to the deal that can be cut. The stronger the evidence, the more likely it is that defendants will find it in their best interest to accept a deal. Because of the increased likelihood of a plea bargain or conviction if a defendant's statements can be used in court, the debate over when such statements can be admitted has been a serious one for some time. It has also been a debate in which the Supreme Court's guidance has been less than consistent. Today, the decision as to whether any type of statement is admissible may involve the examination of two different, constitutionally protected rights, the Fifth Amendment right against self-incrimination and the Sixth Amendment right to counsel.

Early Confession Reasoning

As in many areas of law involving the rights of criminal defendants, courts in the United States first relied on the common law to determine if a confession was admissible in court. The common law rule for the exclusion of confessions emphasized two goals. The first was the need for confessions to be reliable and trustworthy. Out of concern that only reliable confessions be admitted, the common law rule also came to emphasize the need for confessions to be voluntary. The rule was explicitly stated in the 1783 case of *The King v. Warickshall*, which stated:

A free and voluntary confession is deserving of the highest credit, because it is presumed to flow from the strongest sense of guilt, and therefore it is admitted as proof of the crime to which it refers; but a confession forced from the mind by the flattery of hope, or by the torture of fear, comes in so questionable a shape when it is to be considered as the evidence of guilt, that no credit ought to be given to it; and therefore it is rejected.[3]

By 1792 the common law rule of *Warickshall* was accepted by state courts in the United States and became the standard by which all confessions were admitted as evidence.[4] In the first case in which the Supreme Court had to enunciate a standard to be used for the admissibility of confessions, *Hopt v. Utah* (1884),[5] it relied on the common law rule.

In 1908 the Court in *Twining v. New Jersey*[6] established the freedom of state courts to ignore the role of the Fifth Amendment in self-incrimination cases. The *Twining* case did not involve a confession. Twining and a co-defendant were on trial for deceiving state banking examiners as to the fiscal health of their bank. Both defendants refused to take the stand at their trial, as allowed by New Jersey law. While giving instructions to the jury, the judge commented that during its deliberation, the jury could take into consideration the defendants' unwillingness to take the stand and refute the prosecution's case.

After being convicted, Twining appealed his case, making two arguments.

The first was that the right against self-incrimination was among the privileges and immunities protected by the Fourteenth Amendment that states could not infringe upon. The Court quickly rejected this argument, relying on the precedent established in the *Slaughterhouse Cases*.[7] The second argument that Twining relied on in his appeal was that the Self-incrimination Clause of the Fifth Amendment was incorporated through the Due Process Clause of the Fourteenth Amendment. The Supreme Court also rejected this argument since it believed that the Due Process Clause was not meant to require the states to be bound by the same provisions of the Bill of Rights as the federal government. Instead, the Court held that the Due Process Clause only required the Court to examine whether a state's criminal justice procedures provided the defendant with the fundamental fairness required by our system of justice. In this case, it was believed that the process by which Twining was convicted was fundamentally fair.

The decision not to incorporate the Self-incrimination Clause of the Fifth Amendment meant that the Court established two approaches to self-incrimination cases—one for state cases and another for federal cases. The most direct result of *Twining*, however, was that in state cases the state courts—not the Supreme Court—would determine the admission of confessions and other incriminating statements for years to come.

Fundamental Fairness and the State Approach

In the 1930s a number of different social phenomena crystallized, causing the Court to refocus on the need to supervise state cases when it came to confessions. One of the most important of these was a series of documented reports of police abuses in trying to obtain confessions from criminal defendants.[8] Due to the laxness of state judges in supervising third degree tactics used by police, the Supreme Court recognized the need to examine some of the worst abuses in the state courts. Another factor that helped to prod the Supreme Court in this direction was a growing awareness of the role of racial discrimination in America's criminal justice process.[9]

The first case in which the Supreme Court used the fundamental fairness standard to review a state confession case was *Brown v. Mississippi*[10] in 1936. The *Brown* case came to the Court after a white farmer had been found brutally murdered in his home in Kemper County, Mississippi, on March 30, 1934. The investigation first focused on Yank Ellington, a black man, who was arrested by the deputy sheriff on flimsy evidence. Ellington was then taken to the site of the murder, where he and law enforcement officials were met by a number of vigilantes. After the mob was informed of the arrest of Ellington, it accused him of the murder. Ellington protested his innocence to the mob but was taken by the vigilantes. They placed a rope around his neck and hanged him from a tree. Ellington was then taken down and given a second chance to confess. He refused, and was again hanged.

Ellington was once again let down from the tree, this time only to suffer a whipping by the vigilantes. He still refused to change his story. The mob then released Ellington who was arrested again two days later by the same deputy sheriff. The deputy sheriff then drove Ellington into the State of Alabama where he and another law officer subjected him to a severe beating. After this round of beatings was administered, Ellington agreed to sign a statement that the deputy dictated and was then formally arrested and jailed.

Two other suspects, Ed Brown and Henry Shields, were also arrested for the murder and had been placed in jail. While in jail, they too were subjected to beatings. The deputy made them strip and then whipped them with a leather belt and attached metal buckle. Told that the beating would continue until they confessed, both suspects did confess. The beatings did not actually stop until Brown and Shields changed the details of their stories to match the one that the deputy wanted to hear. When the deputy finally got the story that he desired from the two suspects, he reminded them that if they changed or refuted their stories, the beatings would start again. The next day all the prisoners were forced to recite their confessions before witnesses brought in by law enforcement officials. These confessions were then used at trial to convict the three suspects of the murder. The defendants were then sentenced to death. The Mississippi Supreme Court upheld the convictions and sentences on appeal.

What made the *Brown* case unusual was the fact that at the trial the deputy sheriff did not try to hide the mistreatment of the prisoners. At trial no one denied that serious brutalities had taken place during the interrogations of the defendants. The deputy was even asked if he had beaten Ellington and he answered, "Not too much for a negro; not as much as I would have done if it were left to me."[11] Two other witnesses were also called who testified to the beatings that had taken place. On top of this, scars from the rope burns that had been inflicted on Ellington during the attempt to extract a confession by hanging him were clearly visible on his neck during the court proceedings.

Despite Mississippi's claim that the Supreme Court's refusal to incorporate the Fifth Amendment's Self-incrimination Clause meant that the Supreme Court could not review the state proceeding, the Supreme Court did hear the case and unanimously reversed the convictions. Rather than applying the Fifth Amendment to resolve the *Brown* case, the Supreme Court relied on the Fourteenth Amendment's Due Process Clause. The Court reasoned that procedures mandated by the Due Process Clause, which was applicable to the states, were essential for a fair trial of criminal defendants. The Court then ruled that the Due Process Clause prohibited state courts from using confessions that were obtained through the use of physical violence.

In *Brown* the Court began a thirty-year process involving the resolution of over thirty state criminal cases in which it examined what conditions leading to a confession met the requirements of fundamental fairness. During this period, a confession was only ruled admissible if it had been obtained voluntarily. Therefore, the Court reviewed the conditions under which a confession was given to determine if it was coercive and, thus, involuntary. Originally, the definition of coercion only covered physical violence against a suspect and cases were easy to decide. Over time, however, when the police learned that the Court found use of violence unacceptable and switched to other forms of interrogation, the cases become more difficult to resolve. The Court was attempting to determine when a confession was the result of police misbehavior through psychological coercion that overcame suspects' resistance and thus induced them to confess. During the thirty years after *Brown*, the Court further developed the "voluntariness" doctrine for the admission of confessions in state criminal cases.

At first, the impact of *Brown* on state cases was limited because the Supreme Court did not re-enter the field of state confessions until 1940 when it reviewed three state confession cases. The most important of these cases was *Chambers v. Florida*.[12] *Chambers* came to the Court as a result of a Florida case in which an elderly white man had been murdered in the town of Pompano, in Broward County, Florida, on May 13, 1933. Four poor, uneducated, black men, including Isiah Chambers, were arrested for the murder. Upon their arrest, mobs gathered and threatened to take justice into their own hands, so the police removed the defendants to the Dade County Jail for their own protection. While in the Dade County Jail, one of the suspects was purposely held in the death house. The next day the suspects were returned to Broward County. They were questioned on and off for a week about the crime. The suspects were individually questioned by four officers at a time and the interrogation sessions sometimes lasted through the night, making the suspects physically exhausted. Finally, on May 21, 1933, after an all-night interrogation, one of the prisoners confessed. The district attorney, however, did not find the confession to be sufficient, so he ordered the interrogation to continue until the confession was modified to meet his specifications. Confessions and modifications of the original confessions were eventually gained from all of the suspects. These confessions were admitted into evidence because the jury found them to be voluntary. The confessions then laid the foundation for the first-degree murder convictions of the four defendants. The Florida Supreme Court also found that the confessions were given voluntarily.

Upon review, the Supreme Court's decision illustrated its growing concern with state confession cases. Justice Hugo Black wrote the majority opinion in which the Court claimed that it shared with state courts the right to determine whether coercion had been used to extract admissions by examining the record of the case. The examination of the record in *Chambers* revealed that the confessions were not voluntary and should not have been admitted at trial. Even though the physical torture that had been evident in

Brown was missing, the Court found that that police had used coercion in *Chambers*. The coercion was psychological, not physical, and resulted from the incommunicado detention and endless questioning of the suspects. Furthermore, the method by which the confessions were extracted, including the specified modifications of each confession, showed that the confessions were involuntary.

The 1941 case of *Lisenba v. California*[13] brought before the Supreme Court a more difficult set of facts surrounding the admission of a confession. Raymond Lisenba was arrested for the murder of his wife. Before he was arrested or charged, the police illegally detained Lisenba for two days in the house next to his. During this period, he was questioned by a state's attorney and law officers. Furthermore, he was held incommunicado, was not allowed to sleep for a 42-hour period, and was slapped at least once by a police officer. When the police could elicit no murder confession from Lisenba, they charged him with incest and jailed him. Eleven days after Lisenba was jailed, the police confronted Lisenba with the man believed to be his accomplice. The accomplice told Lisenba that he had told the police about Lisenba's complicity in the murder. Lisenba was then taken into the district attorney's office for an 8-hour interrogation, which ended only after he confessed. The charge against Lisenba was then changed to murder. At trial Lisenba pleaded innocent, claiming that he had been beaten by the police during his detention and that his confession was coerced from him in violation of the Due Process Clause of the Fourteenth Amendment. Despite this claim, Lisenba was convicted of murder and the California Supreme Court upheld the conviction.

The *Lisenba* case should not have had results that differed dramatically from the decision in *Chambers*. In many ways Lisenba's treatment by the police was similar to that endured by the defendants in *Chambers*. Both cases involved incommunicado detention, exhaustively long periods of interrogation, deprivation of sleep, and batteries of interrogators against a single suspect. Two factors differentiated the two cases. The first was that in *Lisenba* there was at least one slap of the defendant to which police admitted, which had been lacking in *Chambers*. The second was that in *Lisenba* there was no threat of mob violence, as existed in *Chambers*. Despite all the similarities, the Supreme Court, in a majority opinion written by Justice Owen Roberts, used its discretion to determine the subjective facts and procedural law and found that Lisenba's confession was admissible. Although the Court noted that police conduct in *Lisenba* came close to crossing the line of allowable behavior, the opinion did not indicate what more would have made the confession inadmissible. Instead, the Court pointed out a number of subjective facts that were used to distinguish the result in *Lisenba* from that of *Chambers*. Most of these facts centered around Lisenba's psychological makeup. The Court pointed out that Lisenba did not seem to fear the police during his detention. Furthermore, while Lisenba lacked a formal education, he was described as clever and self-confident. Despite the long interrogations Lisenba did not confess until after his accomplice had told the police about his activities; this showed his ability to not be coerced into confessing. The final difference in Lisenba's case was a belief on the part of the Court that, despite the borderline behavior of the police during the sustained detention and interrogation of Lisenba, his free will had not been overcome and his confession was indeed a voluntary act on his part. Justice Douglas wrote a dissent in which he examined only the facts to resolve the case. In doing so, he found that the facts were sufficiently close to *Chambers v. Florida* to rely on its ruling to find that the confession was not free and voluntary.

The three cases that have been discussed so far all illustrate the increasing difficulty the Court had in determining whether a confession was given voluntarily. These cases also illustrate the Court's embrace of the *totality of the circumstances test*, which required a case-by-case assessment of the facts of every case. Under the totality of the circumstances test, no one feature of a case would necessarily make a confession or statement inadmissible. Instead, the Court examined all the facts surrounding a confession, including suspects' psychological makeup, their mental state and physical condition, and their reaction to police tactics. The Court also examined the factors surrounding the interrogation, including the length of detention, the isolation of the defendant, the possibility of mob violence, and the interrogation methods that were used. After an examination of the facts that led to a confession, the Court would then make the determination of whether the confession was made voluntarily. This approach led to one basic problem: a lack of predictability as to whether a confession would be found to be the product of coercion. Justices could either emphasize differences in cases, as did the majority in *Lisenba* when compared to *Chambers*, or similarities, as did Justice Douglas in his dissent in *Lisenba*. This, at times, made it appear that the Court was inconsistent in its decisions.

During this period, in which the Court used a case-by-case analysis of the totality of the circumstances to determine if fundamental fairness had been denied, the rationale for excluding confessions was three-fold. First, it was considered fundamentally unfair to use a confession at trial that had been wrung from the defendant involuntarily. Second, in order to deter future violations, it was necessary to remove the incentive police had to coerce confessions from suspects. Third, requiring confessions to be voluntary ensured their reliability.[14]

Not all the justices of the Supreme Court were happy with the application of the fundamental fairness standard of the Fourteenth Amendment to state confession cases. In the 1944 case of *Ashcraft v. Tennessee*,[15] the Court momentarily rejected its application. *Ashcraft* involved the admissibility of a confession in the murder trial of E. E. Ashcraft. Ashcraft, who was accused of murder for arranging the killing of his wife, was subjected to a continuous thirty-six-hour interrogation after which he ended up confessing. After his confession was used at trial and a guilty verdict was returned, the Supreme Court reviewed the case and ruled that the confession was inadmissible.

What sets the *Ashcraft* decision apart from other decisions in this era was that the six-justice majority, led by Justice Black, did not review the characteristics of Ashcraft's psychological makeup to determine if he would have been capable of resisting the interrogation techniques used by the police. Instead, the Court held that the thirty-six-hour interrogation was "so inherently coercive that its very existence is irreconcilable with the possession of mental freedom by a lone suspect against whom its full coercive force is brought to bear."[16] *Ashcraft* thus shifted the emphasis from determining whether an individual had voluntarily confessed to a crime—by examining a combination of the police methods and the suspect's characteristics—to the conduct of the police exclusively. While the new "inherently coercive" test highlighted the problems in a criminal justice system that relies on private interrogations and confessions, the opinion did not clearly state what types of interrogation techniques, such as the length of interrogation, being held incommunicado, or being denied counsel, would fail the test in the future.

Ashcraft's inability to permanently change the Court's direction or end the debate over what principles should be relied on to decide state confession cases is illustrated by examining another 1944 case, *Lyons v. Oklahoma.*[17] *Lyons* came to the Supreme Court after a confession in a murder case. The facts were these: A family of three had been killed at home and then the home had been set on fire in hopes of destroying the evidence. Lyons and an accomplice were suspected of the crime, arrested, questioned for two hours, and then held incommunicado for eleven days. At the end of the eleven days, Lyons was interrogated for eight hours ending at 2:30 A.M. During this eight hours, the police brought in a pan of bones they claimed were the victims' and placed it in Lyons's lap to encourage him to break down. Lyons then confessed. Lyons also confessed at the end of a second interrogation session twelve hours after his first confession. During the second interrogation session, Lyons was escorted to the scene of the crime and then to the state penitentiary, where he made the second confession. Lyons's claim that he was subjected to physical violence during both interrogations was supported by a disinterested witness. At trial, Lyons claimed that both confessions were involuntary but the court ruled that the second was admissible. Lyons was convicted and then appealed.

The majority opinion in *Lyons* was written by Justice Stanley Reed and applied the fundamental fairness standard by examining the totality of the circumstances to determine if the second confession was involuntary. The Court ruled that the confession was properly admitted at trial. Justice Reed's opinion discounted the claims that violence had been used in securing the second confession. Therefore, the critical question was whether the coercive tactics used in the first confession were also responsible for the second confession. The Court ruled that even though a confession may have been made after unlawful pressures, force, or threats were applied, it could still be voluntary. The key to determining if it was voluntary was to examine the suspect's mental freedom at the time of the confession. In doing this, Justice Reed found that Lyons did have the mental freedom necessary to make the second confession voluntarily. Justice Reed also pointed out that Lyons was probably guilty, so his confession was most likely reliable. Thus, Justice Reed added to the totality of the circumstances test the probable trustworthiness of a confession as yet another factor to be considered.

In dissent, Justice Frank Murphy protested that police interrogations could not be dissected into distinct and isolated sections. Instead, he argued, "The whole confession technique used here constituted one single, continuing transaction."[18] Justice Murphy went on to argue that the proper standard for determining if a confession should be admitted at trial in state courts should be the Self-incrimination Clause of the Fifth Amendment rather than the Due Process Clause of the Fourteenth Amendment.

The cases that the Supreme Court decided in 1944 show that the justices supported a number of different approaches to the admissibility of confessions in state cases. These included the fundamental fairness approach as determined by the totality of circumstances test, the inherently coercive test which was applied in *Ashcraft*, and Justice Murphy's belief that the Self-incrimination Clause of the Fifth Amendment should be the standard used. Despite the close split that existed between the first two approaches on the Court in 1944, two factors helped to swing the balance in favor of those justices who preferred the fundamental fairness test.[19] The first of these was that both Justice Stanley Reed and Chief Justice Harlan Stone, who had supported the inherently coercive test, began to fear that other justices might use the standard to frustrate police efforts to obtain reliable confessions. Justice Reed's concern with this possibility is seen in his *Lyons* opinion and his inclusions of reliability as one of the totality of circumstances that had to be considered. A second factor curtailed the Court's movement toward the inherent coerciveness standard—changes that took place in the membership of the Court. Membership changes in 1945 and 1946 did not affect the balance on the Court, since newly appointed Justice Harold Burton and Chief Justice Fred Vinson both supported the fundamental fairness standard, as had the justices they replaced, Justice Owen Roberts and Chief Justice Harlan Stone. In 1949, however—with the deaths of Justice Murphy, who had supported applying a Fifth Amendment standard, and Justice Wiley Rutledge, who had supported the fundamental fairness approach but often supported restricting the admission of confessions—a majority on the Court supported a more conservative reading of fundamental fairness, one that was more favorable to law enforcement. Two new justices, Tom Clark and Sherman Minton, supported the fundamental fairness approach and emphasized the need to allow police to use interrogation methods that would result in reliable confessions.

So as the 1950s started, the majority of the Court supported the fundamental fairness approach. What had changed in the application of the test was that the new majority, led by Justice Robert Jackson, included trustworthiness as a major factor to be examined to determine if a confession were admissible. The trustworthiness of a confession was important because it was central to the question of the innocence or guilt of the defendant. This new majority also became increasingly tired of what it saw as the Court's interference in confession decisions that were more properly made in the state courts.

The impact of the new majority was most pronounced in the decision of *Stein v. New York*.[20] One of the basic issues in the *Stein* case was a New York procedural rule that allowed confessions for which the voluntariness was disputed to be put before the jury with all other evidence. The jury then determined the voluntariness and reliability of the confession. If the jury found that the confession had been coerced, it was instructed to disregard its contents in reaching a verdict. The problem was that since juries deliberate in private, it was impossible to know when (1) a jury found that a confession was coerced and (2) the jury ruled that the confession had no influence on its verdict. Stein and his co-defendants had confessed to a murder after a protracted incommunicado detention in which the defendants claimed that they had been subjected to physical violence. The jury heard the confession and was instructed not to take it into consideration in reaching a verdict if it was determined to have been obtained through coercive means. The jury found Stein and his co-defendants guilty and sentenced them to death. Stein and the others petitioned for Supreme Court review.

Justice Jackson, writing for the majority, found that the New York procedure did not violate the Due Process Clause of the Fourteenth Amendment. Jackson went on to look at the totality of the circumstances and found that these confessions were not coerced. This decision was reached by taking into account the fact that the defendants involved were hardened criminals who were not likely to easily break under police pressure. He also pointed out that the defendants confessed only after they were confronted with other evidence that the police had gathered. The emphasis that Justice Jackson placed on the proper verdict and the trustworthiness of a confession could be seen in the last ruling that was made in *Stein*. Justice Jackson stated that even if Stein's confession had been coerced, it would not require the Court to remand the case for a new trial without the confession admitted as evidence. That was because a jury could find that a confession was coerced, but still convict the defendant on the basis of other sufficient evidence. Furthermore, Jackson urged that the only reason that coerced confessions violated the Due Process Clause was because they were untrustworthy. Thus, for the first time in a Supreme Court ruling, if a coerced confession were found to be improperly admitted, it did not require a new trial on the basis that a confession was so probative that it would automatically sway the jury in reaching a guilty verdict.

As should be increasingly clear, the freedom of the justices to exercise their discretion to selectively determine the subjective facts and applicable law means that an approach to constitutional interpretation that is supported by a majority on one day will not necessarily be in vogue sometime in the future. Unbeknownst to its majority at the time, the *Stein* case was the last time that the "other evidence" and "trustworthiness" components of the totality of the circumstances would have the support of a majority on the Court. The new majorities on the Court in the 1950s would still use the fundamental fairness approach of the Fourteenth Amendment, but in weighing the totality of the circumstances they placed more limitations on what types of interrogation methods were acceptable. Once again, one factor that helped change the direction of Supreme Court decisions concerning the admission of confessions in state cases was a change in membership. Specifically, the death of Chief Justice Fred Vinson and the leadership of his replacement Chief Justice Earl Warren.

By the end of the 1950s, the Court—for the first time—started to consider the link between the right against self-incrimination and the right to counsel. Movement in this direction was led by Justices William O. Douglas and Hugo Black, and sometimes with the support of Chief Justice Earl Warren and Justice William Brennan, who had been appointed to replace Justice Sherman Minton in 1956. These justices began to consider the lack of counsel, when requested, as one factor that would cause a confession to be found to violate the requirement of fundamental fairness. In 1959 in *Spano v. New York*,[21] a majority of the Court seemed to support this new position. While the majority found the confession involuntary, based on the totality of the circumstances, which included denial of counsel when requested, Justice Potter Stewart wrote in his concurring opinion that "the absence of counsel when this confession was elicited was alone enough to render it inadmissible under the Fourteenth Amendment."[22] This made Justice Stewart the fifth member of the Court to support the requirement of the presence of counsel when requested in order for a confession to be admissible.

As the 1950s ended and the 1960s began, the Court was less than consistent in its decision, but the overall tone of the decisions was that an increasing number of law enforcement techniques denied individuals the guarantees of due process of law required by the Fourteenth Amendment. The list of factors undermining due process grew, especially new forms of psychological coercion that swayed the Court into finding that the totality of circumstances created coercion. The Court was so adamant about upgrading the standards of interrogation in the states to ensure that confessions were indeed voluntary that between 1959 and 1963, in a series of seven cases, it found that all the confessions were coerced, even though the practices in gaining the confessions were milder than those of earlier cases in which confessions were admitted. *Rogers v. Richmond*,[23] decided in 1961, exemplifies this trend. In *Rogers* the Court ruled that a confession obtained after a six-hour interrogation session in which the suspect was allowed to eat and smoke was inadmissible because the police lied to the defendant and said that they were going to call his wife in for interrogation.

The increasing tendency of a majority of the justices of the Supreme Court to believe that due process did not exist if counsel had been requested and denied during an interrogation moved the Court in the direction of suppressing the admission of confessions in state cases regardless of whether the confession had met the voluntariness standard. It also set the stage for bonding together the Fifth Amendment's Self-incrimination Clause and the Sixth Amendment's Right to Counsel Clause through the decision in *Miranda v. Arizona*.[24]

The Federal Approach to Confession Cases

As the Supreme Court was struggling to develop a coherent fundamental fairness standard in state confession cases, it also had to develop a federal standard. In 1943 in *McNabb v. United States*[25] the Court established a separate standard for the admission of confessions in federal cases than it had in state cases. The *McNabb* case came to be reviewed by the Court after the murder of a federal revenue officer during a raid on a moonshine whiskey business run by the McNabb family. In the two or three days that followed the murder, federal officials brought in and questioned Freeman, Raymond, Benjamin, Emuil, and Barney McNabb about the murder. Although the questioning of the McNabbs took place in the absence of an attorney and they were not allowed to contact family or friends, this case lacked any suggestion of physical coercion. Freeman, Raymond, and Benjamin McNabb subsequently confessed to the crime and their confessions were admitted at trial and used to convict them of second-degree murder. They then pursued the appeal of their convictions to the Supreme Court.

The Supreme Court overturned the conviction of the McNabbs by ruling that the confessions should not have been admitted into evidence. Justice Felix Frankfurter wrote the opinion for the Court and did not base the decision on any provision of the Constitution. Instead, Justice Frankfurter rested the decision on the Supreme Court's supervisory authority over the federal courts. Therefore, rather than trying to determine if the interrogation techniques violated the Fifth Amendment's Self-incrimination Clause or the Fifth Amendment's Due Process Clause, Frankfurter examined congressional law to determine if the confessions were admissible. In doing so, Frankfurter found that federal law required that after people were arrested by federal law officers, they had to be promptly brought before a judicial officer, informed of the charges against them, and informed of their procedural rights. Since this requirement had not been met, it was necessary for the Court to determine if the confession were voluntary. The precedent coming out of *McNabb*, known as the "McNabb rule," was that unless an arrested individual was promptly given an arraignment in federal cases, the detention was illegal, and any confession that resulted would be inadmissible at trial.

One problem that arose out of *McNabb* was the lack of a precise definition of a "prompt" arraignment. Arraignment here refers to an initial appearance. It wasn't until 1957 when the Supreme Court decided *Mallory v. United States*[26] that it clarified what was required to avoid unnecessary delay. *Mallory* came to the Court as a result of Andrew Mallory's conviction for a rape that took place in the basement of an apartment building in Washington, D.C. After the rape, suspicion focused on Mallory, who lived in the basement not far from where the rape took place. Mallory was arrested at around 2 P.M. and immediately questioned for between thirty and forty-five minutes. Six hours after being arrested, Mallory consented to a polygraph test. An hour and a half into the polygraph test, Mallory started talking and then gave a full confession. Mallory was repeatedly interrogated and continued to make statements until 1:30 A.M. In the morning the day after his arrest, Mallory was arraigned and informed of his procedural rights. At trial, Mallory's confessions were admitted as evidence, which led to a conviction and a death sentence. The conviction was upheld by the Court of Appeals for the District of Columbia Circuit prior to reaching the Supreme Court.

The Supreme Court overturned Mallory's conviction, ruling that the confession should not have been admitted since the police failed to arraign him promptly. Justice Frankfurter wrote the majority opinion, which recognized that, in some instances—such as the need to take down volunteered information from a suspect—a slight delay in arraignment may be acceptable. However, delay for the purpose of interrogation was not acceptance. This precedent became the Mallory component of the "McNabb-Mallory rule." In demanding that suspects be brought before a magistrate and informed of their rights prior to interrogation, the Court refused to consider, as it had been doing in state cases, whether certain methods of interrogation were inherently more coercive than others. It is important to note that the Court was not discouraging the use of police interrogations; it only limited such interrogations prior to initial judicial appearance. Once the initial appearance took place, if a suspect decided to cooperate, the Court continued to believe that interrogation did have a proper place in police procedures.

THE RIGHT TO COUNSEL

The history of the Supreme Court's interpretation of the Sixth Amendment's right to counsel is shorter than that of the right against self-incrimination. The protections provided by the right to counsel have come to include two broad rights. The first protection is the right of accused people to retain counsel to defend them in all official proceedings. This category of protection provided by the Sixth Amendment has not been controversial. The second protection provided by the Sixth Amendment right to counsel has been more controversial and has taken longer for the courts to develop. This has been the right of indigents to have counsel appointed to provide a defense on their behalf. The lack of precise language in the Sixth Amendment extending the right of counsel to this class of defendants thwarted its development.

Early Right to Counsel Cases

The first significant contribution that the Supreme Court made in interpreting the Sixth Amendment's right to counsel came in the 1932 case of *Powell v. Alabama*.[27] *Powell v. Alabama* became one of the most celebrated cases of the 1930s.[28] *Powell v. Alabama* involved the arrest, trial, and subsequent convictions of seven illiterate black boys, charged with raping two white women. Because the trial took place in Scottsboro, Alabama, the defendants became known as the Scottsboro boys. The charges grew out of a confrontation between white and black youths on a freight train; the confrontation ended with the charge of rape being brought against the black youths. When the community heard about the charges, people reacted with hostility. As a result, the sheriff called out the militia to help guard the boys. All of the accused were residents of other states, with no families or friends in Scottsboro to help them with their legal problems. Furthermore, the boys were described as poor, ignorant, and illiterate. Despite the fact that rape was a capital crime and that three of the boys, including Ozie Powell, were sentenced to death in separate trials, the boys were not asked whether they had or were able to retain counsel. Noticing the lack of counsel, the trial judge appointed all the members of the local bar to represent the defendants. Regardless of the judge's appointment, no attorney acted as counsel for the defendants until the morning of the trials. After the convictions, the defendants' appeal eventually reached the Supreme Court.

In *Powell v. Alabama* the Court limited its decision to answering the question as to whether the defendants were denied the right to counsel in substance, and, if so, whether that resulted in a denial of due process as required by the Fourteenth Amendment. The Court, in an opinion written by Justice George Sutherland, did not incorporate the Sixth Amendment right to counsel and did not find that the defendant's right to counsel had been violated. Instead, it ruled that the defendants had been denied the due process of law required by the Fourteenth Amendment. The Court reasoned that denial of counsel in these capital trials violated the standard of fundamental fairness necessary to our criminal justice system. The Court's decision was based on its belief that the trials were held too quickly to allow counsel to be secured for the defendants and that the appointment procedures for counsel used by the trial judge were not effective enough to satisfy due process requirements. Justice Sutherland summed up the importance of counsel for a defendant by stating, "Without it, though he be not guilty, he faces the danger of conviction because he does not know how to establish his innocence."[29] Counsel was thought to be so important that it had to be provided at all critical stages of the judicial process. The precedent established in *Powell* was narrow, however, because the Court grounded its decision on the specific characteristics of this group of defendants including their age, ignorance, illiterateness, feeble-mindedness, their lack of friends and family in the Scottsboro area, and the capital charges that made the right to counsel essential to giving them a fair trial. As a result, in future cases, appointment of counsel would depend on the facts of each particular case. Nevertheless, the Court had made a clear statement about the importance of counsel in providing a fair trial within our judicial system.

Six years after *Powell* the Court again indicated the significance of representation by counsel in the case of *Johnson v. Zerbst*.[30] The *Johnson* case was important for two reasons. First, it established the rules of counsel that would be employed in federal criminal trials for years to come. Second, it expanded the right to counsel to indigent federal defendants. *Johnson* came to the Court after two defendants were charged, arraigned, tried, convicted, and sentenced for counterfeiting all on the same day. The defendants in the case had informed the judge that they were without counsel, but were ready to proceed with trial. After conviction, the defendants appealed, claiming that their right to counsel had been violated.

Justice Hugo Black who wrote the Court's opinion in *Johnson*, used the opportunity to create a blanket rule that federal trial courts lacked the power "to deprive an accused of his life and liberty unless he has or waives the assistance of counsel."[31] The right to counsel, the Court ruled, went beyond the right to retain counsel to also include the necessity of appointing counsel in indigent cases. Furthermore, the Court announced that if counsel were withheld at a federal trial, it provided grounds for *habeas corpus* relief. A writ of *habeas corpus* is an inquiry to determine if a person holding another in custody is doing so lawfully. If the detainment is illegal, the person will be released. Finally, the Court stated that although the right to counsel could be waived, any allegation of waiver would be closely scrutinized since waiver required "an intentional relinquishment or abandonment of a known right or privilege."[32] Federal judges had a duty to protect the accused's right to counsel and if they determined that there had indeed been a waiver, the record needed to clearly explain the basis for the judge's determination. The Court then remanded the case, since the trial judge should have taken further steps to ensure that the defendants truly desired to waive their right to counsel.

The comprehensive ruling regarding the right to counsel for the federal courts in *Johnson v. Zerbst* was rejected for state courts six years later in *Betts v. Brady*.[33] Betts, an unemployed farmhand, was convicted of the noncapital felony of robbery. During his trial, he asked for and was denied assistance of counsel. Betts then defended himself to the best of his ability by examining his own witnesses and cross-examining the State's. Despite his efforts, he was convicted and denied *habeas corpus* relief in the state system. Betts then sought review by the Supreme Court, arguing that he was denied due process of law in his trial.

In *Betts*, in an opinion written by Justice Owen Roberts, the Court refused to hold that the Sixth Amendment right to counsel was incorporated by the Fourteenth Amendment's Due Process Clause. Once again, the Court, out of respect for judicial federalism, failed to impose national standards on state criminal justice systems. State courts would thus continue the practice first initiated in *Powell* of deciding on a case-by-case basis which defendants who had been convicted without the help of counsel were denied due process of law under the Fourteenth Amendment. As a result, future cases would require state courts to examine the totality of the circumstances of a case to determine if a fair trial could be conducted when the defendant did not have the assistance of counsel. In *Betts*, the Court ruled that there were no special circumstances that required Betts to have counsel appointed for him, so it upheld his conviction.

As had been the case in self-incrimination cases, the *Betts* decision established two separate standards of constitutional review for right to counsel cases. During the 1940s and 1950s, an examination of the totality of circumstances thus became central to how both the right to counsel and confession cases were handled in state cases. In federal right to counsel cases, courts were to follow the strict waiver policy established in *Johnson v. Zerbst*.

State courts continued to follow the due process requirements first established in *Powell*. One of the difficulties this created was that the Court in *Betts* provided no concrete guidelines for state judges as to what types of factual circumstances would in the future require appointment of counsel. This resulted in separate standards for appointment of counsel in each state. It also left state judges in a quandary about when due process required appointment of counsel. Likewise, defendants had no clear idea of when their special circumstances required the appointment of counsel. All these problems in the implementation of *Betts* made it difficult for state judges to second-guess how the Supreme Court would answer right to counsel cases on appeal. Despite the problems that were created by the *Betts* decision, it remained good law until 1964 when it was re-examined by the Warren Court in *Gideon v. Wainwright*.[34]

The Warren Court Revolution

Prior to the *Gideon* decision, the Supreme Court had sent a number of signals that it believed that the right to counsel had been an undervalued component of our legal system. As a result of the decisions reached by the Warren Court, there were an increasing number of circumstances in which counsel was required in state criminal prosecutions for convictions to be upheld. In fact, the Warren Court was so adamant that the right to counsel was essential to the fundamental fairness of a trial that it never ruled against a defendant's claim that special circumstances required the appointment of counsel. The Warren Court believed that the importance of the right to counsel stemmed from its ability to promote an adversarial system of justice and protect a number of related constitutional rights, such as the right against self-incrimination and the right to confront witnesses. This belief also caused the Warren Court to expand the scope of coverage of the right to counsel to critical stages prior to trial.

This can be seen in *Hamilton v. Alabama*,[35] decided in 1961, which extended the right to counsel to the arraignment stage and *White v. Maryland*[36] decided in 1963, which extended it to preliminary hearings. The purpose behind extending the right to counsel to these stages of the judicial process was to protect the interests of defendants who, without counsel, might make mistakes in their defense that would have the effect of ultimately causing conviction at trial.

Gideon v. Wainwright came to the Court in 1963 after Clarence Gideon was convicted in Florida of breaking and entering with the intent to commit a crime, a felony under Florida law.[37] At his trial Gideon, who could not afford to retain an attorney, asked the judge to appoint one for him. The judge, following the precedent of *Betts v. Brady*, found no special circumstances that required the appointment of counsel. Gideon was then convicted. When the Supreme Court announced that it would hear the case, the discord that surrounded the *Betts* precedent became clear when twenty-two states filed *amicus curiae* briefs, asking the Court to overrule *Betts* and only two states joined Florida in its attempt to see *Betts* upheld.

Justice Black wrote the Court's opinion for *Gideon v. Wainwright*. The Court overruled *Betts v. Brady* and found that the Sixth Amendment's right to counsel was incorporated by the Fourteenth Amendment's Due Process Clause in felony cases. Pointing back to the decision in *Powell v. Alabama*, Justice Black wrote that such a move was possible because "the Court in *Betts v. Brady* made an abrupt break with its own well-considered precedents."[38] Consequently, the Court was only restoring earlier "constitutional principles established to achieve a fair system of justice."[39] Not only did earlier constitutional principles justify the decision to overrule *Betts*, so did proper reason and reflection concerning the adversarial system of justice. Justice Black pointed out that it was an obvious truth that attorneys were essential in protecting legal interests in the judicial system. This was illustrated by the actions of the states that spent large sums of money developing a cadre of professional attorneys to help with the prosecution of those accused of crimes. Furthermore, few defendants who could afford to hire an attorney to help with their defense failed to do so. Because of the complexity of the criminal procedure and the reliance of states on professional counsel to gain convictions, Justice Black went on to reason that "any person haled into court, who is too poor to hire a lawyer, cannot be assured a fair trial unless counsel is provided for him."[40] The final result of the Court's ruling was that indigents had to be granted counsel in state felony prosecutions unless there was a showing of an intentional waiver of the right. After twenty-five years, the states finally had to play by the same rules that the federal government had been subject to since *Johnson v. Zerbst.*

Having established the right to counsel in felony trials in 1963, the Court then set out to define the different situations in which the right to counsel would be extended. At the same time the Court was also in the process of making major changes in the law concerning the Fifth Amendment's right against self-incrimination. The first step in that process took place in *Malloy v. Hogan,*[41] which was decided in 1964. In *Malloy* the Court overruled *Twining v. United States* and incorporated the Fifth Amendment privilege against self-incrimination. Justice William Brennan wrote in his majority opinion that incorporation was necessary because the Fifth Amendment was a vital component in ensuring that the American system of justice was an accusatorial system rather than an inquisitorial one. In fact, this right was so important that it had to be incorporated since "the same standards must determine whether an accused's silence in either a federal or state proceeding is justified."[42]

In 1964 the Warren Court went beyond the parameters established in *Powell v. Alabama*—that the right to counsel extended to critical stages in judicial proceedings—to apply the right to counsel to critical stages in the adversarial process that did not formally take place in judicial proceedings. This indicated a shift in the Warren Court's interpretation of how the right against self-incrimination was affected by the right to counsel. This shift can be illustrated by comparing the Court's 1958 decision in *Crooker v. California*[43] to later decisions like *Massiah v. United States*[44] and *Escobedo v. Illinois.*[45] In *Crooker* a narrowly divided majority ruled that a confession obtained while the defendant was held incommunicado and denied the assistance of an attorney was admissible. The Court refused to reverse the conviction partly due to its fear of the devastating effect on law enforcement if it ordered confessions obtained in absence of counsel to be inadmissible. In 1964, while not ruling that incriminating statements would not be admissible if given without the presence of counsel, the Court in the cases of *Massiah v. United States* and *Escobedo v. Illinois* clearly enlarged the scope of the right to counsel to include situations outside judicial proceedings. The first case in which the Court moved toward a blanket rule to govern admission of incriminating statements rather than examining the totality of circumstances was *Massiah v. United States.*

Massiah came to the Court's attention when Winston Massiah was convicted of smuggling cocaine. The conviction was obtained, in part, through the use of incriminating statements that were gained when Massiah made admissions to an undercover informant. The informant, who was an indicted co-conspirator, was transmitting the conversations to federal agents. The statements were made and recorded after Massiah had already been indicted and arraigned. Based on the conversation between Massiah and the informant, a new and broader indictment was issued against Massiah and twelve others. At trial the informant refused to testify against Massiah so the primary evidence connecting Massiah to the smuggling ring came in the form of testimony from the federal agent who had overheard the conversation between Massiah and the informant. Massiah was then convicted of the charges brought in the second indictment. The Supreme Court then granted review.

In its decision, the Court made a number of significant contributions to law in the areas of both self-incrimination and right to counsel. First, it refused to examine the failure of police to permit an already indicted suspect to have counsel present at the time of interrogation as one factor in the totality of circumstances that should be scrutinized to determine if a statement was admissible under the Fifth Amendment. Instead, the Court's ruling rested on the Sixth Amendment right to counsel. The Court's opinion in *Massiah* also extended the function of the right to counsel beyond preparing for judicial proceedings and trial to that of also representing and counseling individuals under indictment in their interactions with police. The Court then created a blanket rule that in all federal prosecutions post-indictment interrogations were a critical stage in the prosecutorial process to which the right to counsel was attached in order to better guarantee an individual's right against self-incrimination. Therefore, any incriminating statements made by a defendant to the police in between the time of arraignment and trial could not be admitted at trial if the right to counsel had been denied. This was the first time that the Court held that any statements resulting from a denial of the right to counsel would not be allowed. Although *Massiah* was a federal case, this decision became applicable to state prosecutions because of the earlier decision to incorporate the Sixth Amendment right to counsel in *Gideon v. Wainwright*. The overall impact of the decision was, however, narrow. Since it only applied to cases involving post-indictment interrogations, the precedent did not apply to most police interrogations, which take place prior to indictment.

The Court also decided *Escobedo v. Illinois* in 1964. *Escobedo v. Illinois* further asserted that the Fifth Amendment right against self-incrimination was tied to the Sixth Amendment right to counsel. In doing so, the Court also rejected the voluntariness test for admission of incriminating statements. *Escobedo* came to the Court as a result of Danny Escobedo's conviction for murder in Chicago, Illinois. Escobedo was arrested without a warrant for the murder of his brother-in-law and held for over fifteen hours until his attorney obtained his release through a state *habeas corpus* writ. His lawyer then told Escobedo to demand to have his lawyer present if he was again arrested. Eleven days later, after more police investigation plus statements from a man named Benedict DiGerlando about Escobedo's complicity in the crime, Escobedo was arrested again. From the point at which his second arrest was made, Escobedo requested the presence of counsel during any interrogation. The police refused to grant his request and refused his attorney, who had arrived at the police station, the right to see his client. Police admitted that they lied to Escobedo's attorney and told him that Escobedo did not want to consult with him. When Escobedo was confronted by DiGerlando, he accused DiGerlando of firing the fatal shots. Escobedo then made a number of admissions that provided enough information to lead to a conviction for murder. He asked the Supreme Court to review the case since he contended that the admissions should not have been admissible and his request was granted.

In reaching a decision in *Escobedo*, the Court split 5-4 and established a narrow precedent that tied protection of the Fifth Amendment right against self-incrimination to the Sixth Amendment right to counsel. The majority opinion, written by Justice Arthur Goldberg, who had recently replaced Justice Felix Frankfurter, relied on *Massiah* as precedent rather than the long lineage of cases involving the Fifth Amendment right against self-incrimination. In this way the Court did not have to review the totality of circumstances to determine if Escobedo's admissions were the result of some form of coercion. The Court then moved beyond *Massiah* and stated that the point of indictment was not when the right to counsel became effective. Instead, the right became effective at the point at which a person became the "focus" of an investigation and was interrogated based on those suspicions. *Escobedo* was, however, a narrow decision because the majority opinion relied on the specific facts of the case. Justice Goldberg wrote:

We hold, therefore, that where, as here, the investigation is no longer a general inquiry into an unsolved crime but has begun to focus on a particular suspect, the suspect has been taken into police custody, the police carry out a process of interrogations that lends itself to eliciting incriminating statements, the suspect has requested and been denied an opportunity to consult with his lawyer, and the police have not effectively warned him of his absolute constitutional right to remain silent, the accused has been denied "the Assistance of Counsel" in violation of the Sixth Amendment to the Constitution as made "obligatory upon the States by the Fourteenth Amendment," . . . and that no statement elicited by the police during the interrogation may be used against him at a criminal trial.[46]

In making this ruling, the Court again rejected the voluntariness standard of admitting incriminating statements and again decided to use the right to counsel as a shield against the possibility of unacceptable police interrogation methods. The blanket litmus test that would seem to be the natural result of the ruling in *Escobedo* was, however, lost in the insistence that the facts of this case were somehow special and not necessarily applicable to other cases. Yale Kamisar points out that the confusion over the actual precedent of *Escobedo* led to a number of possible applications. The possible applications of when the right to counsel was required included (1) whenever the investigation focused on a particular individual and was no longer a general inquiry; (2) when the suspect was in police custody; (3) when the purpose of an interrogation was to gain incriminating statements; (4) when the suspect had requested and been denied counsel; and (5) when police failed to warn a suspect of his right to remain silent.[47] This confusion over the proper application of *Escobedo* caused many police departments to read it as narrowly as possible and to continue to freely interrogate suspects without allowing them access to legal counsel when it was requested. Clarification of the Court's intent in *Escobedo* would not come for another two years when the Court decided *Miranda v. Arizona*.

Miranda v. Arizona was one of four companion cases—three state and one federal—that were decided at the same time.[48] Each case involved the admission of confessions that came about through police interrogations after the point of arrest, in the absence of counsel, and with no warning by the police of the suspect's Fifth Amendment right against self-incrimination and Sixth Amendment right to counsel. None of the cases had unusual factual circumstances. *Miranda* and the companion cases represented factual cases that were typical of the way that most police departments conducted investigations. The specifics of the *Miranda* case were that Ernesto Miranda was arrested for suspicion of rape. He had retained an attorney who was present at the police station after the suspect's arrest. But Miranda was denied the opportunity to speak to his attorney, as he requested. Miranda was then interrogated while being forced to stand handcuffed in an interrogation room. Within a matter of hours, he gave a confession that led to his conviction.

The Court, through a five-member majority opinion written by Chief Justice Warren, made a ruling that rested on a set of principles, rather than a set of particular facts. The decision had the effect of ending the long history of case-by-case analysis in cases involving self-incrimination and creating a blanket rule: Under *Miranda*, the point at which counsel was required was when a person was subjected to custodial interrogation. The decision also spelled out the repercussions if the proper procedures weren't followed; it specified detailed rules governing police questioning in custodial interrogation situations in both state and federal courts.

According to the Supreme Court, lower courts had to follow eight different procedural guidelines in order for law enforcement officials not to violate the Fifth and Sixth Amendments. The first step that law enforcement officials had to follow prior to subjecting suspects in custody to interrogation was that suspects must first be clearly informed that they have the right to remain silent. When police informed suspects of their right to remain silent, they also had to state that "anything said can and will be used against the individual in court."[49] An individual also had to be "clearly informed that he has the right to consult with a lawyer and to have the lawyer with him during interrogation."[50] The individual was also to be told that if indigent "a lawyer will be appointed to represent him."[51] Furthermore, if "the individual indicates in any manner, at any time prior to or during questioning, that he wishes to remain silent, the interrogation must cease."[52] If an individual being held by police requests to have an attorney present, "the interrogation must cease until an attorney is present. At that time, the individual must have an opportunity to confer with the attorney and to have him present during any subsequent questioning."[53] If the interrogation takes place without an attorney present and a statement is given, "a heavy burden rests on the Government to demonstrate that the defendant knowingly and intelligently waived his privilege against self-incrimination and his right to retained or appointed counsel."[54] And, finally, lower courts were not to make a distinction in the admission into evidence between "statements which are direct confessions and statements which amount to 'admissions' of part or all of an offense . . . no distinction may be drawn between inculpatory and statements alleged to be merely 'exculpatory.' "[55]

In establishing these procedural guidelines for the admission of statements gained through custodial interrogation, the Court grounded its opinion in the Sixth Amendment rather than the Fifth Amendment. It also had the effect of strengthening the belief that only voluntary statements should be admissible at trial, since it was believed that if suspects were made aware of their rights, they would assert those rights unless they waived them knowingly and intelligently. As a result, the government had to demonstrate two things if it sought to introduce statements gathered through custodial interrogation: (1) that defendants not only understood their rights, but also intelligently waived those rights, and (2) that if suspects did waive their rights, they did so freely with no form of compulsion exerted by the state.

The guidelines set down in the *Miranda* decision were designed to place attorneys into the interrogation process more often to act as witnesses to the techniques by which interrogations proceeded. *Miranda* was not, however, meant to end police interrogations and the admission of all statements made by the accused in the criminal justice process. This is demonstrated by the waiver provision that allowed interrogation to continue should suspects waive their rights. Furthermore, the need for a waiver only applied to situations in which the suspect was interrogated while in custody. This left the police free to question individuals in the normal course of a criminal investigation; suspects could even be questioned prior to arrest. Spontaneous confessions, volunteered by suspects while not in custody, would also continue to be allowed into trial.

The point at which law enforcement personnel are required to give *Miranda* warnings was clarified in 1969 when the Court decided *Orozco v. Texas*.[56] Reyes Arias Orozco had been arrested and interrogated at his boardinghouse rather than at the police station. Even though he was not informed of his rights, the prosecution used his statements at the trial. The Court ruled that even though he was not interrogated at a police station, *Miranda* warnings should have been given. The fact that Orozco had been arrested and was in custody was the controlling feature of the case, not where the interrogation took place. Thus, Orozco's statements should not have been admissible at trial. This decision made it clear that if police wanted to use the product of an interrogation, they had to give *Miranda* warnings at the point in which an individual was formally arrested or deprived of her freedom of action, regardless of the location.

The Burger Court

The decisions of the Warren Court concerning the protections of the Fifth Amendment right against self-incrimination and Sixth Amendment right to counsel can be seen as a high watermark. By the end of 1972, Richard Nixon had reconfigured the Supreme Court, starting with the appointment of a new Chief Justice, Warren Burger, in 1969. With the addition of three other justices—Harry Blackmun, Lewis Powell, and William Rehnquist—a new majority emerged. This new majority was shaped in part by Richard Nixon's desire to create a strong "law and order" Court, a Court that would reassert the authority of law enforcement officers to effectively do their job without the Court second-guessing their methods of operation. It was expected by some that this new majority would overrule *Miranda*.

Although it had not overruled *Miranda*, the Burger Court had failed to apply the decision to limit the introduction of a single piece of evidence prior to 1977 when it first reviewed Williams's conviction. During this period, neither the four new justices appointed by Richard Nixon nor Justices Byron White and Potter Stewart, who both dissented in *Miranda*, cast a single vote to exclude any piece of evidence due to a violation of *Miranda*. The Burger Court didn't just refuse to apply *Miranda*, it also weakened *Miranda* in several ways. This was because it believed that *Miranda* warnings were mere "prophylactic rules," designed to preserve the integrity of the Fifth Amendment. As such, *Miranda* warnings could be distinguished from the Fifth Amendment's guarantees.[57] This distinction between the mandates of *Miranda* and the Fifth Amendment was possible because the Burger Court believed that "the fundamental purpose of the Fifth Amendment [was] the preservation of an adversary system of justice."[58] In believing that this was the true purpose of the Fifth Amendment, the Burger Court's strict construction permitted it to reconsider the issue of compelled statements and allowed the admission of statements, which, although taken in express violation of *Miranda*, would after an examination of the totality of circumstances be shown to be voluntary.

The Burger Court thus was capable of narrowing the effect of *Miranda* without overruling the case. It did so by using several primary methods or a combination of these methods.[59] The first method was by limiting the scenarios in which the exclusionary rule would be used to suppress statements from being admitted as evidence when gained through a *Miranda* violation. The second was to limit the *Miranda* decision to specific factual situations by narrowly interpreting the definitions of interrogation and custody.

The first Fifth Amendment case that the new Burger Court majority heard was *Harris v. New York*.[60] *Harris* illustrates how the Burger Court reinterpreted the exclusionary rule to allow prosecutorial use of statements discovered through a violation of the *Miranda* warnings. It also illustrates the weakening of the role that the right to counsel would play in protecting the rights of criminal defendants under the Burger Court. *Harris* came to the Court as a result of Viven Harris's arrest and an interrogation in which police failed to comply with the *Miranda* requirements. Specifically, she was not informed that she had the right to counsel and to have counsel present during any questioning. During the subsequent interrogation, Harris made incriminating statements. At trial, the prosecutor realized that the statements were not admissible and therefore did not seek to introduce them as evidence until after Harris took the stand and testified that she had not been involved in the crime. At that point, the judge allowed the prosecutor to bring in the tainted incriminating statements. The judge then instructed the jury to consider the statements only for the purpose of evaluating Harris's credibility but not as direct evidence of Harris's guilt. Harris was then convicted and the Supreme Court accepted the case on review.

Chief Justice Burger in the majority opinion in *Harris v. New York* found that although *Miranda* could be read to disallow "use of an uncounseled statement for any purpose," it "was not at all necessary to the Court's holding and cannot be regarded as controlling."[61] In effect, the denial of uncounseled statements for any purpose made in the *Miranda* opinion was seen as a nonbinding dictum and not central to the Court's true holding. Therefore, the Burger Court was free to limit the application of a violation of *Miranda* to the prosecutor's case-in-chief. This limitation would stop prosecutors from using the fruit of a *Miranda* violation as evidence in their case against the suspect, but they could use such statements to poke holes in the evidence presented by the defense. In this case, since there was no showing that Harris's will to resist had been overcome by any form of police compulsion, the statement was deemed to be voluntary. Furthermore, since the statement was necessary to assess the credibility of the witness, it did not make sense to deny the prosecution this important piece of evidence simply because of a failure to warn Harris of the right to counsel. The Court also did not believe that admission of tainted statements for this purpose would give police incentive to violate the rights of others in the future.

The Burger Court further facilitated the admission of custodial confessions in the 1972 case of *Lego v. Twomey*.[62] In that case the Court determined that the proper burden of proof in determining if a custodial confession was voluntary when gained in violation of *Miranda* guidelines was that of a "preponderance of the evidence" rather than "beyond a reasonable doubt."[63]

Michigan v. Tucker[64] provides another example of how the Burger Court narrowed the application of *Miranda* by also narrowing the exclusionary rule. Traditionally, the exclusionary rule had been interpreted to deny prosecutors the ability to make use of a direct violation of a person's constitutional rights and the fruits gained through the original violation. In *Tucker* this tradition was not followed. Tucker was arrested and the police failed to warn him of his right to counsel prior to interrogation. Tucker then told police that, at the time of the rape for which he was a suspect, he was with a man named Henderson. When Henderson was brought in for questioning, he discredited Tucker's alibi and told police that Tucker had made incriminating statements to him. At trial, Tucker objected to the use of Henderson as a witness for the prosecution, since police only found out about him because of Tucker's statements, which were obtained in violation of the *Miranda* warnings. The trial judge allowed the testimony and Tucker was convicted. He was then granted *habeas corpus* relief by the Sixth Circuit of the Court of Appeals and the Supreme Court granted Michigan's request for *certiorari*. A writ of *certiorari* is a petition asking the Supreme Court to call a case up for review.

Justice William Rehnquist wrote the majority opinion and stated that the central question that the Court had to determine was "whether the police conduct complained of directly infringed upon [the] right against compulsory self-incrimination or whether it instead violated only the prophylactic rules developed to protect that right."[65] In answering that question, the Court found that in this case the police had only violated the procedural guidelines that *Miranda* had recommended, but "the Court recognized that these procedural safeguards were not themselves rights protected by the Constitution but were instead measures to insure that the right against compulsory self-incrimination was protected."[66] Tucker's Fifth Amendment rights were not violated by the use of Henderson's testimony because Tucker's statements identifying Henderson had not been a product of compulsion. Furthermore, there was no violation of the Fifth Amendment because Tucker's tainted statements were not used to prove the prosecution's case, since they were never used directly at trial.

The way in which the Burger Court narrowed the definition of interrogation, thereby limiting the application of the *Miranda* decision to specific factual situations, can be illustrated by an examination of *Michigan v. Mo-*

sley.[67] Richard Mosley had been arrested in connection with two robberies. Prior to being questioned, he was correctly given his *Miranda* warnings. After being given the warnings, Mosley refused to answer questions but did not request an attorney. The police then cut off the interrogation and took Mosley back to a holding cell. The detective who had arrested Mosley then informed a homicide detective that Mosley had been arrested. The homicide detective moved Mosley to a different floor of the police building and again administered the *Miranda* warnings prior to questioning him about a robbery in which a murder had occurred. Mosley cooperated during this interrogation and made statements that implicated him in the crime. The statements were then used by the prosecutor in his case-in-chief over the protests of Mosley. Mosley was convicted and when the conviction was overturned by the Michigan Court of Appeals, Michigan sought and was granted *certiorari.*

The Supreme Court overruled the decision of the Michigan Court of Appeals. According to Justice Stewart, who wrote the majority opinion, *Miranda* could not be interpreted to act as a permanent bar to all statements defendants make after asserting their rights. Instead, the proper approach was to determine if a defendant's right to cut off questioning had been honored by police. If such a request was honored, then any later statements may be admissible if they were not the product of any form of coercion. In *Mosley*, the statements that resulted from the second round of interrogation were admissible because the circumstances showed that the police had not used the inherent compulsion of custodial interrogation to overcome Mosley's will. The facts showed the opposite. The police did honor Mosley's initial assertion of his rights. Mosley was not questioned by a second officer until over two hours later. At that time, Mosley was again advised of his rights. Furthermore, the second interrogation took place in a different location, and it involved a different crime, so there did not seem to be a purposeful attempt by the police to take advantage of the circumstances to overcome Mosley's will.

As this legal history demonstrates, the decisions that the Supreme Court had previously made concerning the rights against self-incrimination and to counsel left a variety of precedents. These precedents gave any judge or justice who would be asked to rule on Williams's appeal the discretion to exercise a number of legal options. These legal options could allow a number of different resolutions to the case, depending on the subjective facts that were accepted and the procedural laws emphasized. For example, if a judge found that Williams had waived his rights, *Michigan v. Mosley* could be used as a precedent for allowing Williams's statements and the conviction could then be upheld. However, if a judge didn't believe that there was a proper waiver, the judge could find that *Miranda* was violated and rule that Williams's statements were not admissible. This would result in a reversal of Judge Denato's original ruling, allowing the statements and related evidence to be used and forcing Iowa to either release Williams or prosecute him in a second trial. The *Williams* case presented not only a variety of precedents that gave judges the discretion necessary to select between different legal options, it also presented competing versions of the facts. In his appeal, Robert Williams was hoping that the appellate courts would accept different subjective facts and apply different procedural laws than had Judge Denato.

NOTES

1. *Nix v. Williams*, 467 U.S. 431, 451 (Stevens, J., concurring).
2. "Developments in the Law: Confessions,"*Harvard Law Review* 79 (1966): 952.
3. *The King v. Warickshall*, 1 Leach 263–264, 168 Eng. Rep. 234–235 (K. B. 1783).
4. Otis H. Stephens, *The Supreme Court and Confessions of Guilt* (Knoxville: University of Tennessee Press, 1973), p. 23.
5. *Hopt v. Utah*, 100 U.S. 574 (1884).
6. *Twining v. New Jersey*, 211 U.S. 78 (1908).
7. *Slaughterhouse Cases*, 83 U.S. 36 (1873).
8. For examples, see Emanuel H. Lavine, *The "Third Degree," A Detailed and Appalling Exposé of Police Brutality* (New York: Vanguard Press, 1930), and Edwin R. Keedy, "The Third Degree and Legal Interrogation of Suspects," *University of Pennsylvania Law Review* 85 (June 1937): 761–777.
9. The first seven confession cases that the Court reviewed all involved African-American defendants. These cases were *Brown v. Mississippi*, 297 U.S. 278 (1936); *Chambers v. Florida*, 309 U.S. 227 (1940); *Canty v. Alabama*, 309 U.S. 629 (1940); *White v. Texas*, 309 U.S. 631 (1940); *Lomax v. Texas*, 313 U.S. 544 (1941); *Vernon v. Alabama*, 313 U.S. 547 (1941); and *Ward v. Texas*, 316 U.S. 547 (1942).
10. *Brown v. Mississippi*, 297 U.S. 278 (1936).
11. Ibid., p. 284.
12. *Chambers v. Florida*, 309 U.S. 227 (1940).
13. *Lisenba v. California*, 314 U.S. 219 (1941).
14. "Developments in the Law," p. 63.
15. *Ashcraft v. Tennessee*, 322 U.S. 143 (1944).
16. Ibid., p. 154.
17. *Lyons v. Oklahoma*, 322 U.S. 596 (1944).
18. Ibid., p. 606.
19. Stephens, *The Supreme Court and Confessions*, pp. 90–98.
20. *Stein v. New York*, 346 U.S. 156 (1953).
21. *Spano v. New York*, 360 U.S. 315 (1959).
22. Ibid., p. 326 (Stewart, J., concurring).
23. *Rogers v. Richmond*, 365 U.S. 534 (1961).
24. *Miranda v. Arizona*, 384 U.S. 436 (1966).
25. *McNabb v. United States*, 318 U.S. 332 (1943).
26. *Mallory v. United States*, 354 U.S. 449 (1957).
27. *Powell v. Alabama*, 287 U.S. 45 (1932).

28. For an extended examination of *Powell v. Alabama* and the context of the case, see James Goodman, *Stories of Scottsboro* (New York: Vintage Books, 1995).

29. *Powell v. Alabama*, 287 U.S. 45, 69 (1932).

30. *Johnson v. Zerbst*, 304 U.S. 458 (1938).

31. Ibid., p. 463.

32. Ibid., p. 464.

33. *Betts v. Brady*, 316 U.S. 455 (1942).

34. *Gideon v. Wainwright*, 372 U.S. 335 (1963).

35. *Hamilton v. Alabama*, 368 U.S. 52 (1961).

36. *White v. Maryland*, 373 U.S. 59 (1963).

37. For a complete history of this case, see Anthony Lewis, *Gideon's Trumpet* (New York: Vintage Books, 1989).

38. *Gideon v. Wainwright*, 372 U.S. 335, 344 (1964).

39. Ibid., p. 344.

40. Ibid.

41. *Malloy v. Hogan*, 378 U.S. 1 (1964).

42. Ibid., p. 11.

43. *Crooker v. California*, 357 U.S. 433 (1958).

44. *Massiah v. United States*, 377 U.S. 201 (1964).

45. *Escobedo v. Illinois*, 378 U.S. 478 (1964).

46. Ibid., pp. 490–491.

47. Yale Kamisar, "*Brewer v. Williams*, *Massiah* and *Miranda*: What is 'Interrogation'? When Does It Matter?" *Georgetown Law Review* 67 (1978): 25 n. 145.

48. The companion cases were *Vignera v. New York*, *Westover v. United States*, and *California v. Stewart*.

49. *Miranda v. Arizona*, 384 U.S. 436, 469 (1966).

50. Ibid., p. 471.

51. Ibid., p. 473.

52. Ibid., p. 473–474.

53. Ibid., p. 474.

54. Ibid., p. 475.

55. Ibid., p. 476.

56. *Orozco v. Texas*, 394 U.S. 324 (1969).

57. *Michigan v. Payne*, 412 U.S. 47, 53 (1973).

58. *Garner v. United States*, 424 U.S. 648, 655 (1976).

59. Cynthia Picou, "Miranda and Escobedo: Warren v. Burger Court Decisions on 5th Amendment Rights," *Southern University Law Review* 4 (1978): 176.

60. *Harris v. New York*, 401 U.S. 222 (1971).

61. Ibid., p. 224.

62. *Lego v. Twomey*, 404 U.S. 477 (1972).

63. Ibid., p. 489.

64. *Michigan v. Tucker*, 417 U.S. 433 (1974).

65. Ibid., p. 439.

66. Ibid., p. 444.

67. *Michigan v. Mosley*, 423 U.S. 96 (1975).

Chapter 5 _____ ‘____

The First Appeals

> To experienced lawyers it is commonplace that the outcome of a law-
> suit—and hence the vindication of legal rights—depends more often on
> how the fact finder appraises the facts than on a disputed construction
> of a statute or interpretation of a line of precedents.
> —Justice William Brennan[1]

When the *Williams* case first came to the Supreme Court, Justice Powell
commented that "resolution of the issues in this case turns primarily on
one's perception of the facts."[2] Justice Powell's comment is absolutely correct. The determination of which version of the facts was believed was central to what evidence was presented to the jury and thus influenced its
verdict. If a separate version of the facts had been accepted by Judge Denato,
he may have ruled that Robert Williams's incriminating statements and related evidence was not admissible, and this may have resulted in a different
verdict. The debate as to which subjective facts should be accepted and how
the procedural law of the Fifth and Sixth Amendments should apply to them
became the basis of the appeal of Williams's first trial. In determining both
the facts and the law, discretion plays a major role. By examining the appeals
process in the state and lower federal courts, this chapter illustrates why
competing versions of the facts and law led to delay in the final administration of justice in Williams's murder conviction.

Our federal and state judicial system allows people who are convicted of
crimes to appeal their convictions to an appellate court. While many people

see the appeals process as a tactic used by those convicted to delay justice, appeals courts do play an important role in our system of justice. The primary function of appellate courts is to correct errors of either the substantive or procedural law as they were applied to the subjective facts at trial. Because individual judges are capable of erring in their interpretation of the law, judicial review helps to ensure that justice will not necessarily suffer. One key advantage that appellate courts have over trial courts in interpreting the law is time. Trial judges are forced to shoot from the hip and quickly make rulings on procedural law with little chance for contemplation. Appellate judges, on the other hand, consider these same issues after having read extensive written briefs and heard oral arguments. They then have the luxury of taking time to consider the issues. Another advantage appellate judges have is that they make decisions in panels comprising a number of judges, so the chance of an idiosyncratic error by an isolated individual is limited.

Appeals in state cases go to either the intermediate court of appeals, if one exists, or to the state supreme court. Unsuccessful appellants at state intermediate courts can then request review by state supreme courts. In the *Williams* case, the first state appeal went directly to the Iowa Supreme Court. If the case involves a federal constitutional issue and the state supreme court either refuses to review the case or resolves it, then the party that lost may petition the U.S. Supreme Court to review the case. Finally, if unsuccessful in this attempt for U.S. Supreme Court review, a defendant also has the opportunity to attack the conviction collaterally through the *habeas corpus* process, if the case involves a right protected by the U.S. Constitution.

Although appeals can be filed in almost any case, they will only be ruled on favorably when a serious error of law was made at trial. Serious errors of law are distinguished from harmless errors. Serious errors are ones that may have led to a reversal of the verdict by the judge or jury had the defendant had a fair trial. To appeal a verdict, a defendant must file a notice of appeal and submit supporting documents such as the transcript of the trial. In 1956, in *Griffin v. Illinois*,[3] the Supreme Court held that states had to cover the costs of the trial record for indigent defendants. This was followed in 1963 by *Douglas v. California*,[4] in which the Supreme Court ruled that states had to provide representation for indigent defendants in their appeal. These two decisions have increased the number of defendants who appeal their convictions. Currently, about one-third of all individuals convicted of crimes do appeal their cases.[5]

Appellate courts do not hold new trials or review the factual determinations leading to a verdict. Appellate courts do not accept new evidence or listen to new testimony. Appellate courts only examine the legal issues in the trial record that counsel argues denied the defendant a fair trial. Appellate courts are limited to hearing arguments about how the law—as applied in the decisions of the lower court judge through the record of the trial—was misapplied in a harmful manner.

THE STATE APPELLATE PROCESS

After Williams's conviction, Henry T. McKnight filed an appeal on behalf of Williams before the Iowa State Supreme Court. In his brief, he argued that Williams's conviction should be reversed for two reasons. The first was that, in accordance with the Supreme Court cases of *Escobedo v. Illinois*[6] and *Miranda v. Arizona*,[7] the state had failed to sustain its burden in showing that the defendant voluntarily, knowingly, and intelligently waived his Fifth Amendment right to remain silent and his Sixth Amendment right to counsel when he gave the police admissions against his interests on the trip from Davenport to Des Moines. The second was that the trial court had erred in overruling his motion to suppress the evidence resulting from the automobile trip between Davenport and Des Moines while Williams was in police custody. Richard C. Turner, Iowa's attorney general, filed a brief responding to McKnight's appeal.

On December 15, 1970, the Supreme Court of Iowa issued its opinion in the case of *Iowa v. Williams*.[8] In a 5–4 decision the court upheld the conviction of Williams. In his majority opinion, Justice Robert Larson first pointed out that almost all protections of the Constitution, including the right to counsel and the privilege against self-incrimination, may be relinquished by a citizen. Waivers could be made during a period of custodial interrogation after the accused has been given the required warnings. A waiver may come prior to or after an accused has consulted an attorney. If, however, an accused person chose to exercise his rights, further interrogation had to cease until an attorney was present. Should the accused waive his rights, he may limit the scope of an interrogation by announcing that he would like to forgo further interrogation until an attorney is consulted. In such a circumstance, the interrogation should not proceed until the accused has given consent to be questioned or voluntarily and willingly gives the police further information. Suspects may waive their rights when they are not in the presence of an attorney. A waiver of *Miranda* rights may not be presumed from a silent record. However, an oral or written waiver is not required. Rather, the court indicated that a waiver may be found from an examination of the totality of circumstances of the record.

The majority opinion noted that, in determining the totality of circumstances regarding a motion to suppress, the trial court, subject to review, had to make determinations concerning the credibility of the witnesses and the evidence. In other words, the trial court must determine the subjective facts of the case. The function of the appellate court, in this particular case, was to review the decision of the trial court to determine if it erred in its ruling that there had been a proper waiver of Fifth and Sixth Amendment rights. In making this judgment, the Supreme Court of Iowa was to give weight to the trial court's findings of fact, but was not bound by them, since it was incumbent on the State to show to the court's satisfaction that the defendant was advised of his rights and that he voluntarily, knowingly, and intelligently waived them while not subject to force, threats, promises, deception, or trickery.

In effect, what this analysis of the procedural law of the case means is that the Iowa Supreme Court had several discretionary choices to make regarding the outcome of the *Williams* case. The first was to once again examine the record of the case and make a determination of what were the facts. In doing so, it gave weight to the subjective facts as determined by the lower court, but stated that it was not bound to accept them. The Iowa Supreme Court also had the discretion to determine if the trial court had properly interpreted the procedural law of the Fifth and Sixth Amendments.

In applying its understanding of the procedural law to the totality of circumstances of the subjective facts, the Iowa Supreme Court found that Williams had been properly warned of his rights prior to the trip from Davenport to Des Moines. He had also consulted with counsel prior to the trip and been told not to talk to the police during the trip. The court believed that, despite Williams's testimony that he had been interrogated during the trip, there was no evidence supporting his claim. The suggestion made by Detective Leaming concerning the desirability of finding the body due to weather conditions was not thought to be so improper as to make Williams's statements inadmissible if there was a voluntary waiver. As a result of the totality of these attendant circumstances, the court ruled that Williams had effectively waived his rights and volunteered statements concerning the whereabouts of the victim's body.

The four dissenting justices in *Iowa v. Williams* believed that the subjective facts in the totality of circumstances did not support a finding that the waiver requirements had been met by the State. In his dissenting opinion Justice William Stuart stated:

It seems to me the only reasonable conclusion is that Captain Leaming embarked on a psychological campaign to obtain as much information from this mentally weak defendant as possible before letting him talk to his counsel. The fact that he was able to get the information by implanting ideas in defendant's mind without direct questioning is unimportant. If it were not for the agreement made with defendant's counsel, I personally would have no objection to this technique. However, I believe the law to be otherwise. There was no claim of verbal waiver of counsel. I do not think it was shown by the totality of the circumstance.[9]

The opposite findings of the majority and dissenting justices shows that, at times, the outcome of a case is highly dependent on the subjective facts and procedural law that are accepted. It also illustrates that neither the facts nor the law is as clear as it seems because of the discretionary choices of judges.

HABEAS CORPUS AND THE FEDERAL COURT PROCESS

District Court

The decision by the Iowa Supreme Court to affirm the conviction of Williams did not end that case's odyssey through the judicial system. On October 12, 1972, Williams filed a petition for a writ of *habeas corpus* in the U.S. District Court, Southern District of Iowa, against Lou Brewer, the warden of the Iowa State Penitentiary at Fort Madison, Iowa, where he was imprisoned.

The writ of *habeas corpus* is a procedural device that sets in motion a judicial inquiry to determine if a person who holds another in custody can demonstrate to a court's satisfaction that there is a legal justification for restraining that person's liberty. Since 1867, federal *habeas corpus* relief has been available to individuals convicted of state criminal charges who want to challenge the conviction on federal constitutional grounds. The Warren Court acted to broaden the rules for petitions of *habeas corpus* to make them available to a wider range of state prisoners. In *Fay v. Noia*[10] the Court ruled that *habeas corpus* proceedings could be used to review how state courts had resolved federal issues. In the same year, in *Townsend v. Sain*,[11] the Court held that if a petitioner did not receive a full and fair hearing on a constitutional claim made in a *habeas corpus* proceeding, then the federal courts were required to conduct an evidentiary hearing.

Habeas corpus review has generated animosity between state and federal courts because the state courts dislike the ability of the federal courts to redecide issues that have already been settled in state courts. The Burger Court acted to cut back on the number of petitions of *habeas corpus* and restore a sense of finality in the decisions of the state courts.

In *Williams v. Brewer*,[12] Williams's petition, which was handled by Robert Bartels of the University of Iowa School of Law, was based on his particular view of the facts and the procedural law. Williams claimed that the procedural law had been misinterpreted in two areas. First, he claimed that evidence used against him at trial was obtained in violation of the Fifth Amendment in that "such evidence was obtained from me after I had invoked my privilege under the *Fifth Amendment* to remain silent."[13] Second, he claimed that he was denied assistance of counsel during the interrogation and, thus, evidence used against him "was in violation of my *Sixth Amendment* right to the assistance of counsel."[14]

These claims that the procedural law had been misapplied were based on

Williams's understanding of the facts. To support his claims, he stated that the trial court had found as a matter of fact that an agreement existed between his attorney and the police not to question him until he was returned to Des Moines and his attorney was present. Furthermore, even though Williams had invoked his rights by telling Detective Leaming that he would not talk until he was in the presence of his attorney, Leaming continued conversing with him. The petition also pointed out that Detective Leaming testified that he was hoping to get all the information he could out of Williams prior to allowing him to consult with his attorney in Des Moines. Finally, Williams stated that he did not waive his right to counsel and he was not afforded the possibility of having counsel present during the period in which he was transported.

On behalf of Lou Brewer, the warden of the Iowa State Penitentiary, Richard Turner, Iowa's attorney general, responded to the petition for the State of Iowa. They made the argument that both the trial court and the Iowa Supreme Court had properly interpreted the procedural law with regard to the Fifth and Sixth Amendments, given the facts of the case.

The case of *Williams v. Brewer* was heard by District Court Judge William C. Hanson. There was agreement by the attorneys for both parties that the case would be submitted on the record of the facts and proceedings of the trial court, with no new testimony or evidence presented. On March 28, 1974, Judge Hanson made his decision. While working off the same record as the state courts, Judge Hanson used his discretion and identified areas of the procedural law that he believed had been inadequately developed based on his views of the subjective facts that were developed at the trial court.

According to Judge Hanson, the following facts were established in the record. First, there was an agreement between the police and McKnight that Williams would not be questioned until he was back in Des Moines and had a chance to consult with McKnight. Hanson further stated that the record showed that Detective Leaming had refused to allow Thomas Kelly to ride with Williams from Davenport to Des Moines. Judge Hanson also declared that because Detective Leaming knew about Williams's religious beliefs, his questions concerning the whereabouts of the body and the desirability of a Christian burial for the victim constituted an interrogation, even though Williams had asserted his rights. Furthermore, even though they were conducting an interrogation, the police did not re-advise Williams of his rights after his first incriminating statement.

Judge Hanson also reviewed whether Williams's statements were voluntary, as the Iowa courts had determined. According to Judge Hanson, this issue was a question of law, not of factual correctness, and thus could be re-examined. Judge Hanson therefore examined the procedural law of what constituted a waiver and a voluntary confession. He first ruled that the question as to whether there was a waiver of rights was related to, but still distinct from, the question of the voluntariness of a statement. The prosecution in such cases has the burden of demonstrating the voluntariness of a statement by at least a preponderance of the evidence. If there is a question concerning the timing of a defendant's incriminating statements in relation to an officer's questions, it is the State's burden to clearly illustrate through an examination of the timing that the admissions were voluntary. Furthermore, when a trial court makes a constitutional error, unless it can be shown beyond a reasonable doubt that the error did not prejudice the defendant, the case must be reversed.

In assessing the facts to determine if Williams had waived his rights and his statement was voluntary, Judge Hanson made the following findings. First, just because Williams had been warned of his rights and indicated that he wished to wait until after consulting with his attorney and then had cooperated with the police, this did not mean that the state had met its burden of proving that Williams had waived his rights. Furthermore, because Williams was denied counsel on the trip, and was questioned in an attempt to take advantage of both his religious views and history of mental illness with the purpose of obtaining incriminating statements, his statements were ruled involuntary.

In making a further determination, Judge Hanson examined the record and found that not only were the statements not voluntary, but they came about through a violation of *Miranda*. According to the *Miranda* decision, statements that were the result of police interrogation could not be used unless the suspect had clearly waived the protections of Fifth and Sixth Amendment rights. Since Judge Hanson had ruled that no such waiver could be found in the record, the statements obtained from Williams on the trip from Davenport to Des Moines should have been suppressed at trial.

Judge Hanson also found that Williams's statements were a direct result of a violation of the Sixth Amendment right to counsel. In doing so, he relied on the precedent of *Massiah v. United States*.[15] *Massiah* was applicable because judicial proceedings, in the form of Williams's initial appearance in Davenport, had already began against him. According to Judge Hanson, this meant that the automobile trip from Davenport to Des Moines was a pretrial event, protected by the right to counsel. Breaking new ground in the case, Judge Hanson stated that when police have agreed with a defendant's attorney not to question the defendant in his absence and the defendant has asserted his desire not to talk without counsel, the police are not permitted to interrogate further until notice is given to counsel. In such a situation, the defendant cannot waive his right to counsel and be interrogated until notice is given to his attorney.

Having found that Williams's statements were not voluntary, that he had not properly waived his Fifth and Sixth Amendment rights as required by *Miranda*, and that there was a further violation of Sixth Amendment rights by interrogating him without his counsel after judicial proceedings had already began, Judge Hanson ruled that Williams's statements should not have been admitted into trial where they were prejudicial against Williams. Judge Hanson then ordered that Williams's writ of *habeas corpus* be granted but that it should not go into effect until sixty days "pending an appeal or the pursuit of a new trial by the State of Iowa."[16] In the case of an appeal or a trial, Hanson ordered that the writ should be stayed until sixty days after the judgment of the last court was submitted.

COURT OF APPEALS

On the same day that Judge Hanson issued his decision, Richard Turner gave notice that Lou Brewer and the State of Iowa were going to appeal Judge Hanson's decision to the U.S. Court of Appeals for the Eighth Circuit. The appeal, which was handled for Iowa by Richard Winders, an assistant attorney general, was submitted on September 12, 1974. Robert Bartles again acted as the attorney on behalf of Williams. The basis of the State of Iowa's appeal was that Judge Hanson had overstepped his discretionary boundaries by misinterpreting the procedural rules of *habeas corpus*. That caused Judge Hanson to rely and rule on his own view of the relevant facts rather than those accepted by the trial court.

On December 31, 1974, a three-judge panel consisting of Circuit Judges Charles Vogel, Donald Ross, and William Webster issued their opinions in *Williams v. Brewer*.[17] Their decision was split 2–1, with Judges Vogel and Ross in the majority and Judge Webster in dissent. The critical issues that the court had to settle involved the procedural law of *habeas corpus* and *Miranda*. The majority's findings were as follows. First, it is possible for a district court in *habeas corpus* proceedings to base its decision on the record of the state trial court without further evidentiary hearings. Normally, when a case is decided based on the existing record, the federal court should presume as correct the factual findings of the state court. However, this presumption of correctness does not extend to constitutional questions such as whether a state prisoner had properly waived his *Miranda* rights. Instead, a federal *habeas* court is obligated to fully review the state record in order to determine if the totality of circumstances does show that there was a constitutional waiver of rights.

In examining the totality of circumstances, it is incumbent on federal *habeas* courts to find that the state has met its burden of showing that the prisoner waived his rights prior to making incriminating statements. Even though such a waiver does not have to be oral or written, it cannot be assumed from a silent record. The Court of Appeals, quoting from *Miranda* emphasized that "If the individual indicates in any manner, at any time prior to or during questioning, that he wishes to remain silent, the interrogation must cease."[18]

In resolving the legal issues, Judge Vogel, speaking for the panel, affirmed the district court's decision. Judge Vogel ruled that the state trial court's finding that Williams waived his rights was a constitutional question that could be re-examined. Furthermore, since there were inconsistencies and ambiguities in the record that were relied on by the state trial court, the district court could rely on a differing version of the facts as long as it could be supported by the record. The district court's finding that there was no waiver could be supported because the state trial court had applied an incorrect constitutional standard in allowing evidence to be presented in court without first requiring the state to demonstrate that Williams had waived his rights prior to making incriminating statements. The district court, not the state court, had therefore reached the proper conclusion under the totality of circumstances test. This was because, despite an indication by Williams after he had been warned of his rights that he did not wish to make any statements until he had consulted with an attorney, the police continued to engage Williams in conversations with the stated intent of obtaining information from him. Only after this subtle form of interrogation was the state capable of soliciting from Williams statements and further incriminating evidence. All such statements and evidence should therefore have been excluded from trial because of its potential for prejudicing the case against Williams.

Having lost its attempt to have the three-judge panel of the Court of Appeals for the Eighth Circuit overturn Judge Hanson's order sustaining Williams's petition for *habeas corpus*, the State of Iowa on January 14, 1975, petitioned the Court of Appeals for the Eighth Circuit to hear reargument *en banc. En banc* is a procedure by which all of the Court of Appeals judges for the circuit sit together on a panel to decide a case. In its petition, Iowa notified the Court of Appeals for the Eighth Circuit that if it was denied a rehearing of the case, it intended to petition for a writ of *certiorari* to the U.S. Supreme Court. On January 30, 1975, the U.S. Court of Appeals for the Eighth Circuit denied the petition for a rehearing *en banc.* Therefore, on February 6, 1975, over six years after the case began, Iowa petitioned the Supreme Court to review the district court's decision through a petition for writ of *certiorari.*

The decisions made at each level of the appeal demonstrate that the judges who heard the case often accepted competing versions of the facts. It also shows that once the subjective facts were determined, there were enough legal options for judges to use their discretion to select precedents that applied the procedural law in divergent ways. The different results that were reached by the Iowa Supreme Court and the lower federal courts exposes the weakness in the myth perpetuated by mechanical jurisprudence that the law is clear and a source of stability within the legal system. Instead of clarifying the issues involved in the case, the line of precedents concerning the rights against self-incrimination and to counsel created enough legal options so that a variety of legal rulings could all be considered soundly reasoned, even though they supported opposite conclusions. This situation also meant that, if the U.S. Supreme Court heard the case, the subjective facts it accepted and the precedents it relied on in making its decision could differ from those of the lower courts.

NOTES

1. *Speiser v. Randall*, 357 U.S. 513, 520 (1958).

2. *Brewer v. Williams*, 430 U.S. 387, 409 (1977).

3. *Griffin v. Illinois*, 372 U.S. 12 (1956).

4. *Douglas v. California*, 372 U.S. 353 (1963).

5. Robert A. Carp and Ronald Stidham, *Judicial Process in America* (Washington, D.C.: Congressional Quarterly Inc., 1993), p. 18.

6. *Escobedo v. Illinois*, 378 U.S. 478 (1964).

7. *Miranda v. Arizona*, 384 U.S. 436 (1966).

8. *Iowa v. Williams*, 182 N.W.2d 396 (Iowa 1970).

9. Ibid., p. 408.

10. *Fay v. Noia*, 372 U.S. 391 (1963).

11. *Townsend v. Sain*, 372 U.S. 293 (1963).

12. *Williams v. Brewer*, 375 F.Supp. 170 (S.Dist. Iowa 1974).

13. Joint Appendix, p. 19, *Brewer v. Williams*, 430 U.S. 387 (1977).

14. Ibid.

15. *Williams v. Brewer*, 375 F.Supp. 170, 178 (S.Dist. Iowa 1974).

16. Ibid., p. 186.

17. *Williams v. Brewer*, 509 F.2d. 227 (8th Circuit, 1975).

18. Ibid., p. 233, quoting *Miranda v. Arizona*, 384 U.S. 436, 473 (1966).

Chapter 6

Brewer v. Williams

> No litigant is entitled to more than two chances, namely, to the original
> trial and to a review, and the intermediate courts of review are provided
> for that purpose. When a case goes beyond that, it is not primarily to
> preserve the rights of the litigants. The Supreme Court's function is for
> the purpose of expounding and stabilizing principles of law for the ben-
> efit of the people of the country, passing upon constitutional questions
> and other important questions of law for the public benefit.
> —Chief Justice William Taft[1]

The success of Williams's petition of *habeas corpus* before the Eighth Circuit
Court of Appeals did not mean that Williams was automatically released
from the Iowa State Penitentiary at Fort Madison, Iowa where he was serving his sentence. On February 6, 1975, the court of appeals issued an order
staying its mandate that Williams be released until after the State of Iowa's
request that the Supreme Court review the case was resolved. Williams's fate
was thus placed into the hands of the Supreme Court in the case of *Brewer
v. Williams*.[2] Because the Supreme Court is asked to review thousands of
cases each year, its schedule does not allow it to hear all of the cases that it
is petitioned to review. Therefore, just because the State of Iowa was requesting the Supreme Court to review the *Williams* case did not guarantee
it a hearing before the High Court.

By 1977 when *Brewer v. Williams* was granted *certiorari*, the Court, under the direction of Chief Justice Burger, had shown a willingness to narrow

the application of *Miranda v. Arizona*,[3] but had not overruled that land-
mark decision. According to the Court's rulings, the core of *Miranda* remained and prosecutors were still denied use in their case-in-chief admission
of statements taken from defendants who were in custody and who had been
subjected to a violation of the guidelines established in *Miranda*. In other
factual situations, the Court had developed alternative approaches to what
due process required, since the Burger Court believed that *Miranda* was
not a requirement of the Fifth or Sixth Amendments. Central to this re-
structuring of *Miranda* was a return to the totality of circumstances test to
determine if statements that resulted from a failure to comply with *Miranda*
were involuntary. Under this approach, statements that were tainted could
be used for impeachment at trial and ones gained when police renewed
efforts to interrogate an individual after an initial assertion of rights could
also be used at trial if they were not compelled. These changes in the application of *Miranda* and the fact that the Burger Court had never suppressed any evidence based on *Miranda* set the stage for the state of Iowa
and twenty-one other state attorneys general to request that the Court overrule *Miranda* in *Brewer v. Williams*.

AGENDA BUILDING ON THE SUPREME COURT

Clerk of the Court and Docket Keeping

The need to maintain the building and offices of the Supreme Court and
to keep up with the large volume of requests to review cases has resulted in
the development of a Supreme Court bureaucracy that employs several hun-
dred people. One member of the Supreme Court bureaucracy essential to
the smooth operation of the Court is the Clerk of the Court. The Clerk
of the Court is responsible for maintaining order in the flow of legal papers
that flood into the Supreme Court. The office of the Clerk of the Court
collects and records all the petitions, motions, legal briefs, and statements
of jurisdiction that are sent into the Supreme Court. The Clerk also is
charged with collecting the fees for filing a case before the Supreme Court.
Another of the Clerk's responsibilities is to maintain records on the actions
of the Supreme Court in granting review of cases. In this capacity, the Clerk
of the Court is the contact point for attorneys with business before the
Supreme Court. The Clerk of the Court also schedules cases for oral argument before the Court.

The office of the Clerk of the Court acts as the first weeding point for
petitions sent to the Supreme Court. A weeding process is necessary because
the Court does not have the capacity to hear the approximately 7,000 requests for review it currently gets each year. The staff members of the Clerk
of the Court examine all the petitions sent to the Court to determine if they
have followed the requirements for style, format, length, and payment of

fees. Petitions that have been filed by indigents, also known as *in forma pauperis* petitions, do not have to comply with most of the style and format requirements developed by the Clerk's office. They also do not have to pay the filing fees.

After the Clerk's office has screened the petitions, all acceptable petitions will be placed on the Court's docket and given a docket number to make it easier to track its progress. For petitions that are given a docket number, the Clerk will inform attorneys for the other party to the case that they have thirty days to file a brief in response. When the respondent's brief arrives, the Clerk then sends each justice's chamber a complete set of briefs for their further consideration. After screening the State of Iowa's brief, the Clerk of the Court assigned it the docket number of 74–1263.

In the petition for writ of *certiorari* that Iowa filed on behalf of Lou Brewer, the warden of the Iowa State Penitentiary, Iowa presented four questions to the Supreme Court that it believed warranted the Supreme Court reviewing the case. The first was whether the federal district court had exceeded its authority in the *habeas* proceeding by disregarding the state court's findings on the facts by resolving disputed facts without conducting an additional evidentiary hearing. The second question that Iowa presented was whether an accused person who had retained counsel could waive his constitutional rights absent the presence of his attorney. A third question was whether the district court had erred by disregarding relevant facts in the record that showed that Williams had waived his constitutional rights. A final question that Iowa put before the Supreme Court was whether a more flexible standard should be adopted to replace the requirements of *Miranda v. Arizona*, which Iowa believed were too restrictive.

Court Jurisdiction

After the members of the Court receive a copy of the petitions that have been forwarded to them by the Clerk of the Court, they begin their own screening process. One of the first things that the justices will determine is whether the Supreme Court does indeed have jurisdiction and, if so, what type of jurisdiction exists. Jurisdiction refers to the authority of a court to hear a case. The jurisdiction of a court basically defines what types of cases it can hear. If a court, even the Supreme Court, lacks jurisdiction, it will not hear a case. The Supreme Court has two different types of jurisdiction—original and appellate. The Constitution grants the Supreme Court original jurisdiction in a variety of cases. The great majority of the Supreme Court's cases come to it through its appellate jurisdiction.

There are three different methods by which appellate cases come to the Supreme Court: appeal, certification, and writ of *certiorari*. By law, the Court must decide appeals cases, since it represents the appeal as a right. Due to acts of Congress, however, the only type of cases that provide a direct appeal to the Supreme Court are those that have originally been heard by a three-judge district court. As a result, direct appeals to the Supreme Court are now rare.

Certification of a case to the Supreme Court is also rare. Certification requires that the review process be initiated by a lower appellate court which must file a writ of certification asking the Supreme Court to clarify federal issues in order to allow it to reach a decision in a case before the lower court. Because certification requires the lower court to admit that resolving the legal issues is beyond their grasp, this method is rarely used. When a case is certified, the justices of the Supreme Court have several possibilities in disposing of the case. They can dismiss the case, they can answer the limited questions that were certified and then return the case to the lower court, or they can elect to take over the case and give it a final resolution.

The most common method by which the Court receives cases is through the writ of *certiorari*. As with the majority of cases that are now decided by the Supreme Court, the *Williams* case came to the Court through the *certiorari* process. All cases that come to the Supreme Court through writ of *certiorari* are discretionary, allowing the Court to pick and choose which cases it will decide. If the Court rejects a case, the decision of the lower court stands. The Court does reject most cases. In the year that Iowa's petition for a writ of *certiorari* was filed with the Supreme Court there were 4,068 other petitions filed and the Court only granted 181 a full hearing.[4] The ability to select which cases to hear allows the Court to fulfill its role as the primary policy-making body in the federal judiciary. The selectivity of the justices not only allows them to pick which areas of law they will shape, but it also allows them to wait for a case with a specific factual situation that will better lend itself to a clearer declaration of law than others might. The types of cases that the Court selects also sends signals to the legal community and interest groups as to those areas of law the Court believes need to be further developed.

Sifting through all the petitions for writ of *certiorari* to find the ones the Supreme Court deems worthy of its time and effort requires a great deal of work in itself. The reading load necessary for a justice to make an informed decision on whether to grant review for all the cases they must screen is enormous. It has been estimated that it amounts to more than 375,000 pages of material a year.[5]

Justiciability

Prior to deciding the merits of each of the petitions, the justices also screen the petition to make sure that the case is *justiciable*. A justiciable case is one that the judiciary is capable of resolving. As with a lack of jurisdiction, lack of justiciability will also cause the Court to reject review of a case. Justiciability is largely a series of self-imposed rules that define what types of cases are capable of judicial resolution. The rules concerning justiciability are subject to wide interpretation by the justices. This gives the justices latitude in determining when a case is justiciable. Generally speaking, however, the Court will refuse to hear cases if any of the following requirements of justiciability are lacking: (1) the suit is brought by an individual who has not been injured or in which the court can provide no remedy for the injury; (2) the suit lacks adverseness because there is no real controversy between the parties; (3) the case would result in the Court giving an advisory opinion; (4) the case isn't ripe because the facts haven't been fully developed; (5) the case is moot or has resolved itself; or (6) the legal issue involves a political question that can be best resolved by a separate branch of the federal government.

Law Clerks and Petition Screening

In order to dispose of petitions in a timely fashion, the justices have come to rely on the help of their law clerks. During the tenure of Chief Justice Burger, each justice was allowed to hire four law clerks and the Chief Justice was allowed five. Each justice is responsible for hiring his or her own clerks. Although no formal qualifications are specified for the position, most clerks share a common background of a sound education at one of the premier law schools in the country.

Law clerks work for individual justices rather than for the Court as a whole. As a result, their duties differ depending on which justice they serve. Despite these differences, the task of being a law clerk does involve similar duties. One of the most time-consuming tasks of law clerks is to screen the petitions for writ of *certiorari* that flood into the Court. In 1972 Justice Powell suggested creating a *certiorari* pool in which the justices could contribute the time of their clerks to review the thousands of petitions for writ of *certiorari* that come to the Court each term.[6] Implementation of Justice Powell's idea created a pool of clerks who divided the petitions among themselves. The clerks now write memos on each petition assigned to them. These memos are then circulated to all the justices in the pool. Justices who do not use the *certiorari* pool still use their own clerks to write memos on the petitions that come in for review. At the time that *Brewer v. Williams* came before the Court, all the justices except Brennan, Marshall, and Stevens participated in the *certiorari* pool.[7]

The *Certiorari* Decision

The actual decision as to whether to grant *certiorari* happens in a conference attended by all the justices. Throughout the term the justices meet in weekly conferences to decide which cases will be granted review. The groundwork for the *certiorari* decision is laid by the Chief Justice who, after study of all the writs of *certiorari*, puts together a discuss list. All cases placed on the discuss list are considered for possible review by the Court. The development of the discuss list plays a further screening role in the selection process. This is because only about 20–30 percent of those cases given a docket number are placed on the discuss list.[8] All other cases are placed on the dead list and will not be considered for review. A few days before each *certiorari* conference, the Chief Justice distributes the discuss list to the other justices. Since not being included on the discuss list means a denial of review, other justices then have the ability to move cases from the dead list onto the discuss list if they believe them important enough to merit consideration by the Court.

Only the justices themselves are allowed to attend the *certiorari* conference. As a result, while we have a general understanding of the process, the particulars of what has happened at specific conferences remains somewhat of a mystery. It is known that all conferences start with a customary handshake between the justices. The justices then sit at the conference table. Seating arrangements are not random. Tradition mandates that the Chief Justice sit at the head of the table and the senior associate justice at the other end. In between these two justices, the other associate justices sit in order of seniority. Because no one except the members of the Court are allowed into these conferences, the junior justice sits closest to the door and is responsible for acting as the doorkeeper, sending and receiving messages to and from the outside.

The actual discussion of the merits of the cases placed on the discuss list is less of a collegial discussion than a statement of the individual decisions that the justices have already made independent of each other. Rather than making decisions after an open discussion of the issues, the modern Supreme Court operates more like nine independent law offices that make independent decisions and only come together to count votes.[9] The conference process begins with the Chief Justice, who presents a short statement of the facts of the case and an assessment of the issues. The discussion then proceeds to the associate justices, moving from the senior justice down to the junior justice with all the justices presenting their views of the case. Normally, due to the workload of the Court, the discussion is brief and perfunctory, with each justice having already made up his or her mind prior to the conference. At the same time that they present their view of the issues of each petition, the justices also normally indicate which way they are planning to vote. Those petitions for which review is supported by four justices are granted a hearing. This is known as the *rule of four*. At the end of the conference, the votes on each petition discussed are reported to the Clerk of the Court, who then informs both parties to the case whether review was granted. In the vast majority of cases, the Court offers no reasons as to why it acted the way that it did. When the Court refuses to grant *certiorari*, it simply means that it has decided not to disturb the decision of the lower court. It neither creates precedent nor approves any statement of principle made by the lower court.

When the Court votes to hear a case, it reserves the right to reframe the issues that are brought before it. Exercising its discretion, the Court can ask the lawyers to address legal questions that were not raised in the writ of *certiorari*. This may be done in complex cases to provide the justices with more information and allow a more thorough examination of the issues. The Court also has the power to narrow the range of issues in a case to more sharply focus on what the justices believe are the more critical issues. When the Court votes to hear a case, the Public Information Officer makes available to the media the filings and briefs for the case. On December 15, 1975, the Supreme Court voted to grant Iowa's request for *certiorari*.[10]

THE DECISION PROCESS

Legal Briefs

The first step after the Court grants review is the filing of written legal briefs. The party bringing the case before the Supreme Court has 45 days after notification by the Clerk of the Court that the case has been granted review to file a written legal brief arguing the merits behind why the Court should upset the lower court decision. Forty copies of the brief must be sent to the Court; another copy goes to the opposing party. Upon receipt of this legal brief, the opposing party has 30 days to file 30 copies of a brief explaining why the lower court decision should be upheld.

The rules of the Court specify both the format and content requirements of the legal briefs. Rule 34 of the Supreme Court specifically states that an appellant's brief must include the following:

1. A description of the questions presented for appellate review.
2. A list of all the parties to the proceedings in the court whose judgment is being reviewed.
3. A table of contents and list of legal authorities.
4. Citations to the opinions and judgments issued by the courts below.
5. A statement describing the Supreme Court's jurisdiction over the case.
6. A description of all the constitutional provisions, treaties, statutes, ordinances, and administrative regulations, relevant facts, and other matters material to the appeal.
8. A summary of the appellant's argument.
9. The detailed argument of the appellant, including the points of fact and law presented.
10. A conclusion stating the relief the appellant is seeking.[11]

The responding brief must cover the same points. In order to lighten the workload of the justices, the responding brief does not have to include material in which there is agreement between the parties.

The attorneys writing the briefs are in control of the actual arguments made in the briefs. Due to the nature of oral argument before the Supreme Court, attorneys must take care to include all of the relevant points that they believe may sway the justices. This is the last opportunity in which the attorneys will be able to have total control of their arguments. As a result, they must strive to concisely state their arguments and show that they have a complete understanding of how the relevant existing law should be applied in their case in order to yield the outcome that is desired.

Brief for the Petitioner

In *Brewer v. Williams,* the central component of the argument that the State of Iowa made in its Brief for the Petitioner was that the Court should overrule its decision in *Miranda v. Arizona* and declare that the sole constitutional requirement for the admissibility of an incriminating statement should be whether it was made voluntarily. While police should not be allowed to coerce confessions from suspects, Iowa argued that spontaneous and voluntary confessions should be admissible. Iowa stated that *Miranda* had shifted the rules guiding the criminal justice system too far in favor of the criminal over the police officer. Iowa believed that police interrogations were essential to police being able to do their duty, which was finding the truth. It also pointed out that "it is unreasonable to insist that police must advise suspects not to give them evidence they sorely need to do that duty."[12]

Iowa urged the Court to adopt a totality of circumstances approach to the admission of voluntary incriminating statements, which would be similar to those found in 18 U.S.C., section 3501. Under this law, passed by large majorities in Congress and signed by President Lyndon Johnson on June 19, 1968, trial judges were to consider the following circumstances when determining if an incriminating statement should be admissible at trial:

(1) the time elapsing between arrest and arraignment of the defendant making the confession, if it was made after arrest and before arraignment, (2) whether such defendant knew the nature of the offense with which he was charged or of which he was suspected at the time of making the confession, (3) whether or not such defendant was advised or knew that he was not required to make any statement and that any such statement could be used against him, (4) whether or not such defendant had been advised prior to questioning of his right to the assistance of counsel, and (5) whether or not such defendant was without the assistance of counsel when questioned and when giving such confession.[13]

Iowa argued that if *Miranda* were overruled and this preferred standard were used to determine the admissibility of Williams's statements, the statements would be admissible.

The Brief for the Petitioner also argued that the harmful effects of the *Miranda* ruling were enlarged by the Court's application of the exclusionary rule to the states. The exclusionary rule disallows the use of illegally seized evidence at trial. Iowa's position was that "Criminals are the *only* real beneficiaries of the exclusionary rule. The rights of innocent citizens are very rarely protected by it."[14] The State criticized the effect of what it considered to be the liberal decisions regarding the exclusionary rule, which allowed criminals to go free by stating, "We in the heartland of America ask this Court to reassess the situation and give a little less emphasis to rights and a little more to duty."[15] In Iowa's opinion, the Court should allow the police more leeway during police interrogations. Iowa argued that police should be allowed to use trickery and deceit during interrogations as long as the purpose was to find the truth rather than inducing false confessions.

A second argument made in the Brief for the Petitioner centered around Iowa's position that the Sixth Amendment right to counsel could, as they believed happened in this case, be waived in the absence of counsel. Iowa argued that since the right to counsel was a personal right of the suspect, the suspect could waive it at any time. This was true even if—and Iowa argued that it was questionable—there had been an agreement between the police and attorney McKnight not to interrogate Williams on the trip from Davenport to Des Moines. It was also true even if Detective Leaming had denied Attorney Kelly permission to accompany Williams on the trip back to Des Moines. The Sixth Amendment, Iowa argued, did not require an attorney to be present at the time that a suspect waived his rights. As long as suspects are informed of their right to counsel, the Sixth Amendment allowed them to effectively waive their right to counsel.

Iowa's Brief for the Petitioner went on to argue that the federal courts had ignored relevant evidence that helped to illustrate that Williams had waived his Fifth and Sixth Amendment rights. Elements in the record that allowed such a conclusion to be drawn included Williams's initiation of conversations concerning the process of the investigation. It also included the spirit of cooperation that Williams showed from the time of his decision to voluntarily surrender through the point at which he led the police to the body of Pamela Powers. Iowa pleaded for the Court to reassess the issue of waiver in favor of the State and to downplay the federal court's finding that Williams had been tricked into cooperating with the police through some form of subtle interrogation.

To bolster its argument that the federal courts had been mistaken in their decision that there was no waiver by Williams of his rights, Iowa also argued that the ruling law of *habeas corpus* found in 28 U.S.C., section 2254 (d) provided that findings of fact that the trial jury had ruled on, such as the existence of a waiver, had to be respected unless there was an evidentiary hearing by the federal district court. This argument was based on *Townsend v. Sain*.[16] Iowa pleaded that the trial court was in the best position to judge the credibility and demeanor of witnesses and the conclusions reached at trial should therefore be deferred to. Furthermore, the jury at the trial had been instructed that it could only make use of Williams's statements to the police if it found that they were made voluntarily. Iowa also submitted that this case presented a good example of a case in which the federal courts should abstain from issuing writs of *habeas corpus*, since the combined wisdom of nine state supreme court justices should be respected by federal judges.

Brief for the Respondent

Williams's Brief for the Respondent, filed by Robert Bartels, discussed the same issues presented in Iowa's brief, but reached different conclusions. It began, however, with one additional reason for why the Supreme Court should rule in favor of Williams. This argument stated that the issue of whether Williams's incriminating statements were voluntary had not been properly presented before the Court in the petition for *certiorari*. Therefore, the Brief for the Respondent argued that since the federal courts ruled that the statements were involuntary, "the voluntariness issue disposes of the entire case and requires reversal of Respondent's conviction, regardless of what resolution may be made of the issues raised in the petition for *certiorari*."[17]

The brief went on to argue that Williams's Sixth and Fourteenth Amendment right to counsel had been violated, regardless of the requirements of *Miranda v. Arizona*. This was due to a number of factors. One of these factors was Detective Leaming's actions to isolate Williams from his attorney and then disregard his desire not to be interrogated without counsel present. A second factor was the Respondent's belief that the factual context of this case presented a situation in which no waiver of Williams's right to counsel was possible. This was because the police had agreed not to interrogate Williams and the police had purposely engaged in misconduct for the purpose of depriving Williams of his right to counsel. A third factor that demonstrated that Williams's right to counsel had been violated was that the State had failed to meet its burden of showing that there had been a tacit waiver and that there had not been, as argued by Iowa, a spirit of cooperation between Williams and the police. Instead, the record supported the opposite conclusion—that Williams had asserted his right to counsel and did not desire to be questioned until he had the opportunity to consult with his attorney.

The Brief for the Respondent also argued that Detective Leaming violated the requirements of *Miranda v. Arizona*. This was done in two ways. According to the Respondent's argument, when Williams indicated that he wished to assert his right to counsel, *Miranda* required that all interrogation cease until his attorney was present. Furthermore, *Miranda* also required that when a suspect indicated the desire to remain silent, further interrogation—with or without the suspect's attorney present—had to cease. In this case, Detective Leaming did not honor Williams's desire to assert either of his rights; instead, the detective engaged in further interrogation for the purpose of depriving Williams of his rights.

The Brief for the Respondent further argued that this was an inappropriate case to use to overrule *Miranda v. Arizona*, as argued by Iowa and the *amicus curiae* briefs. Two primary reasons were given. The first was that this case did not demonstrate the type of technical mistake on Detective Leaming's part that represented the heart of Iowa's arguments in favor of overruling *Miranda*. Instead, this case provided an example of a purposeful violation of a suspect's constitutional rights, which should never be tolerated by the Court. Second, most of the legal commentaries used in the briefs that supported overruling *Miranda* were outdated; the reality was that the *Miranda* procedures had not had an overall detrimental effect on the effectiveness of law enforcement.

The final argument presented in the Brief for the Respondent was that the federal courts had properly applied 28 U.S.C., section 2254(d) in resolving factual issues before the courts, since the parties had agreed to forgo an evidentiary hearing. Respondent pointed out that all the factual conclusions that had been reached by the federal courts could be supported by the record of the state trial. Furthermore, because the State had given its approval not to hold an evidentiary hearing when the *habeas corpus* petition was heard by the federal district court and had failed to ask for reconsideration on the issue at the district court level or appealed the issue to the court of appeals, neither lower court had been given the opportunity to rule on this claim, so it was improperly before the Supreme Court.

After the Brief of the Respondent was filed with the Court, the State of Iowa was given the opportunity to submit a Reply Brief for the Petitioner. In its Reply Brief, Iowa made two primary points. The first was to clarify that the issue of voluntariness had been properly presented before the Court. The second was to emphasize once again that Williams's incriminating statements were not the result of police interrogation. Instead, they were spontaneously volunteered.

Amicus Curiae Briefs

The Court also allows the submission of *amicus curiae* or "Friend of the Court" briefs. These are briefs submitted by individuals, organizations, and representatives of governments who are not a party to the case but who have been given permission by either the parties involved or the Court to submit a brief. Neither the federal government nor the states need permission to file *amicus curiae* briefs. The purpose of *amicus curiae* briefs is to broaden the Court's understanding of how its decision could impact society beyond the parties to the case. The number of *amicus curiae* briefs filed in a case varies widely, as does their influence on the Court.

In *Brewer v. Williams*, there were two *amicus curiae* briefs submitted. One was submitted by the State of Louisiana and the other was a combined brief submitted by two organizations—(1) Americans for Effective Law Enforcement, Inc. (AELE), a national, nonprofit, nonpolitical, nonpartisan interest group that sought to inform the public about the need to facilitate effective enforcement of criminal laws; and (2) the National District Attorneys Association, Inc. (NDAA), a nonprofit, nonpolitical corporation composed of members from all 50 states. The members of the NDAA included the twenty-one state attorneys general who signed the brief. Both briefs supported Iowa's position that *Miranda v. Arizona* should be reconsidered.

The joint AELE–NDAA brief gave four reasons why *Miranda* should be overruled in favor of a more flexible standard for evaluating the admission of incriminating statements. First, the crime involved in the *Williams* case was of the most heinous and reprehensible nature. A second reason was the overwhelming guilt of Williams. Third, the brief also tried to influence the Court by stating that a successful retrial of Williams would be quite difficult, or even impossible, if the questioned evidence were not admissible. The final reason given by the brief was that Captain Leaming's conduct was not in any way oppressive. The brief argued that the combination of all of these features of this case proved that the mandates of *Miranda* were unworkable and should be overruled in favor of a set of guidelines that would be more flexible and allow incriminating statements to be admissible in a wider variety of circumstances. The State of Louisiana's brief argued that the only issue the Court should consider in the case was the voluntariness of the defendant's confession.

Oral Argument

After the justices have had adequate time to read the legal briefs and study them, the next step in the review process is oral argument. The primary function of oral argument is to allow the justices to have another method of gathering information prior to making a decision.

Oral argument represents the only time that the attorneys to the case will have direct access to the justices who will decide the case. It is also the only time that the work of the Supreme Court is conducted in public view. On the day of oral argument the Marshall of the Court announces the sitting of the justices by stating "Oyez! Oyez! Oyez! All persons having business before the Honorable, the Supreme Court of the United States, are admonished to draw near and give their attention, for the Court is now sitting.

God save the United States and this Honorable Court." [18] When the Court is in session, it is also the duty of the Marshall to maintain order in the courtroom. The justices make their appearance dressed in the black robes that have been traditional since John Marshall was Chief Justice. The justices sit at their bench with the Chief Justice in the middle and the other justices sitting according to seniority. After the justices are seated, oral argument begins.

Preparation is the key to successful oral argument. Oral argument allows the attorneys to isolate for the Court those issues, from the many contained in the legal brief, which ones they believe are crucial to allowing the Court to decide the case in their favor. Due to the time limit for each attorney, the attorneys must keep their presentations concise. In 1970, Chief Justice Burger convinced the Court to limit oral argument to a half-hour for each party to the case. When attorneys begin their presentations, the clock starts and when the half-hour is over a red light will give notice that time is over. Only the attorneys who represent the parties to the case are normally allowed to argue the case; those filing *amicus curiae* briefs are generally restricted from participation. The one exception to this rule has been a willingness by the Court to allow an attorney for the federal government to argue before the Court when desired.

The attorneys must clearly understand the issues of the case, since the Court frowns on attorneys who read during presentation. The Court prefers a conversational presentation in which the justices have the discretion to interrupt the attorneys to guide the discussion to those points they consider crucial to the resolution of the case. It is not uncommon for the justices to interrupt one attorney more often than the other. Any interruptions by the justices come out of the attorney's half-hour, so it is crucial for attorneys to know the case well enough to move smoothly and quickly from one issue to another without being rattled. Because the justices can interrupt at will, attorneys who plan long presentations may not get to make all their points. This underscores why the written briefs need to be complete.

The justices must also be prepared for oral argument. Each justice approaches oral argument differently. Most justices will have read the briefs that have been submitted and familiarized themselves with bench memos that identify the facts and relevant issues involved in the case. These memos are usually drafted by their law clerks. Some justices ask few questions of the attorneys; others dominate the questioning. Some will only ask questions seeking clarification of an issue, while others ask more argumentative questions. Likewise, some justices treat the attorneys with the utmost respect, while others project an attitude bordering on contempt. Often, the purpose of a question asked by a justice may be to communicate concerns to other justices rather than the attorney. Justice Felix Frankfurter, for example, often used oral arguments to pontificate to other justices his specific views of the law.

After the Supreme Court granted *certiorari* in the *Williams* case and all the briefs were filed, it heard the case on October 4, 1976. Richard Turner and Richard Winders argued the case for Iowa and Brewer and Robert Bartels argued the case for Williams.

Case Conference

On Wednesday afternoons and all day Friday, case conferences are held to discuss the cases that were argued during the week. As with the conference in which granting *certiorari* is considered, case conferences are held in private with only members of the Court in attendance. No formal record of the discussion is made. Prior to the arrival of the justices, the conference room will be made ready for them by staff members who will bring in carts filled with the records, briefs, documents, and related law books for the cases under consideration.

When the justices arrive, the conference will again start with the traditional handshake before they begin their business. The Chief Justice is in charge of the deliberations and begins the discussion of each case. Normally, the Chief Justice's presentation includes an introduction of the case under consideration, his assessment of the legal issues involved, and how he would resolve the case. The discussion then moves from the most senior justice to the junior justice, who all give an assessment of the case. In order to take pressure off the junior justices, voting goes in reverse order from junior to senior to Chief Justice. In reality, the votes of most justices are known after their discussion of the case. This vote is a tentative vote and the justices are free to change their vote until the final vote is taken after opinions are written.

Despite the belief by many people that the Court discusses the merits of each case in depth and then forms some sort of consensus through a collegial process, this no longer accurately reflects how the Court makes decisions. In most cases today, the discussion and deliberation ends after each justice gives an assessment of the case and a tentative vote is taken. Rather than making the decision as a body, the justices make nine independent decisions based on individual study of the case and come together to inform each other of how they would resolve the case. The justices are more likely to spend time discussing the merits of each case with their own law clerks than with each other. This does not mean that the case conferences are useless. At times they may influence individual justices, and they are also important in giving the justices cues about where their colleagues stand and what will be necessary to write an acceptable majority opinion.

Opinion Assignment and Writing

The way that the Court communicates its decisions to the legal community and the public is through its opinions. The opinion seeks to justify and rationalize the Court's decision. When the opinion is supported by the majority, it must also strive to produce a clear precedent of law that can be followed by lower courts. The decision as to who makes the assignment of the opinion depends on the outcome of the vote at the case conference. When the Chief Justice is in the majority, he decides who will write for the Court. If the Chief Justice is not in the majority, then the seniormost justice in the majority makes the assignment. The Chief Justice, however, makes the assignment in more than four-fifths of all cases.[19] Since Chief Justice Warren Burger was in the minority in *Brewer v. Williams,* assignment of the opinion was made by the seniormost justice in the majority, Justice William Brennan. Justice Brennan assigned the opinion to Justice Potter Stewart.

After the assignment of the opinion, the writing begins. Writing opinions is the most difficult task for a justice of the Supreme Court. Writing the majority opinion is a difficult task because the author is not trying to simply please him- or herself, the justice is trying to please all the members of the majority. Each justice approaches the job differently. All justices are concerned with the opinions that they produce, since this creates part of their legal legacy and will set the tone for how they will be remembered and respected in history.

Increasingly, draft opinions reflect a collaborative effort between a justice and his or her law clerks. After consulting with clerks about the case conference, justices often rely on their law clerks to compose a first draft of their opinions. The Court's library and its librarian may also prove to be of assistance during the process of writing opinions. All opinions should contain some basic items. These include a summary of the facts of the case, a statement of the issues involved, a review of the relevant laws and/or constitutional provisions, a review of the applicable precedents, a statement of the Court's decision and order, and the Court's reasoning process. After reading through the draft, getting comments on it from other law clerks, and making any corrections the justice believes are necessary, the justice will then circulate the draft to the other justices.

In the offices of the other justices, the law clerks and justices will examine the draft opinion and send suggestions back to the author. At this point, any or all the justices may seek to change the reasoning in the draft opinion, so negotiation may take place between the different offices. Negotiations may get tough, as separate justices press the author of the opinion to go in divergent directions. Justices may threaten to hold out their support for the opinion unless their demands are taken into consideration. The need to hold onto a majority can be a realistic threat that causes a justice to alter the opinion. This process of negotiation may continue through several drafts. Justice Brennan commented that he once had an opinion that went through ten drafts.[20] The end result of the negotiation process is that if there is a change in the size of the majority from the initial conference, it usually causes the size of the majority to grow.[21]

One reason that justices work so hard to retain majority support for their opinions is that failure to present a united front could either cause a change in the outcome of the case—since all votes are tentative until the majority opinion is accepted—or prompt the Court to issue a plurality opinion. Plurality opinions explain the decision that the Court reaches, but, since they lack majority support, they do not have weight as precedent. This causes problems for lower courts in applying plurality opinions.

While the majority opinion is being drafted, other members of the Court may be either threatening to or actually drafting concurring or dissenting opinions. Concurring opinions may be written by justices who agree with the decision of the majority, but disagree with the reasoning. Dissenting opinions may be written by justices who disagree with the majority decision. While concurring and dissenting opinions may create animosity between the justices and take away from the weight of a majority opinion, they may also serve a useful purpose. Separate opinions advance alternative reasoning for what the Court has done or should have done, sometimes prompting the author of the majority opinion to sharpen his or her own arguments and craft a clearer opinion, which is easier for lower courts to implement.[22]

The give and take of the drafting process can be very time consuming. It took the Burger Court an average of 52 days to complete an opinion.[23] The process ends when all the justices indicate their satisfaction with one of the draft opinions by signing onto that opinion. When this is done, the final votes are tallied specifying the support for each opinion and the size of the majority. The opinions are then sent to the Supreme Court's printing department, where the Reporter of Decisions is responsible for compiling the official record of Supreme Court decisions and opinions that are published in the *United States Reports*. The Court uses an in-house publisher because it is concerned about maintaining the secrecy of its decisions until it is ready for the public announcement. Prior to publication, the Reporter of Decisions must go through the drafted opinions and check all the references and citations to make sure they are accurate, look for grammatical and spelling errors, and make sure that all the opinions are uniform in style and reflect the *United States Reports* requirements. The Reporter of Decisions is also responsible for writing a summary of all decisions, which includes a summary of the facts, legal issues, and the Court's holding for each issue.

When all the opinions are finalized, the Court announces the decision to the public. Chief Justice Burger convinced the rest of the Court in 1971 to abandon the practice of allowing the author of each opinion to read the opinion at the time of announcement. Since then, the author of the majority opinion has simply given a short summary of the decision and the reasoning. Justices who have written concurring or dissenting opinions can also summarize their reasoning at the public announcement. Usually the whole process is completed in less than five minutes.

THE DECISION AND OPINIONS

On March 23, 1977, the Supreme Court handed down its decision in *Brewer v. Williams*. In a 5–4 decision the Supreme Court upheld the district court's grant of *habeas corpus* to Williams. Justice Potter Stewart wrote the majority opinion, which was joined by Justices William Brennan, Thurgood Marshall, Lewis Powell, and John Paul Stevens.

Before addressing the issues confronted by the Court in the case, Justice Stewart's opinion began by reviewing the facts of the case leading up to Williams's conviction. The Court then ruled on Iowa's claim that the district court had overstepped its authority by disregarding the rules of *habeas corpus* requiring federal courts to defer to the factual findings of state courts. It was the Court's opinion that the district court had not violated the rules governing *habeas corpus*. This was because both parties to the case had waived their right to an evidentiary hearing before the district court and agreed to allow the district court to decide the case on the facts in the record. In exercising this grant of power, the district court made no findings of fact that were in conflict with the state courts. The new findings made by the district court included the declaration that Detective Leaming had denied attorney Kelly the opportunity to ride back to Des Moines with Williams. The Court believed that the district court came upon the new findings after careful study of the record.

Justice Stewart's opinion went on to declare that even though the district court had found three grounds for reversal and the court of appeals had found two to affirm the district court's opinion, the High Court only needed to consider one. Accordingly, the Court did not confront the issue of whether there was a violation of *Miranda v. Arizona* or the Fifth Amendment right against self-incrimination. So the issue left to resolve was whether Williams's Sixth Amendment right to counsel, as applied to the states through the Due Process Clause of the Fourteenth Amendment, had been violated.

Justice Stewart stated that the history of the Sixth Amendment had evolved so that there was a clear understanding of the extent of the protections it granted. Justice Stewart noted that:

Whatever else it may mean, the right to counsel granted by the Sixth and Fourteenth Amendments means at least that a person is entitled to the help of a lawyer at or after the time that judicial proceedings have been initiated against him—"whether by way of formal charge, preliminary hearing, indictment, information, or arraignment."[24]

Based on this understanding of the requirements of the Sixth Amendment's right to counsel, the Court had no trouble declaring that Williams's rights had been violated. This was because it was clear that judicial proceedings had begun against Williams prior to the trip from Davenport to Des Moines. As a result, Justice Stewart believed that *Massiah v. United States* [25] was the applicable precedent. Williams was therefore entitled to the assistance of counsel during the trip. There was also no doubt that Detective Leaming deliberately tried to elicit statements from Williams during the trip. This was done by giving Williams the

Christian burial speech which was tantamount to interrogation. The method of interrogation, open or covert, does not matter if an individual has been denied the right to assistance of counsel. Detective Leaming did this despite his knowledge that Williams was being represented by counsel on both ends of the trip. [26]

The Court next addressed the issue of whether Williams had waived his right to counsel. The state trial court had ruled that there was a waiver by Williams, and the Iowa Supreme Court had agreed and ruled that, based on an examination of the totality of the circumstances, it was clear that Williams had waived his right to counsel. After finding that this was a constitutional issue, rather than a factual one, both of the federal courts had disagreed and declared that there had been no waiver. The Supreme Court agreed with the federal courts stating that when the state makes a claim that there has been a waiver of rights, it has the burden of proof.

Justice Stewart wrote that since *Johnson v. Zerbst* the standard to judge if a waiver existed has been that the state had to prove "an intentional relinquishment or abandonment of a known right or privilege."[27] The majority, relying on the subjective facts it accepted, believed the State had failed to meet this standard. This was evident by all of Williams's efforts to ensure that he would be protected through the assistance of counsel. These efforts included calling an attorney, Henry McKnight, prior to giving himself up for arrest and then speaking to the same attorney shortly after being booked. Furthermore, Williams consulted with another attorney, Thomas Kelly, after his initial appearance and again prior to being transported back to Des Moines. Each time that Williams conferred with an attorney, he was told not to make any statements to the police. Williams was also assured by his attorneys that the police would not question him during the trip. Before the trip began, it was understood that Williams had asserted his rights based on his arranging for counsel on both ends of the trip and those attorneys making an agreement with police that Williams would not be questioned during the trip. After the trip began, Williams repeatedly asserted his rights, saying that he did not want to talk until he was returned to Des Moines and had the chance to talk to his attorney. Despite these indications that Williams wished to assert his rights, Leaming proceeded to purposely try to elicit incriminating comments from Williams without further advising him of his rights. At no point did the record show that Williams had willingly and knowingly relinquished his rights.

The final section of the opinion addressed the reservations the Court had in making its ruling in light of the crime involved. Despite these reservations, the Court went on to explain why it was necessary to grant the writ of *habeas corpus* in this case. It stated:

The pressures on state executive and judicial officers charged with the administration of the criminal law are great, especially when the crime is murder and the victim a small child. But it is precisely the predictability of those pressures that makes imperative a resolute loyalty to the guarantees that the Constitution extends to us all.[28]

The Court then suspended the issuance of the writ of *habeas corpus* for 60 days to allow Iowa the opportunity to initiate new trial proceedings against Williams.

In most cases if the government decides to retry an individual granted a writ of *habeas corpus*, the trial will not be marred by questions regarding the proper procedural laws because the Court had clarified the rules in its decision. Due to a footnote that was attached to the Court's final ruling, this was not the case in *Brewer v. Williams*. In the footnote, the Court did not directly address the issue as to which evidence, if any, beyond the incriminating statements made while Williams was transported from Davenport to Des Moines would also have to be excluded as "fruit of the poisonous tree." The fruit of the poisonous tree doctrine extends the exclusionary rule to disallow not only direct evidence found through a legal violation, but also additional evidence found as a result of the violation. The body of Pamela Powers is an example. Instead, Justice Stewart gave Iowa an opportunity to attempt to test the development of a new procedural law concerning the exclusionary rule of justice by stating:

While neither Williams' incriminating statements themselves nor any testimony describing his having led the police to the victim's body can constitutionally be admitted into evidence, evidence of where the body was found and of its condition might well be admissible on the theory that the body would have been discovered in any event, even had incriminating statements not been elicited from Williams. . . . In the event that a retrial is instituted, it will be for the state courts in the first instance to determine whether particular items of evidence may be admitted.[29]

Through this footnote and an unwillingness to specify which evidence should have been suppressed because of the violation of Williams's Sixth Amendment rights, the Supreme Court put into motion a sequence of events that would delay for seven more years the final resolution of the *Williams* case.

Justice Thurgood Marshall filed a concurring opinion to allow him to address some of the issues raised in the dissenting opinions. Justice Marshall wanted to clarify that, unlike the dissenters, he believed that the facts showed that Detective Leaming had not performed his duties in a proper manner. Instead, despite being told that Williams would show police where the body was after consulting with McKnight, Detective Leaming purposely isolated Williams from his attorneys to persuade him to incriminate himself. Justice Marshall also pointed out that he did not believe that the majority's decision would result in Williams's freedom because the State of Iowa would either have a retrial ending in conviction or have Williams committed through a civil proceeding.

Justice Powell wrote a concurring opinion that drew attention to the fact that the resolution of the case was highly dependent on an individual's perception of the facts. The most important fact cited by Powell was whether Williams had voluntarily waived his right to counsel; this fact, in turn, was dependent on whether there had been any interrogation. Justice Powell believed that Detective Leaming's actions on the trip from Davenport to Des Moines did constitute a highly effective form of interrogation that was psychologically coercive by taking advantage of a young man with a history of mental disorder and deep religious views on the day after Christmas while being isolated from his attorneys by the police. He also criticized the dissenters for implying that the majority's ruling made it impossible for a suspect to waive his rights unless an attorney was present. He emphasized that the majority opinion had not established such a precedent. It explicitly stated that suspects could waive their rights after they had asserted the need for counsel to be present. The problem that the dissenters failed to recognize was that in this case there was no waiver that was free of interrogation within a coercive environment. Justice Powell also commented that the rationale of *Stone v. Powell*,[30] which forbid *habeas corpus* petitions on Fourth Amendment grounds when the issues had been given a fair hearing in state courts, may apply to Fifth and Sixth Amendment claims such as this. He believed, however, that the answer to this question should wait until the Court had a case properly before it that addressed that issue specifically.

Chief Justice Burger wrote a dissenting opinion, the tone of which was set by the first few sentences. They read:

The result in this case ought to be intolerable in any society which purports to call itself an organized society. It continues the Court . . . on the much criticized course of punishing the public for the mistakes and misdeeds of law enforcement officers, instead of punishing the officer directly, if in fact he is guilty of wrongdoing. It mechanically and blindly keeps reliable evidence from juries whether the claimed constitutional violation involves gross police misconduct or honest human error.[31]

Chief Justice Burger went on to complain that Williams was undoubtedly guilty of a horrendous crime, and that no member of the Court suggested he was not. Furthermore, even though the facts showed that Williams was warned of his rights five times before voluntarily relinquishing his rights and leading the police to the body, the Court was going to suppress reliable evidence that was necessary for a proper prosecution. Chief Justice Burger warned that the plausible result of this case was that an individual could only waive their rights in the presence of an attorney, even though those rights were personal rights.

The bulk of Chief Justice Burger's dissent was then directed at discrediting the Court's application of the exclusionary rule. He stated that in this decision the Court had interrupted a recent movement on the Court to reinterpret the exclusionary rule as a judicially conceived rule, which should be applied only when it could effectively act as a deterrent to police violations, rather than as a personal constitutional right. As a result, rather than automatically excluding evidence, the Court should have balanced the competing interests of the harm exclusion does to the truth-seeking process of a trial with the imperative to safeguard constitutional rights.

In this case Chief Justice Burger reasoned that the evidence should have been admitted for several reasons. All of these reasons were tied to the subjective facts he accepted. In his view, the facts showed that there had been no purposeful attempt by the police to deny Williams his constitutional rights. Therefore, Chief Justice Burger argued that in cases where incriminating disclosures were voluntarily made and no coercion was involved there may be a violation of the *Miranda* rules, but not the Fifth Amendment, so there was no need for automatic exclusion. He also believed that since the right to counsel was fundamentally a trial right, there was no reason to automatically exclude evidence if there was a violation of the Sixth Amendment in a pretrial setting. What should have been done in this case was to admit all the evidence because of its reliability and trustworthiness, since Williams's statements were voluntary and uncoerced. Admitting the evidence would still ensure Williams a fair trial while promoting the integrity of the fact-finding process. It would also have no harmful effect on future police infractions of constitutional rights, since there were no purposeful violations in this case.

Chief Justice Burger then advanced the argument that *Stone v. Powell* should be the ruling precedent for the case. He believed that since *Stone v. Powell* placed a moratorium on federal *habeas corpus* review of Fourth Amendment cases when the defendant had a fair trial and appeal in the state judicial system, it could also be expanded to other cases involving the exclusionary rule. Chief Justice Burger then suggested that the proper method of disposing of the case was to vacate the judgment of the court of appeals and remand the case for reconsideration in light of *Stone v. Powell.*

Justice Byron White also wrote a dissent that was joined by Justices William Rehnquist and Harry Blackmun. As was true of the other opinions, the conclusions Justice White drew were based on his subjective view of the facts of the case. White's dissenting opinion began by noting that the majority's decision would probably make it impossible to retry Williams. It went on to state that this circumstance had come about because the majority had made a mistake in its determination that Williams had not waived his rights. The majority, Justice White believed, had misinterpreted *Massiah* to mean that a suspect had a right not to be asked any questions in the absence of counsel unless the right were waived prior to questioning. Justice White argued that the reality of *Massiah* and *Miranda* was that the Court had only meant to give suspects the right not to answer questions in the absence of counsel. For Justice White, the facts of this case showed that Williams not only had been informed of his rights, but that he understood them. Williams's decision to cooperate with the police was a choice of his own free will and the record indicated that he had knowingly and intelligently waived his rights. All his statements and the resulting evidence should have been permitted at trial because Detective Leaming's conduct did not jeopardize the fairness of the trial or add to the possibility of convicting an innocent man, which was the circumstance the Sixth Amendment was designed to prevent.

Justice Blackmun also wrote a dissent, which was joined by Justices White and Rehnquist. It started by stating that this was the wrong case to consider overruling *Miranda v. Arizona*, as urged by Iowa and 21 other states in the joint *amicus curiae* brief of the AELE and NADA. The opinion went on to state that he also believed that *Massiah v. United States* was a flawed case on which to settle the issues of this case. The reason was that Justice Blackmun did not believe that the police had purposely set out to deny Williams counsel after judicial proceedings began. Justice Blackmun argued that Williams's isolation during the trip was necessary due to the need to transport Williams back to Des Moines. He also pointed out that Detective Leaming had a greater concern than simply trying to elicit incriminating information from Williams during the trip. Detective Leaming, who could not be sure that the victim was dead, had to be concerned about her possible condition after two days. Justice Blackmun further argued that not all attempts to gather information, such as the discussions between Leaming and Williams, should be regarded as being equivalent to interrogation. Based on his belief that Detective Leaming had not purposely tried to violate Williams's right to counsel, Justice Blackmun stated that it was unfortunate that the majority had elected to widen the scope of *Massiah* to exclude the evidence gained as a result of any effort of police to gather information in the absence of counsel after arraignment even when it was gained through volunteered statements. Justice Blackmun then ended his opinion by marking his disappointment that, due to the Court's decision, Williams would probably go free.

As could have been predicted prior to the Court's decision, the resolution of the case depended on the subjective facts believed to be true by the justices. The different sets of subjective facts that were accepted by the justices led them to emphasize different legal options in their opinions. No justice who wrote an opinion had to be creative and develop a new approach to the law. Instead, each justice was capable of firmly supporting his opinion by relying on the line of precedents that had previously been decided by the Court. The ability of all the justices to be able to ground their opinions in precedent illustrates the importance that discretion plays. As the justices demonstrated in *Brewer v. Williams*, discretion to exercise legal options allows justices to continue to guide the direction of the law to reflect their own preferences. In this particular case, it also resulted in the need for Iowa to either put Williams on trial a second time or let him go free.

NOTES

1. David O'Brien, *Storm Center*, 3rd ed. (New York: W. W. Norton and Co., 1993), p. 249.

2. *Brewer v. Williams*, 430 U.S. 387 (1977).

3. *Miranda v. Arizona*, 384 U.S. 436 (1966).

4. Harvard Law Review, "The Supreme Court, 1975 Term," *Harvard Law Review* 90 (1976): 279.

5. O'Brien, *Storm Center*, p. 232.

6. Stephen Wasby, *The Supreme Court in the Federal Judicial System*, 3rd ed. (Chicago: Nelson-Hall, 1988), p. 207.

7. O'Brien, *Storm Center*, p. 236.

8. Gregory A. Calderia and John R. Wright, "The Discuss List: Agenda Building in the Supreme Court," *Law and Society Review* 24 (1990): 809.

9. O'Brien, *Storm Center*, p. 153.

10. *Brewer v. Williams*, 423 U.S. 1030 (1975s).

11. This summary of Rule 34 is provided by Thomas G. Walker and Lee Epstein, *The Supreme Court of the United States: An Introduction* (New York: St. Martin's Press, 1993), p. 103.

12. Brief for Petitioner, *Brewer v. Williams*, 430 U.S. 387 (1977), p. 16.

13. Ibid., p. 25.

14. Ibid., p. 32.

15. Ibid., p. 33.

16. *Townsend v. Sain*, 372 U.S. 293 (1963).

17. Brief for the Respondent, *Brewer v. Williams*, 430 U.S. 387 (1977), p. 11.

18. O'Brien, *Storm Center*, p. 148.

19. Walker and Epstein, *The Supreme Court*, p. 108.

20. William J. Brennan, Jr., "State Court Decisions and the Supreme Court," *Pennsylvania Bar Association Quarterly* 31 (1960): 405.

21. David Danelski, "Explorations of Some Causes and Consequences of Conflict and Its Resolution in the Supreme Court," *Judicial Conflict and Consensus*, Eds. Sheldon Goldman and Charles M. Lamb (Lexington: University Press of Kentucky, 1986), p. 29.

22. Wasby, *The Supreme Court in the Federal Judicial System*, p. 233.

23. O'Brien, *Storm Center*, p. 317.

24. *Brewer v. Williams*, 430 U.S. 387, 398 (1977).

25. *Massiah v. United States*, 377 U.S. 201 (1964).
26. *Brewer v. Williams*, 430 U.S. 387, 401 (1977).
27. Ibid., p. 404, citing *Johnson v. Zerbst*, 304 U.S. 458, 464 (1938).
28. Ibid., p. 406.
29. Ibid., p. 406 n. 12.
30. *Stone v. Powell*, 428 U.S. 465 (1976).
31. *Brewer v. Williams*, 430 U.S. 387, 415–416 (1977) (Burger, C. J., dissenting).

Chapter 7

The Second Trial

Society has police to protect it from thieves and murderers, and it has lawyers to protect it from the police. No one has yet discovered how to protect society from the lawyers.

—Phillip E. Johnson[1]

The day after the decision was made in *Brewer v. Williams*,[2] interest in the decision was so high that the *Des Moines Register* took the unusual step of publishing the entire majority opinion in its pages. Reaction in Iowa to the Supreme Court's decision was quick. Police Chief Nichols said the Court's decision was "asinine."[3] Cleatus Leaming said that he was disappointed in the verdict, but added that the fact that the case was heard by the Supreme Court showed the system worked. Vincent Hanrahan, who had been the chief prosecutor in Williams's trial, was unhappy with the decision and had hoped the Court would change the *Miranda* rule. Richard Turner, Iowa's attorney general, called the decision "a bitter pill."[4] District Judge Glanton, the judge who had allowed Williams's statements on the trip from Davenport to Des Moines to be used as evidence at the preliminary hearing, thought the decision was a good one, which made clear that a person's right to counsel could not be taken away through subterfuge. Deputy Warden Paul Hedgepeth said that Williams had heard the Court's announcement over the radio and was pretty happy but was refusing to comment based on the advice of his attorney. Pamela's parents, who now lived in Washington, Michigan, were, of course, disappointed with the decision. Merlin Powers,

Pamela's father, told reporters, "I was kind of expecting it to go this way, the way judges and society in general are today. . . . I'm just really too broken about it to say anything."[5]

Discussing the implications of the decision, Dan Johnston, Polk County district attorney, said that he wasn't sure if the State would be able to successfully prosecute Williams a second time. "The problem as I see it," said Johnston, "is that a good deal of the evidence in the first trial resulted from the conversation between Williams and the Des Moines police officer."[6] Despite the problems involved in a second prosecution, Johnston said that since the murder charge still stood on Williams, his office would try to keep Williams in jail until a course of action was decided on. He also mentioned that if they did proceed against Williams, they would be helped by Cleatus Leaming, who had resigned from the police department and was working as an investigator in his office.

Within two days of the Supreme Court's decision, the State of Iowa was weighing its options. Dan Johnston stated that he assumed that Polk County would retry Williams, but was frustrated because his office could not locate the case file. Johnston noted that he was also looking at other options. These included a plea bargain and the filing of sexual psychopath charges, under which Williams would be confined to a mental hospital until it was determined that his release would not be detrimental to society. Iowa Attorney General Richard Turner stated that if Polk County did not proceed with charges against Williams, his office would. A final option officials were considering was returning Williams to Missouri to the state mental hospital at Fulton from which he had escaped. Fulton Police Chief W. W. Lewis told the press that "as far as I'm concerned [Williams] is still wanted down here."[7]

Amid all of the County and State's planning on how to proceed against Williams, the *Des Moines Register* editorialized: "It would be appalling if the U.S. Supreme Court ruling overturning the conviction of Robert Williams causes Williams to go free because of the loss of evidence ruled inadmissible by the court weakens the case against him." The editorial went on to state that despite this possible turn of events, the Court had made the right decision because of the importance of counsel in protecting the rights of the accused and ensuring the fair administration of justice. It continued by pointing out "If the high court condoned police conduct in this case, it would be an invitation to police to deceive attorneys and to try to break down their clients."[8]

The fact that Robert Williams's conviction had been overturned did not mean that Williams would be automatically released from prison. Instead, the State sought and secured an order to continue to hold Williams at the state penitentiary until a verdict was reached in a second trial. Dan Johnston announced on March 31, 1977, that Polk County would proceed with another murder trial against Robert Williams. Johnston explained that he was convinced to proceed by the footnote in Justice Stewart's opinion indicating that while Williams's statements could not be used at trial, the body and other physical evidence might be admissible under the theory that they would have been found anyway. Johnston added, "We are prepared to go into court and show . . . the body probably would have been found within 48 hours."[9]

PRETRIAL MANEUVERS

Pretrial Motions

Prior to the second trial, Williams filed an affidavit of indigency requesting appointment of counsel for his upcoming trial. The affidavit stated that, due to his financial situation, Williams could not afford to hire his own attorney and was thus requesting that one be appointed for him. The affidavit explained that Robert Bartels, who had handled the appeal and *habeas corpus* filing on his first case was not available to represent him due to prior commitments. Williams then requested that Shelton Otis, a San Francisco attorney, be appointed to represent him. Williams noted that Shelton Otis had indicated to him that he was both willing and able to represent Williams. Shelton Otis, a member of the bar in California and Michigan, had tried cases previously in Iowa and had extensive experience in criminal trials. Williams also stated that Gerald Crawford, a Des Moines attorney, was willing to act as co-counsel. The affidavit did not request a hearing to determine appointment of counsel.

On April 21, 1977, District Judge Ray Hanrahan made a decision regarding the appointment of counsel for Williams. After discussing the matter with Robert Bartels, who assured the judge that Williams was indeed indigent and that Bartels himself could not continue representing him, Judge Hanrahan decided that both Williams's interest and the court's interest in the orderly processing of pretrial matters and the trial would be better served by the appointment of local attorneys. As a result, Judge Hanrahan appointed two members of the Polk County Offender Advocate's Office— Roger P. Owens and John C. Wellman—along with Gerald Crawford, as co-counsels.

Before the trial began Williams's attorneys sought to protect him from the adverse influence of the publicity surrounding his case by filing a motion requesting three types of relief: a change of venue, individual voir dire examination of each potential juror, and the sequestration of the jurors after they were selected. The prosecution argued that there was no need for a change of venue because there was less publicity over the circumstances leading to the second trial than there had been over the first trial. Both sides submitted affidavits from citizens who gave opinions regarding whether they believed Williams could get a fair trial in Des Moines.

On May 27, 1977, Judge Denato granted the request for a change of venue and moved the trial to Cedar Rapids, Iowa. He denied a defense request to conduct public opinion polls to find an unbiased venue to which the trial should be moved. He also granted the request for the attorneys to individually question prospective jurors during the voir dire, since he believed that this would aid in selecting an impartial jury. Judge Denato did not, however, grant the request for sequestration of the jurors. He believed it unnecessary and gave three reasons supporting his decision. The first reason was that allowing individual questioning of jurors during voir dire would help to ensure that the jurors would remain unbiased throughout the trial and capable of reaching a nonbiased verdict. His second reason was that the trial was expected to last as long as two weeks and sequestration would drastically limit the number of people who could expect to remain in the jury pool. His final reason was that juror isolation for as long as the trial was expected to take could cause them to lose the "common sense of balance" necessary to reaching a reasoned decision.

Prior to trial, Williams's attorneys made several motions to suppress evidence. The most important of the suppression motions included the desire to suppress all of Williams's statements during the trip between Davenport and Des Moines, which the Supreme Court had ruled resulted from a violation of his Sixth Amendment right to counsel. Included in the motion was a request to suppress all evidence gathered as a result of the tainted statements including "articles of clothing, and photographs of articles of clothing, found on the body, evidence concerning the condition of the body, and the results of medical, chemical, or pathological tests performed on the body."[10] The defense also sought to suppress hair samples that had been taken from Williams while he was being held at the Polk County Jail.

The suppression hearing was held on May 31, 1977, before Judge Denato. Robert Blink, the assistant county attorney presided over the State's case while Roger Owens, Gerald Crawford, and John Wellman acted on behalf of Williams's defense. Williams was transferred to the Polk County Jail from the State Penitentiary in Fort Madison for the hearing. The hearing was closed to the public and tight security was maintained. Judge Denato also reminded court employees that they were not to discuss the proceedings with members of the press or with anyone who was likely to divulge information about the proceedings to the press.

Both sides had specific things they were hoping to prove to the judge's satisfaction in the hearing. On the first issue—admission of the body and related evidence—the prosecution's goal was two-fold. First, to present credible evidence that, despite Detective Leaming's violation of Williams's right to counsel, the body of Pamela Powers would inevitably have been found by alternative lawful means. Second, to present credible evidence that the body would have been found in a condition similar to that in which it was actually found. If this could be done and Judge Denato accepted the prosecution's evidence, he could apply Justice Stewart's footnote to the subjective facts he accepted and allow the body and other physical evidence to be presented at trial.

The defense team wanted to demonstrate just the opposite. It was hoping to convince the judge that the subjective facts proved that the body would not have been found for a considerable period of time, if at all. If the defense attorneys failed in this strategy, they wanted the judge to accept a version of the facts that the body would not have been found in the same condition. In a strategic move to make the prosecution's job more difficult, the defense requested a ruling, which was granted, to formally separate the State's witnesses so they would not hear each other's testimony.

Prior to calling any witnesses, the State's exhibits—consisting of photographs and maps of the location where the body was found—were all marked for identification. During the suppression hearing the prosecution offered three recently taken photographs that were used to give the judge a view of the road and ditch where Pamela Powers had been located. Two photographs taken of the body at the time of the discovery were also introduced as exhibits to help demonstrate that if the police search had continued, the body would have been discovered. The State's witnesses testified that these photographs showed that, before it was disturbed, the body was readily discernible and that the snow that had fallen had not hidden the body.

The first witness called by the prosecution was John Jutte, a special agent for the Iowa Bureau of Criminal Investigation. Jutte testified that he was the person who had first found Pamela Powers's body when Williams led the police to the site where it had been dumped. After direct examination, Jutte was cross-examined by John Wellman. In the cross-examination, Jutte was initially pressed to testify that even though he had found the body, it was only because Williams had led the police to the body. After some roundabout testimony in which Jutte testified that he had not spoken to Williams, Judge Denato asked if it could not be stipulated that the body was found through the actions of Detective Leaming and Williams. Both sides accepted this stipulation as fact. On redirect examination Jutte described the bright clothes that first caught his attention upon locating the body. He also testified that the face was partially exposed and had not been covered by snow.

The prosecution next called Carroll Dawson, who was in charge of the Identification Section of the Des Moines Police Department on the night that the body was located. Officer Dawson had been called out to take charge of the body for the Des Moines Police Department. He testified that he was one of the individuals who had physically removed the body from the crime scene. He stated that Pamela was originally partially covered with snow. The snow wasn't brushed off until after a picture was taken. He also identified a picture presented by the prosecutor as accurately showing the body as he initially found it. He said her whole body was frozen stiff and her back was stuck against the side of a cement culvert from which she had to be broken loose. Upon cross-examination, Officer Dawson admitted that he had no knowledge as to whether anyone other than himself may have cleared snow from the body prior to pictures being taken. Judge Denato, hoping to clarify the situation then asked about the snow on the body. Officer Dawson told him that he had to brush snow off to be able to completely see the body, but he didn't remember anyone else doing so.

The State then called Dr. Jack Hatchitt, who in 1968 had been a Des Moines Police Department medical examiner and had helped to carry the body out of the culvert. Dr. Hatchitt testified that the body was completely frozen when it was found. His testimony also revealed that at the time the body was found it was getting dark and snowing. He said that a light snow was falling when he was at the crime scene, but that the snow got heavier as the night went on. After the testimony of Dr. Hatchitt, the State introduced two exhibits that were climatological charts showing the temperatures, precipitation, and winds for the Des Moines area for the months of December 1968 and January 1969.

Thomas Ruxlow of the Iowa Bureau of Criminal Investigation was called to the stand next by the State. He testified that he had been placed in charge of the search operation, which began on December 26, 1968. He explained that on Christmas Day a call had gone out over a Grinnell, Iowa, radio station asking for volunteers to assemble the morning of December 26 at the Grinnell Police Department. This request for volunteers resulted in a search party composed of around 200 individuals. Officer Ruxlow then testified that the search concentrated on Jasper and Poweshiek counties because articles of clothing had been found at the Grinnell rest area on Interstate 80 and it was surmised that the clothes were probably the last articles of evidence that would have been discarded. Therefore, the search first concentrated on Poweshiek County and then moved westward into Jasper County. Officer Ruxlow explained that the search was conducted systematically. Maps of Poweshiek and Jasper counties were marked off in grid fashion with an area roughly seven miles north and south of Interstate 80 being searched. The volunteers were split into teams of four to six people and assigned specific grids to be searched. The instructions given to the volunteers when they began the search at 10 A.M. were:

when searching, to check all the roads, the ditches, any culverts; they were instructed to get down and look into any culverts. If they came upon any abandoned farm buildings, they were instructed to go into the property and search those abandoned farm buildings or any other places where a small child could be secreted.[11]

Officer Ruxlow's testimony then explained that the search was suspended at 3 P.M. when he was called away from headquarters. At that time, he followed Leaming's vehicle as Williams led them to the location of the body.

He also testified that the pictures did indeed demonstrate the condition of the body prior to disturbance. He went on to state that before the searchers quit, all the grids in Poweshiek and Jasper counties had been searched. He pointed out that had the search been reinstated, the same techniques would have been used in Polk County, where the body was actually located. He estimated that, using those techniques, it would have taken between three and five hours to search the 2½ miles west from where the search was disbanded to where the body was located and that it would have been found.

John Wellman's cross-examination of Officer Ruxlow attempted to point out the improbability of the searchers actually finding the body. Wellman got Officer Ruxlow to testify that the only place where the ditches were actually driven in for sure was on Interstate 80, where snowmobiles were used to cover the ditches and median. On other roads, the ditches were visually inspected from vehicles on the road. Officer Ruxlow added that his reports showed that searchers were following instructions and getting out of their vehicles to search culverts and other places where a body could have been hidden. He added that if a ditch was weedy, searchers were instructed to walk through the weeds. In response to his questioning, Wellman was told by Officer Ruxlow that the searchers did not have maps showing where all the culverts were located.

Wellman then pressed Officer Ruxlow as to the reasons why the search was cancelled. Officer Ruxlow explained that he was instructed to meet Detective Leaming at a Grinnell truck stop at 3 P.M. and that because this left no one to supervise the search, it was suspended. Officer Ruxlow stated that there was no way to communicate to the searchers that the search was ended. This left some searchers in the field finishing up their last grid assignments. When they reported back to headquarters, there was no one to give them new assignments. Officer Ruxlow also testified that the search was never resumed after 3 P.M. because the body was found. When pressed, he testified that he did not know when the search would have been resumed had the body not been found.

The next witness that the State called was Dr. Earl Rose, a physician who specialized in pathology. Dr. Rose testified that freezing temperatures stopped decomposition of human bodies by stopping enzymatic actions. When questioned as to whether being exposed to an additional three to five hours of freezing temperatures would affect the decomposition of a body, he answered *no*. He added that a body kept in continual freezing temperatures would be preserved for a postmortem autopsy until it was thawed and that, according to temperature charts for the time in question, the body would not have thawed until April of 1969.

In cross-examination, Dr. Rose was questioned about a report filed by Dr. Leo Luka, who did the postmortem on Pamela Powers. The postmortem report stated that Pamela's face was blue when it was found. Dr. Rose testified that the face was cyanotic, causing it to turn blue. He further tes-

tified that the blueness in the face would have persisted as long as the body
was frozen. He added that the blueness in the face was not caused by its
being frozen. Instead, as Dr. Luka had reported, it was probably an indication of suffocation or strangulation. The bluing, Dr. Rose explained, was
blood in the face that did not have oxygen.

Dr. Rose next testified, in response to the defense's questions, that fluid
samples, which Dr. Luka had taken from the mouth, rectal, and vaginal areas
of the victim's body showing a positive test for acid phosphatases, would
also have been preserved due to the freezing temperatures. He noted that
the positive acid phosphatase test was an indication that seminal fluid was
present, even if there was no presence of spermatozoa.

During cross-examination, Dr. Rose was questioned about the possibility
of the body being disturbed by animals. Dr. Rose admitted that Dr. Luka's
original report on the condition of the body indicated that the face had
been disturbed by some sort of animal. He also admitted that it was not
uncommon in rural areas for a body to be subject to such abuse by animals.
When questioned, he told the court that if the face had been eaten away, it
could not have been determined that the face was cyanotic.

Beyond its cross-examination of the State's witnesses, the defense only
introduced two items to demonstrate that the body would not inevitably
have been found without a violation of Williams's rights. To demonstrate
that the sun set on December 26, 1968, at 4:50 P.M., a full 55 minutes
before the body was located, the first defense exhibit was a chart giving the
time of sunrise and sunset for Des Moines, Iowa. The second was transcripts
of the testimony of Detective Leaming from the first trial relating to the
weather conditions at the time the body was found and the fact that it still
took the police five minutes to discover the body, even when they had been
led to its location.

Judge Denato moved on to consider whether the hairs that had been
gathered from Williams while he was in custody were admissible. The State
first called Officer Carroll Dawson of the Des Moines Police Department.
He testified that on December 27, 1968, while Williams was being held at
the Polk County Jail, he requested some hair samples from Williams, who
willingly gave them. During cross-examination, Officer Dawson admitted
that he had known of Williams's mental history, but had not informed him
of his *Miranda* rights prior to requesting the hair samples. Gerald Limke,
another Des Moines police officer who assisted in getting hair samples from
Williams, was called next. He corroborated Officer Dawson's story that the
samples had been given willingly, with no threats of danger or promises of
better treatment.

The defense then called Williams himself. Williams testified that at the
time when the officers asked him for hair samples he was fearful for his
safety. He also told the court that it would be more accurate to say that he
didn't give the officers any hairs. An accurate portrayal of the event would

be that the officers took hair samples from him. He went on to state that he allowed the hairs to be taken because he believed that they had gotten his attorney's permission. He said that he couldn't believe that after Detective Leaming had already broken one agreement with McKnight that the police would do anything else to him without consulting his attorney. On cross-examination, Williams told the prosecutor that at the time that the hair samples were taken the police had not threatened him or promised him anything in return for the samples.

Judge Denato ruled on the suppression motions on June 1, 1977. Although the rulings had a mixed result, overall it was a victory for the prosecution. This was because, even though none of Williams's statement during the trip between Davenport and Des Moines could be used at trial, the body and all of the physical evidence associated with its discovery *was* ruled to be admissible because of an *inevitable discovery exception* to the exclusionary rule. Judge Denato stated that guidance for his decision was found in the footnote of Justice Stewart's majority opinion in *Brewer v. Williams.* Judge Denato went on to note that in inevitable discovery cases, the burden of proof, by a preponderance of the evidence, is on the State to show that the evidence would have been discovered without legal violations. After examining the evidence and determining the subjective facts, Judge Denato ruled:

The Court concludes that the searchers would have arrived at the site of the body within a short time of its actual finding, had they continued the search after dark. The culvert in question was itself uncovered and readily visible and in getting down to look into it as the searchers were doing the depression on either side of it would have been obvious—the body was in one of these depressions. Had the searchers stopped due to the snow and the dark the next day was a Friday and a weekend was upcoming—the search would clearly have been taken up again where it left off, given the extreme circumstances of this case and the body would have been found in short order. . . . Accordingly, the Court concludes that the body of Pamela Powers would have been found in any event even had the incriminating statements not been elicited from the defendant and that decomposition would not have taken place so as to alter the medical examination findings of Dr. Luka and thus there held admissible in evidence.[12]

Judge Denato allowed the samples of body hairs taken from Williams to be used because Williams had consented. There had been no compulsion, so Judge Denato ruled that Williams had knowingly waived his constitutional rights. At the hearing Judge Denato also granted a defense request to have Williams tested at Mercy Hospital to determine if he had the ability to produce sperm.

Trial Strategies

As the date for trial drew closer, both parties to the case continued to maneuver to advance strategies that would benefit their view of the case at trial. One thing that had changed since the first trial was the rules governing discovery. The new rules promulgated by the Iowa Supreme Court allowed the defense to have access to all police files and reports regardless of whether the prosecution would rely on them at trial. The new rules also allowed the defense to take sworn depositions from all prosecution witnesses prior to trial.

As the trial grew closer, the defense began a search for alternative suspects. The reason the defense believed that other suspects should be considered was that a police report made available to them through the broadened discovery process showed that the police once theorized that Williams was sterile. The defense also possessed a prosecution report that had not been shared in the first trial, which showed that, according to the autopsy report, there was no spermatozoa found in the semen taken from the body of Pamela Powers. Since the sterility test done on Williams showed that he was not sterile, the defense believed that someone other than Williams was responsible for the attack on Pamela.

The possible suspect that the defense began to point a finger at was Albert Bowers, who, it claimed, had a history of child molestation. Like Williams, Bowers was a black male who lived in the Y.M.C.A.; he was employed there to clean washrooms at the time of Pamela's disappearance. Defense lawyers contended that a towel covered with human blood had been found in Bowers's room the day after the crime. It also claimed that Bowers left Des Moines shortly after Williams was arrested, despite requests by police that he remain in town. The defense further believed that some of the pubic hairs discovered in the investigation could have come from Bowers. Bowers, however, had died in 1971. Based on these facts, the defense requested and Judge Denato granted an order to exhume the body. After the body was exhumed on June 24, 1977, an autopsy was done by Dr. Garry Peterson who was able to find signs of sperm. The defense informed that prosecution of this finding. Due to the positive results of the test for spermatozoa on Albert Bowers revealed by the autopsy and its theory that the crime was committed by a sterile man, the defense never made mention of his name as a possible suspect during the trial process.

The prosecution also continued to try to influence the trial process. Prior to trial, prosecutors informed the court that they could not produce any of the records of the medical tests that had been conducted on the fluids taken from Pamela Powers's body. The prosecution said that these tests, which had been stored at Wilden Hospital in Des Moines, had been destroyed when the basement flooded. Due to this situation, the prosecutors motioned for a ruling that the defense could not make mention at trial that, even though acid phosphatase had been found on the body, there was no sign of sperm. The prosecutors argued that since Dr. Luka, who had performed the autopsy, had not been present when the fluids were tested, he could not testify as to what particular tests were performed or the competency of the individual who conducted the tests. Such a ruling would prevent the defense from entering its theory that the crime had been committed by a sterile man. Judge Denato denied this motion and allowed both sides to the case to work off the record with regard to the test results.

Jury Selection

The trial process got started on July 5, 1977. Dan Johnston handed control of the prosecution over to an assistant in the Polk County Prosecutor's Office, Robert Blink. The first order of business was to select a jury. The entire trial process was widely covered by the press. More than a dozen reporters attended the jury selection process. A panel of about 100 people were called in the venire. After introductory comments by Judge Denato, he separated the individuals into a number of panels and instructed some to stay for questioning and others to return the next day. A panel of 12 potential jurors were then brought into the courtroom. Judge Denato began the voir dire process by asking the prospective jurors a number of general questions. The attorneys for both parties then subjected individual jurors to questioning. It took the attorneys about 45 minutes to question the first few prospective jurors, but by the end of the process the time decreased to between 15 and 30 minutes each. The questions ranged from the need to prove a case beyond a reasonable doubt, the differences between direct and circumstantial evidence, and racial prejudices. Williams's attorneys told the possible jurors that Williams would be implicated in the crime and that some of the evidence did indicate that Williams was at the scene of the crime. The defense also questioned some jurors to make sure that they did not believe that the "Perry Mason" television show, in which the killer was always revealed in court, was an accurate reflection of reality.

After two days of voir dire, both sides had used their eight peremptory challenges and the jury was seated. It was composed of eight women and four men with three alternates. After the jurors were selected, Judge Denato asked reporters to consider not reporting the names of the jurors to prevent them from possibly receiving calls, which could affect the fairness of the trial. Despite this request for anonymity for the jurors, the names and hometowns of all the jurors were reported in the *Des Moines Register* on July 8, 1977. Later, other papers and the wire services followed suit.

THE TRIAL

Opening Statements

On July 8, 1977, the State, represented by lead counsel Robert Blink and co-counsel Rodney Ryan, began to present its case, which would take 2½ days and would involve calling 18 witnesses and presenting 41 exhibits.

Robert Blink's opening statement, which lasted only about five minutes, provided a narrative of the events involved in the case that the jurors would learn about. It told the story of the Powers family going to the Y.M.C.A., how Pamela disappeared, and Williams's departure from the building shortly thereafter while carrying a bundle. It then told of Williams's flight across the state as he discarded pieces of evidence. Blink ended by reading the following indictment against Williams:

The grand jurors of the County of Polk in the name and by the authority of the State of Iowa accuse Robert Anthony Williams also known as Anthony Erthell Williams of the crime of murder as defined in sections 690.1 and 690.2 of the code of Iowa and charge that Robert Anthony Williams also known as Anthony Erthell Williams in the County and State aforesaid did with malice aforethought, premeditation, deliberation and intent to kill, murder Pamela Powers in Polk County, Iowa.[13]

When the defense began its opening statements, which also lasted about five minutes, Mr. and Mrs. Powers walked into the hall, choosing not to hear once again a recitation of the evil that had befallen their child. John Wellman, Williams's lead attorney, told the courtroom that Williams had indeed carried Pamela Powers out of the Y.M.C.A. on December 24, 1968, and disposed of her in a rural area. The defense went on to assert that, despite this admission, Williams had not killed the girl. Wellman explained that Williams had found the body in his seventh floor room at the Y.M.C.A. Upon doing so, he panicked and removed it, hoping not to be implicated in the crime. Williams did this because of the facts and circumstances surrounding his life at the time. To help Williams's defense, Wellman did not explain that at the time of the crime he was an escapee from a mental hospital, where he had been sent for statutory rape. The defense admitted that Pamela Powers had met a terrible death and been sexually molested shortly before or after her death, but stated that those actions had to be separated from Williams's actions after he discovered the body. Wellman went on to explain the defense's theory that the crime had been committed by a sterile man, which excluded Williams as a suspect, since he was not sterile.

Following the opening statements, Judge Denato offered all the jurors and alternates pencil and paper to take notes during the trial. Each juror accepted the offer. Judge Denato then decided that it would be better to recess for lunch than to allow the prosecution to start its case. Before recess, the judge admonished the jury to keep the notes to themselves and to destroy them after the trial. He then told them that the purpose of the admonishment was to reinforce the oath that they had undertaken as jurors. He reminded them that they were bound by the law, which he would instruct them in at the end of the trial. In their deliberations, they should use the law as provided by the court and apply it to the evidence that was presented at trial in order to reach a verdict. He emphasized the importance of the jurors only relying on the evidence that was presented at trial and told them to avoid talking about the case with others, even their spouses. He also informed them that they should not pay attention to any media accounts of the case.

The Prosecution's Case

When court reconvened, the State called the first of its witnesses, which included Nelda Powers, Merlin Powers, Kevin Sanders, and Donald Hanna. All these witnesses provided the same testimony that they had at Williams's first trial. They told the story of Pamela's disappearance, followed by Williams's departure from the Y.M.C.A. The defense did not cross-examine any of these witnesses, causing the State to exhaust its supply of witnesses who were available to testify. After both sides stipulated, at the request of the prosecution, that Pamela Powers had Blood Type O, Rh factor negative, Judge Denato released the jury for the evening, reminding them of his admonishment.

After the jury was dismissed, the defense made a motion requesting that the jury be sequestered during its deliberation. Judge Denato denied the motion explaining that the voir dire showed that each of the jurors had an open mind concerning the case and was willing to resolve the case based on the evidence submitted at trial. Furthermore, there was no indication that any of the jurors would violate their oaths as jurors.

On the second day of the trial, the State called two more witnesses, Lurine McMahan and Fred Thompson, who testified that they had seen Williams carrying a bundle wrapped in a blanket through the lobby of the Y.M.C.A. Lurine McMahan, who worked at the front desk and sold candy from the desk, also testified that she had sold Pamela Powers some candy. The only cross-examination of these two witnesses concerned some questions for Mrs. McMahan about the switchboard of the phone system for the Y.M.C.A., which she had operated.

The State also called a group of witnesses to demonstrate Williams's efforts to dispose of evidence of the crime. The first was Merle Killinger. Killinger had been employed by the Iowa State Highway Commission in December of 1968 and assigned the duty of maintaining Interstate 80 rest areas. He testified that, on December 25, 1968, he found a number of items in the men's restroom at the rest stop near Grinnell, Iowa. These items were presented as exhibits 1 through 10 for the prosecution. These items included a blanket, a man's suit jacket, a man's suit trousers, a man's yellow shirt, a man's light jacket, a man's handkerchief, a girl's sweater-type blouse, a Y.M.C.A. towel, a pair of girl's socks, and a pair of girl's slacks. Especially damaging to Williams were the last two items, which were Pamela's and had been identified as such during the testimony of Merlin Powers. On top of this damaging evidence, Mr. Killinger told the court that the trousers had the name "Anthony" written inside the right-back pocket.[14] Mr. Killinger then told the court that he had taken all the items, bagged them together, and given them to Officer Gates of the Grinnell Police Department.

Andrew Newquist, who worked as a special agent for the Iowa Highway Department in 1968, was then called by the State. Officer Newquist testified that he had been present when Williams's car had been searched. He identified State exhibits 19 and 20 as photos of Williams's car. Officer Newquist was asked if he could identify state exhibits 13 through 17 as items that had been gathered when the car was searched. These items included a necktie, a pair of socks, a rear-seat floor mat, rear-seat covers, and a rug from the front-seat area. Officer Newquist did identify all of the items except for the necktie and a pair of socks, neither of which carried his identification mark. He did comment, however, that he remembered a necktie and pair of socks being taken from the car, but he could not be sure that these were the identical ones. Officer Newquist then explained that these items were turned over to Chief Wendell Nichols of the Des Moines Police Department on December 27, 1968.

The State then called Thomas Ruxlow of the Iowa Bureau of Criminal Investigation as a witness. Agent Ruxlow testified that on December 26, 1968, he had observed the body of Pamela Powers where it was found. The prosecutor then produced two maps and asked Agent Ruxlow to draw an *X* on the approximate place where the body was found. Agent Ruxlow was then taken through a series of aerial photographs, which were marked State exhibits 27 through 41. He testified that the photos clearly depicted the roads that connected the Y.M.C.A. to the location where the body was discovered.

The next two witnesses for the prosecution were called to demonstrate a clear chain of custody for some of the exhibits that were used as evidence. Charles Gates testified that in 1968 he worked for the Grinnell Police Department and that, in that capacity, Merle Killinger had given him all the articles that he had found in the men's restroom at the Grinnell rest area. He then told the court that he had turned all the found items over to Officer Forrest Speck of the Des Moines Police Department. Officer Speck was then called and testified that he had received the items, originally found at the rest area and that he had turned the articles over to Officer Charles Soderquist, who worked in the Identification Bureau of the Des Moines Police Department.

To demonstrate Williams's eastern flight, the State next called Mark Cupples. Cupples was working at Cupples' Skelly gas station in Grinnell, Iowa, on Christmas Eve of 1968. He testified that on that night Williams had stopped at the station and bought two dollars worth of gas. The Court then broke for lunch.

In the afternoon, the first witness called by the State was the Reverend Robert Kem. Reverend Kem was the director of St. Andrew's Episcopal

Church, the church to which the Powers family had belonged. He testified that he had baptized Pamela and knew her well. He also stated that he had been the one to identify the body after its discovery on December 26, 1968.

Next the State called Cornelius McWright, an FBI laboratory technician from Washington, D.C. In response to a question, McWright told the court that the FBI had received a package of evidence from the Des Moines Police Department, which was tested for the presence of semen. After explaining to the court how such tests were conducted, he gave the results. McWright stated that he had tested the man's shirt and pants that had been found at the Interstate 80 rest stop. The tests revealed signs of semen, but no sperm. McWright also testified that he had tested several items for blood typing. These included the man's shirt and towel found at the rest stop on Interstate 80, which both proved to contain type O blood, the same type as Pamela Powers. A child's undershirt, also found at the rest stop, had blood stains, but the blood type could not be determined.

During cross-examination, McWright testified that he had tested a sock and tie, which Davenport police officers Clarence Yeager and Andrew Newquist had found inside the glove compartment of Williams's car. The test indicated the presence of traces of sperm. McWright was then asked if the presence of sperm on some of the articles tested, but only semen on others, would indicate that the samples came from different persons. McWright replied that there was a possibility that this conclusion could be drawn, but that sperm cells do break down and may have in this case before tests were conducted. When pressed, McWright admitted that one conclusion that could be drawn from the lack of sperm in some semen stains but not in others was the possibility that the two semen samples came from different sources. He also stated that he found no blood stains that were Type A blood. (Williams's blood was Type A.) When asked, McWright informed the court that neither the bedspread taken from Williams's room nor the blanket found at the rest stop had blood, semen, or any other type of biological stains. At the end of McWright's testimony, the prosecutor asked for and received a stipulation from the defense that the chain of evidence was intact and that all the exhibits testified about were indeed the real items and had been returned from the FBI to the Des Moines Police Department.

One of the most powerful witnesses for the State was Dr. Leo Luka, the Polk County medical examiner who had performed the autopsy on the body of Pamela Powers. Dr. Luka testified that the external examination of the body showed numerous abrasions and lacerations on the head, face, and legs. The face was cyanotic and it looked like part of the nose had been chewed off by a small animal. The probable cause of death given by Dr. Luka was asphyxiation, most likely from being smothered. He also testified that there were signs of sexual abuse at or shortly after the time of death due to disturbances of the rectum, mouth, and vagina, but there had been no penetration. The rectum was dilated and the vagina was separated in an unnatural position, but the hymen was intact. Dr. Luka went on to explain that fluid taken from the rectum, vagina, and the mouth had tested positive for acid phosphatase, indicating the presence of semen, but that no traces of sperm were found.

On cross-examination, Dr. Luka told the court that he believed that the sexual molestation had taken place after death. He said that there was no sign of bleeding in either the rectum or vagina. In Dr. Luka's opinion, the only likely injury that would have bled prior to death was on the forehead. Dr. Luka was also questioned about whether a person's bladder empties at the time of death, and he replied that it did sometimes. This was done because the lack of such a stain on the sheets from Williams's room advanced the defense theory that Pamela had been killed elsewhere and placed in Williams's room by the murderer. He was then asked about the effect that freezing would have on any sperm that may have been present in the fluids found on the body. He answered that the lack of sperm could be explained by the freezing temperatures, which would destroy any sperm that was present. The defense reminded him of a deposition he had given on June 7, 1977, in which he said that under the freezing conditions the body was subjected to, one would expect to see sperm in seminal fluid. Despite this reminder, Dr. Luka stuck to his statement that freezing could cause the breakdown of spermatozoa in seminal fluid.

After Dr. Luka's testimony, the prosecution had exhausted its witnesses for the day. On Monday morning, July 11, 1977, Sam Bailey, Jr., a member of the jury, requested a meeting with Judge Denato prior to the start of court. He told Judge Denato that a friend of his had called him over the weekend and voiced surprise that he was placed on the jury since he, Bailey, had met Mark Powers, Pamela's brother. Bailey had told his friend that he didn't think that he had met him, but, later, as he tried to remember, he recollected that he had been introduced to him on a pheasant-hunting trip. Judge Denato then asked Bailey if he had any recollections of Mark Powers other than just having hunted with him. Bailey answered *no*. In answer to another question, Bailey told the judge that this revelation would not have any effect on his ability to fulfill his duties as a juror. Judge Denato then told Bailey that it would be okay to continue as a juror. After his meeting with Bailey, Judge Denato informed the attorneys for both sides about his discussion and decision.

The first prosecution witness called on Monday morning was Gerald Limke, a police officer who had been assigned to the Des Moines Identification Bureau in December of 1968. The primary purpose of Officer Limke's testimony was to demonstrate an unbroken chain of custody of the evidence that had been gathered at the rest stop and from Williams's car between the Des Moines Police Department and the FBI laboratories, which conducted tests on the items.

The final witness called to complete the prosecution's case against Williams was Morris Clark, a special agent of the FBI, who in 1969 was the chief of the Microscopic Analysis Unit. Agent Clark quickly established his credentials as an expert in identifying hair samples. He then verified the chain of possession for the evidence sent to him from Des Moines and for the hair samples collected from Williams and Pamela Powers. Next, Agent Clark proceeded to explain how hairs found on the various pieces of evidence compared to the hair samples that had been provided by the Des Moines Police Department. Agent Clark then testified that several pieces of evidence contained hairs similar to samples of hair from both Williams and Pamela Powers. Agent Clark then was led through the various pieces of evidence that had been sent to the FBI and explained what the individual findings were. He first discussed the evidence found at the rest stop on Interstate 80. On the blanket he found several negroid head hairs and a few negroid pubic hairs, which were all microscopically similar to the sample hairs provided by Williams. The blanket also contained several caucasian head hairs which were like those of Pamela's. On the suit coat, there were negroid limb hairs that were similar to the limb hairs of Williams. The yellow shirt held a head hair like that of the defendant. The light jacket also contained head hairs like Williams's. The blouse contained one head hair that was similar to Williams's. It also contained a few negroid body hairs that were not similar to Williams's and a few white colored head hairs for which the race of the person they came from could not be determined, but which differed from Williams's. The towel held two head hairs similar to Williams's and one head hair similar to Pamela Powers's. The slacks contained two head hairs similar to Williams's and two pubic hairs the race of which could not be determined, but which did not match Williams's. Agent Clark then went on to discuss his findings on the evidence gathered from the search of Williams's car. The rear floor mat contained a few hairs that matched Pamela Powers's; it also contained a negroid head hair that was not like Williams's and a few caucasian pubic hairs that did not match any samples. The rear seat cover and the left front floor mat only contained hairs that could be matched with the defendant and victim. The final hairs examined by Agent Clark had been taken from the body of Pamela Powers. He found that of the two hairs that were found, one head and one pubic, they both were similar to those of Williams. Robert Blink then tried to ask Agent Clark the probability of the hairs that were similar actually coming from Williams, but the defense raised an objection on the grounds of a lack of foundation for the witness to provide an opinion. The objection was sustained. It must be remembered that in 1977, when Williams's second trial was held, accurate DNA testing of hair and blood was not possible.

On cross-examination, Agent Clark was pushed to admit that even though some of the hairs were similar to Williams's it was only a probability that they had actually come from him. Upon being questioned about the bedspread that had been taken from Williams's room at the Y.M.C.A., he told the court that he had examined it and found no biological stains, but he did find two negroid pubic hairs which did not match Williams's. The next information solicited in cross-examination was an indication of the relative ease by which hairs fall off the human body and are transferred from one article to another. Then Agent Clark was asked if all of the items found at the rest stop on Interstate 80 were mingled together in one bag whether one could assume that hairs would be transferred from one item to another. His answer was, "They very well could be."[15] After being asked, Agent Clark admitted that this could also be true for all of the items found in Williams's car. The defense wanted to reinforce its theory that the possibility remained that someone other than Williams had committed the crime, so a final line of cross-examination concerned the unidentified hairs that were found. Agent Clark told the court there were ten hairs that remained unidentified. When asked about those unidentified hairs, he stated that he had not examined any of them to determine if they had come from a common source. In a brief redirect examination, Robert Blink elicited a response that it was not unusual to have hairs from a crime scene that remained unidentified.

The Defense Case

The primary defense strategy during the trial was to admit to Williams's role in disposing of the body of Pamela Powers, but to deny any greater role in the crime. To accomplish this, the defense conceded that Williams was responsible for removing Pamela's body from the Y.M.C.A. It went on to argue that this admission did not mean that Williams was responsible for the death. Instead, the defense claimed that someone else, who was not named at trial, had killed Pamela Powers and, in order to cast suspicion on Williams, had placed her body in Williams's room in the Y.M.C.A. The theory continued that upon discovery of the body, Williams panicked, carried the body out of the Y.M.C.A., disposed of it by the roadside, finally realized the gravity of his actions two days later, and gave himself up. In presenting its view of the case, the defense only called four witnesses.

To support the defense's theory of what actually happened, it used part of the prosecution's theory of how the crime happened to its advantage. This was because the prosecution claimed that Pamela had been murdered while she was being sexually molested. To prove this, the prosecution had tests conducted to determine if spermatozoa could be found on Pamela's body or on her clothing. These tests revealed that while acid phosphatases— a component of semen—were found in the body, there were no traces of spermatozoa found on the body or on Pamela's clothing. The defense used this information to put forward the theory that whoever had attacked Pamela was sterile, which removed Williams from suspicion, since he was not sterile.

Due to the defense's admission of the complicity of Williams in the removal and disposal of the body, those facts were not in contention. The key to the defense case, then, became its claim that a sterile man committed the crime. To win the case the defense version of the disputed facts—that freezing preserved, rather than destroyed sperm cells—would have to be the subjective facts that the jury accepted. One problem that the defense faced at the beginning of its case was Dr. Luka's testimony that the freezing temperatures that the body had been subjected to would have destroyed any sperm that had been present in the body. This testimony contradicted the prosecution's own position at the suppression hearing when it argued that the condition of the body was unaffected by the weather because it was preserved due to the freezing temperatures. The defense also believed that Dr. Luka had changed his earlier testimony, that freezing would not affect the composition of spermatozoa, once he found out that Williams was not sterile. As a result, at the start of its own case, the defense called Officer Don Knox of the Des Moines Police Department to impeach the testimony of Dr. Luka.

The testimony of Officer Knox was heard without the jury being present in order to give Judge Denato a chance to rule on its acceptability without the possibility of tainting the jury's deliberating process. Officer Knox testified that in either December of 1968 or January of 1969, Dr. Luka had informed him of the autopsy results, which were negative for male sperm. When asked, he told the court that the sterility theory of crime had been his and not Dr. Luka's. He then examined two defense exhibits, which were police memos indicating that the police were trying to determine if Williams had ever had a vasectomy. In reply to a question, he then admitted that the police probably would not have followed up on their sterility theory if Dr. Luka had told them that freezing destroyed signs of sperm.

The prosecution objected to Officer Knox's testimony on the grounds of relevancy and on the grounds of Officer Knox's lack of qualification as an expert witness in the field of male reproductive systems or cell decomposition. The defense replied that they were not suggesting that Officer Knox was an expert in the field, they merely believed that it helped to shed light on the veracity of Dr. Luka's testimony that freezing destroyed sperm. Judge Denato ruled that Officer Knox's testimony could not be put before the jury. He pointed out that the defense had interpreted Dr. Luka's testimony too narrowly because he had stated that freezing was only one possibility to explain the absence of spermatozoa. Furthermore, Officer Knox demonstrated that the sterility theory had not originated with Dr. Luka.

The jury was then brought back into the courtroom and the defense called its first witness Dr. Earl Rose, a pathologist, as an expert witness. Dr. Rose had testified at the suppression hearing that freezing under the conditions in which the body was found would not have an effect on any sperm that might have been present. Dr. Rose testified after looking at a defense exhibit of a climatological chart for the time in question that the temperatures would have stopped any decomposition of sperm cells. He further testified that the time between when the abduction happened and the body was discarded would not have been enough to destroy any sperm cells that may have been present. In answer to a hypothetical question, Dr. Rose also testified that it would not be uncommon, considering the conditions under which Pamela Powers had died, for the body to empty the contents of its bladder. Dr. Rose next testified that in 1968 it was possible to do a blood test on semen stains, thus allowing you to know the blood type of the individual from whom the semen came. The last piece of information solicited from Dr. Rose was an admission that he had previously testified in this case as a witness for the State and that his current testimony was unchanged from his original. Upon cross-examination Dr. Rose informed the court that he had no personal knowledge of the autopsy of Pamela Powers.

The defense's second witness was Dr. Dennis Boatman, a urologist who specialized in the male reproductive system. Dr. Boatman was asked about Defense exhibit H, which was a report on a semen analysis done on Williams. He explained that the report showed that Williams was not sterile and was within the normal range of sperm production, with a sperm count of 26 million per cc. He went on to state that this basically meant that Williams would have a sperm count of 26 million in one-fifteenth of a teaspoon. Dr. Boatman was then asked to comment on various explanations that might allow a man who was sterile at one time to later have a normal sperm count. He answered that one thing would be if he had a vasectomy reversed. He then told the court that he had examined Williams and that he had not had this procedure performed. Temporary sterility could be caused by some diseases, such as malaria, but the disease would incapacitate the man at the same time that he was sterile. He went on to explain that seminal fluid only contained 2 percent sperm. That was true, he told the court, whether it was a man's first ejaculation or his tenth in one day. Regardless of the number of ejaculations, one would expect to find 2 percent sperm in the seminal fluid, although there would be less seminal fluid overall with each new ejaculation. You would, however, expect to find the sperm count still in the millions, he added. In cross-examination, the prosecution brought out the fact that Dr. Boatman had not conducted the sperm test on Williams himself and that he was instead merely working off the report.

The defense next called Clarence Yeager, who had been a Davenport police officer in 1968. In reply to questioning, he informed the court that he was responsible for keeping Williams's car under observation after it was discovered in Davenport. He testified that the car stayed outside in the cold until 5:30 P.M. on December 25, 1968, when the car was seized and the warrant served. It was at that time that the necktie and sock were found in the car. When Clarence Yeager was done testifying, the defense requested that a climatological chart for Davenport showing the high temperature on December 25, 1968 as 15 degrees Fahrenheit and a low of 3 degrees be stipulated to and offered as evidence. The request was granted. The defense then moved to offer its other exhibits into evidence. These included a number of things from Williams's room, including a bedspread, a pillowcase, and a set of sheets. There was no objection from the prosecution. The defense then received a stipulation that if Jack Sullivan, the chief security officer for Northwestern Bell Telephone of Des Moines, was called, he would testify that phone records indicated that on December 24, 1968, a Reverend Robert Anthony at the Des Moines Y.M.C.A. received a call from Mount Pleasant, Iowa, at 12:28 P.M. and that the call lasted until 12:40 P.M.

The jury was dismissed for the afternoon. The attorneys then met in Judge Denato's chambers at which time the defense again requested that the jury be sequestered during its deliberations. The defense cited all its earlier arguments in favor of sequestration and the additional argument that the names of the jurors had been printed in the prominent papers in the state and had been carried by the Associated Press and United Press International. In their opinion, this greatly increased the possibility of inappropriate contact with the jury. The prosecution objected to the motion because the purpose of sequestration was to keep the jurors from seeing information about the trial, not to protect them from inappropriate contact. Judge Denato denied the request, stating that thus far there appeared to be no inappropriate attempts to influence the jurors. He did note that the jurors could be polled to ensure that this was true before the start of its deliberations.

Before the start of trial on the morning of July 12, 1977, the defense counsel and the defendant had a discussion recorded by the court reporter. The reason that a record of the conversation was made was to preempt possible problems that may have come up on appeals regarding the quality of Williams's legal counsel. The purpose of the meeting was to discuss whether Williams should testify at the trial. At the meeting, the attorneys reinforced Williams's understanding that he had a right to testify at the trial and that, should he desire to testify, his attorneys would not stop him from doing so. Williams then stated for the record that after hearing the pros and cons as described to him by his attorneys he did not want to testify.

Prior to the meeting, Williams's attorneys explained to Williams in confidence that in most trials the jurors liked to see the defendants take the stand and proclaim their innocence. If he did take the stand, however, information that could be damaging to his defense could also come out. One piece of information that the defense feared was that Williams had been confined to a mental institution in Missouri for a sexual offense. An even more damaging piece of evidence that they feared might come out if he testified was the content of Williams's sanity and competency hearing, held prior to his trial in 1969. During that hearing, Williams had discussed a story that he had told McKnight, his attorney at the time, about how he had lured, molested, and killed the young girl. In balancing these competing interests, all three of his attorneys, with Williams agreeing, believed that the best strategy was not to have Williams testify, even though they had conducted a number of practice cross-examinations with Williams.

When the trial was reconvened, the defense called its final witness, Dr. Garry Peterson, a forensic pathologist. Dr. Peterson stated that in his position in the Medical Examiner's Office of Hennepin County, Minnesota, he reviewed approximately 1,500 sexual assault cases a year and that normally he was called to testify for law enforcement in such cases. He also told the court that he did have experience in detecting sperm in the bodies of women who had been frozen. He was then questioned about the viability of detecting sperm under a variety of conditions. He testified that, after normal intercourse, sperm was detectable for between 12 and 24 hours. If a person died after intercourse, the sperm would be detectable for a longer period of time because the secretions of the female reproductive system would cease and the body temperature would go down, stopping enzymes from causing decomposition of the sperm. He added that the freezing of a body at the time of or shortly after death would preserve any sperm indefinitely until the body was thawed. Dr. Peterson was then asked if a girl died under the same conditions as Pamela Powers and her body were frozen within the same time span as hers, whether he believed any sperm present would have been preserved. He answered that he believed it would. After being questioned, Dr. Peterson told the court that he had reviewed Dr. Luka's autopsy report and that he believed that there had been no attempt to insert a penis into the vagina because the hymen was intact, even though the lips of the vulva area had been spread, and there was no internal or external trauma to the vaginal area.

The final piece of evidence that the defense provided in its case was a stipulation that Robert Anthony Williams had surrendered himself to the Davenport Police Department on December 26, 1968, at approximately 8:40 A.M. The defense then rested its case.

Rebuttal Evidence

The prosecution then called one rebuttal witness to try to strengthen Dr. Luka's contention that freezing would destroy rather than preserve any sperm cells that may have been present on Pamela Power's body. If this testimony could be propped up by supporting testimony, it would make it easier for the jurors to accept the prosecution's version of the facts that freezing would have destroyed any sperm cells present and thereby make it easier to believe that Williams had committed the crime, even though he was not sterile. The witness was Dr. David Culp, a urologist. Dr. Culp was a specialist in the reproductive system and had done research involving freezing sperm cells for later insemination. In the most technical testimony of the trial, Dr. Culp tried to explain the difference between slow freezing, such as would have happened to Pamela Power's body, and quick freezing, which takes place at much colder temperatures, and their varied effects on sperm. He told the court that slow freezing tends to kill live sperm cells and may cause them to be destroyed altogether. He also testified that certain diseases, such as chicken pox, mononucleosis, and herpes, could also cause a man to be temporarily sterile for a period of time. Drug use could also have the same effect. He pointed out that continual ejaculations could deplete a man of enough sperm to make them almost undetectable. When asked if one would expect to find signs of sperm under the conditions in which Pamela Powers met her death and her body was then discovered, Dr. Culp did not provide an answer. Instead, he pointed out that there were too many variables that were unknown to be able to give a definitive answer. Upon cross-examination by the defense, Dr. Culp admitted that he had never performed an autopsy and that he had never had the opportunity to observe sperm living or dead inside a dead woman's body.

When Dr. Culp's testimony was finished, the state again rested its case. After consulting with the defense and finding that it had no other evidence, Judge Denato closed off any further evidence in the trial. The jury was then dismissed for the rest of the morning while Judge Denato met with the attorneys to discuss the instructions that he would give to the jurors. Before the discussion of the instructions began, the defense motioned for a directed verdict on the first-degree murder charge to the extent that it required premeditation or deliberation. Defense counsel argued that the State had presented no competent evidence that in any way supported the element of premeditation or the element of deliberation necessary for the charge to be proven. Judge Denato denied the motion. Prior to the discussion, Judge Denato had distributed to the attorneys for both parties his intended instructions. The prosecution offered no objections to the instructions. The defense, however, had several changes that it desired. The first involved dropping the premeditation or deliberation portion of the indictment for first-degree murder. A second was an instruction to impeach Dr. Luka's testimony. The defense was not successful in these motions. It was successful in getting Judge Denato to add an instruction that presented the defense theory of the crime. This instruction stated that if the jury found that the defendant did indeed do all of the things to which the defense had admitted, including carrying a body out of the Y.M.C.A., but did not otherwise participate in the crime, he should be found not guilty.

Closing Arguments

The trial then moved on to the closing arguments. In the closing arguments both sides presented dramatic appeals as they conveyed their theories of the crime. Robert Blink, the prosecutor, placed all blame for the murder of Pamela Powers on Robert Williams. Blink first reminded the jury that he represented the State of Iowa in the case. He went on to explain that the jury had to make its decision based on two elements—the law and the facts. He first sought to explain the law of the case. He explained that the judge would strictly define the law for the jurors and that if the jury found that the defendant had taken the life of little Pamela Powers willfully and intentionally with malice aforethought, premeditation, deliberation and with the specific intent to kill, it was their duty to convict. He next told them that it was their duty to determine the facts of the case. He then walked them through what he considered to be the facts of the case. Through both the testimony of the witnesses and the exhibits that were introduced, he reviewed Williams's flight from the Y.M.C.A., dumping evidence as he traveled, until he surrendered.

Blink then summarized the case against Williams. After telling the jury that Williams had killed Pamela Powers during an attempted rape, Blink continued:

The problem then becomes to get rid of the evidence. Now, why, why, if Mr. Williams did not in fact kill her, did he go to such an extensive means to as much as possible ensure that he would not be connected with the crime? He went to those extensive means because he knew that he had to get rid of the evidence. It pointed at him. And rightfully so, for it is absolutely consistent with the acts of a man who committed murder and it is no way inconsistent with the acts of a man who did not commit murder. Now, we don't have an eye witness, Pamela Powers is dead. But I think Pamela Powers speaks to us in a certain respect. She tells us about what happened. She tells us through the clothing, through the bloodstained towel, the postmortem examination. And I submit to you that the muffled cries of Pamela Powers in Room 724 of the Y.M.C.A. in Des Moines, Iowa, on Christmas Eve of 1968, which were but a whimper and whisper at that time are reverberating in these halls. And they speak to you, and they speak to all of us. And they say that "I was killed, my life was taken into the adult world, something I didn't even understand—I couldn't comprehend, only to leave it in a violent fashion." Who took out the body? He did. Who dumped the body? He did. Who disposed of the clothing? He did. Who ran away? He did. Who killed the girl? He did.[16]

When Robert Blink finished the State's closing argument, it was the defense's turn. In its closing argument, the defense again admitted that Williams had disposed of the body of Pamela Powers, but tried to clear him of any involvement in the murder. Gerald Crawford told the jury that, in order to find Williams guilty, the jury had to answer *yes* to one of two questions. Referring to Williams's alias, "Anthony," he said the first question was whether "Anthony Williams willfully killed Pamela Powers, with malice aforethought, with deliberation, with premeditation and with the specific intent to kill."[17] He believed that after hearing all the evidence the state had failed to demonstrate this. Therefore, a guilty verdict depended on the answer to a second question—whether Anthony Williams killed Pamela Powers in attempting or perpetrating a sexual assault. Gerald Crawford then told the jury, "The evidence is clear. Pamela Powers, at the time of her death or shortly thereafter, was sexually molested by a sterile man"[18] He added that the killing and molestation happened before Pamela's body was ever removed from the Y.M.C.A. He noted that all the facts of the prosecution's case were consistent with this conclusion.

Crawford also went over the facts and testimony that were revealed during the trial, but he added items that he believed favored the defense. For example, he raised questions about whether Williams had enough time to commit the murder. He told the jury:

The evidence also shows that from 12:28 until 12:40 Mr. Williams was on the telephone and you have that evidence before you. They have seen him leaving at 1 o'clock. He was on the telephone until 12:40 and, ask yourself, in 20 minutes, does a man go from the 7th floor of the Y.M.C.A. downstairs, spot a little girl and abduct her, go back upstairs with her to Room 724, suffocate her and sexually assault her three times, put a bundle together around her, put some clothes on top of the bundle and carry the bundle downstairs to the main floor and out the lobby in 20 minutes?[19]

Crawford then attacked the prosecution's case, calling everything beyond what the defense itself stipulated as a fact to be circumstantial. He went on to explain the weaknesses that he believed existed in the prosecution's case. He first pointed out the difficulties in believing the prosecution's position that the freezing of the body would have destroyed any signs of sperm cells that may have been present in the seminal fluid taken from the body. In doing so, he noted that Williams's car was also subject to freezing temperatures before it was seized and searched. He went on to say that the two socks and necktie that were found in the car were not tested by the FBI for signs of sperm until almost an additional month had gone by. He found it curious that despite the freezing temperatures and delay in time, those sperm cells had not been destroyed. He also found it odd, in light of the testimony, that no urine stain had been found on Williams's sheets if the crime had taken place in his room as the prosecution contended. Likewise, if a struggle had taken place in Williams's room, one would expect to find at least a partial fingerprint of Pamela Powers. Instead, all indications were that she had been attacked somewhere else and placed in Williams's room after she was dead. He next attacked the prosecution's view that the hairs of Williams that were on Pamela's clothes found at the rest stop pointed the finger of guilt at him. Crawford reminded the jury that all the items had been placed in a common bag and that some of Williams's hairs may easily have been transferred from his articles to hers. He said that what he found informative was that a total of twelve hairs were of unknown origin, including two pubic hairs that were found on the little girl's slacks. He also expressed disappointment that the prosecution had not thought to compare these unidentified hairs to one another to see if they could have come from the same person.

Gerald Crawford told the court that he believed that the crime was committed by a sterile man and that they had presented adequate evidence to show that Williams was not sterile. Crawford next told the jurors that they would have to sort through the testimony given by all the doctors as to the effects that freezing would have on the decomposition of sperm cells. To help them with this process, he reviewed the inconsistencies in Dr. Luka's testimony, reading from the depositions in which he had gone on record to say that freezing would preserve sperm cells and comparing that to his contradictory comments at trial that freezing would destroy them. He told the jurors to use their own common sense as to what effect freezing has in the preservation of something. He reminded the jurors that the State's other witness on the matter, Dr. Culp, worked with living sperm in the area of artificial insemination and had never examined a dead female for traces of sperm. Next, he drew the jury's attention to Dr. Rose, who had testified that freezing would preserve any sperm present. He pointed out that Dr. Rose had entered the case as a witness for the prosecution, but was uncalled by the State when it was realized that Williams was not sterile and his testimony was no longer helpful to their case. He also reminded the jurors that Dr. Rose had told the court that you could distinguish a person's blood type from a sample of seminal fluid. He stated that if such a test had been done, it could have conclusively shown that the seminal fluid had not come from Williams, but the State had failed to conduct such a test. Finally, he reminded the jurors that Dr. Peterson, who was a specialist in sexual assaults, had also testified that freezing would preserve, not destroy, any sperm that had been present. Based on all of the contradictions and discrepancies in the State's case, Gerald Crawford then suggested that there was enough doubt for Williams to be found not guilty.

Roger Owens then continued with the defense's closing argument. He explained to the jurors that those items that the defense had not admitted to in the prosecution's case were based on circumstantial evidence. He told the jury that in a circumstantial case, such as this, all the evidence must be consistent in order for the jury to convict. All the evidence was not consistent in this case because Williams was not sterile. Furthermore, there had not been a showing by the state that there had been actual penetration to indicate a rape. Owens also told the jury that it was preposterous to consider Williams as a cold, hard, calculated killer, as the prosecutor portrayed him. He questioned how anyone who walked out of a Y.M.C.A. in broad daylight with a body, left the clothing in a rest stop on the interstate, parked his getaway car on a public street, and then turned himself in after contacting an attorney, could be called calculated.

In a bit of drama, Owens told the jurors that a verdict of innocent "is going to take a lot of guts, and we think you have got it."[20] He reminded them of John F. Kennedy's book *Profiles in Courage* and said that they would have to show the same type of courage in finding Williams not guilty. He then told the jurors that they had taken an oath to uphold the law. Then he threw a lawbook 20 feet across the courtroom, stating that the book was worthless when the laws were not upheld. He ended the defense team's closing arguments by stating, "And by God, now, everyone at this table wants you to uphold that law. Not just Mr. Crawford, Mr. Wellman and Mr. Williams, but Mr. Blink and Mr. Ryan also, and so do I. . . . I think you will find Mr. Williams not guilty."[21]

As is traditional, the prosecution was then given a rebuttal and the last word in the trial. Robert Blink told the jury that Pamela Powers was like "a rose, not yet blossomed." Williams, however, was the type of man who sees such a rose "and steps on it, crushes it into the ground . . . and indeed we found what was left of that rose in a ditch near Mitchellville."[22] Robert Blink said the defense theory that Williams could not have committed the crime since he was not sterile was much ado about nothing. He said that all the expert witnesses were dealing in theories and that their conclusions were influenced by a wide variety of variables. The variable that could not be explained away was that the semen on the body and the pants found at the rest stop on Interstate 80 were similar. For dramatic effect, Blink then wrote the word "body" on the courtroom chalkboard, followed by the word "pants." He then emphasized the point by holding up a pair of pants with the name "Anthony," Williams's alias, on them and saying what was on the girl was on these pants. The link between the pants and the semen could not be denied and Blink told the jury that this, perhaps more than any other piece of evidence, haunted Williams.

He warned the jury about falling into the situation that the defense desired. That being, speculating about what may have happened rather than concentrating on what the evidence actually showed. Blink explained, "I think they want you to speculate. I think they want you to guess. I think they want you to imagine."[23] An example, he believed, was the defense's attempt to make a big deal out of the lack of a urine stain on the sheets from Williams's room. Blink told the jurors that rather than speculating on why, they should remember that Pamela had originally shown up missing when she left to go to the washroom, which provides its own explanation. Robert Blink ended his summation by asking for the jury to bring in a verdict of guilty and added, "It is your common sense that must lead to your conclusions."[24]

Instructions, Deliberations, and the Verdict

After the closing arguments, Judge Denato had to give instructions to the jury. Judge Denato's instructions informed the jury that, before they could find Williams guilty of first degree murder, the state had the burden of proving the following elements:

A. That on or about December 24, 1968, in Polk County, Iowa, the defendant did willfully and unlawfully kill Pamela Powers.

B. That such action on the part of the Defendant was done with malice aforethought.

C. That such action of the Defendant was done with deliberation, premeditation and with a specific intent to kill Pamela Powers; or,

Was done in the perpetration of the crime of Attempted Rape.[25]

The jury was also given instructions on the possible verdicts of second-degree murder, manslaughter, and innocent. After receiving its instructions, the jury retired for its deliberations at 9:17 A.M. on July 13, 1977. As the jury filed out of the courtroom Williams was overheard to remark, "I feel good."[26] Williams was then taken to the top floor of the Linn County Jail to be held as the jury deliberated. Jury deliberations went much slower than in the first trial, which convicted Williams in only 90 minutes. Deliberations continued until 5 P.M., when the jury quit for the day. On July 14, 1977, the second day of jury deliberations, the jury made a request for the testimony of two witnesses, Dr. Luka and Dr. Peterson, to be read back to them. The attorneys were informed of the request. In a meeting in Judge Denato's chambers, Robert Blink objected to allowing the testimony to be read. He argued that it unduly emphasized particular evidence and might possibly cause the jury to ignore the body of other evidence in the case that would not be in the best interest of the State. The defense counsel indicated that they had discussed the request with Williams and that they had no objections. Judge Denato decided to accede to the request so Jeffrey Faust, the court reporter, spent 40 minutes reading back the testimony of the State's witness, Dr. Leo Luka, and the defense's witness, Dr. Garry Peterson. Both had given conflicting testimony as to whether sperm cells would be destroyed by freezing temperatures.

It is interesting that the indication from the jury deliberations at this point was that the verdict in the case might hinge on whether freezing temperatures would have affected the condition of the evidence. This is ironic, because, in the suppression hearing involving the inevitable discovery of the body, both parties to the case had made arguments in favor of the opposite conclusions they sought at trial. At that hearing, the State had argued in favor of admission of the body because even if it would have been found at a later point in time it would have been in the same condition due to the freezing temperatures. The defense, on the other hand, had argued that the body would not have been in the same condition if discovered later, and, therefore, should not be allowed as evidence. This change in arguments shows that, in a trial situation, consistency in the positions of the parties is not as important as the need to advance a strategy to win the case.

On July 15, 1977, at 10:02 A.M., after deliberating for 13 ½ hours, the jury returned a verdict of guilty of first-degree murder against Robert Williams. Williams sat silently and displayed no emotion when the verdict was read. He did glance at Pamela Power's brother, Mark, who was sitting in the second row. After discussing the verdict with Williams, Gerald Crawford told the press, "He's awfully disappointed. His belief is in himself, and his knowledge that he's innocent, is not new to him—he's lived with it for 8½ years."[27]

Despite making a pact between themselves not to discuss the case with reporters, several jurors did agree to discuss the case anonymously. The jurors said that they had taken six or seven ballots by late in the afternoon of July 14. They believed at that point that they were close to an agreement and considered coming back at 7 P.M. to try to reach a decision. Instead, they decided to take the night off to think over their positions. When they returned on the morning of July 15, they were able to reach consensus. The jurors who spoke said that there was no animosity between the jurors over the verdict, and one said that they were "glad it's over" since they "just want to forget about it."[28]

The jurors did not explain what facts were most influential in reaching their verdict. Robert Blink told reporters that he believed that the most devastating single piece of evidence were the pair of pants with Williams's name on them that contained semen stains. Blink said, "The pants were cold and irrefutable evidence. Everything else was in the abstract," including "all the medical testimony."[29] The Powers family did not have much to say after the verdict came in. Mark Powers simply stated, "I'm pleased it's over," but declined further comment.[30] Mr. and Mrs. Powers, who were not in court for the verdict, met with prosecutors later in the afternoon. They were described as being "very calm" and reminisced about Pamela's life. They were said to be "very pleased . . . because they thought justice was done."[31] The emotional relief the Powers family felt when the verdict came in was probably dealt a severe blow the next day when Gerald Crawford announced after a discussion of the verdict with Robert Bartels that there would be an appeal.

On August 19, 1977, Williams was again sentenced to life in prison. Prior to sentencing, Judge Denato told Williams that he had a right of elocution, or to make a final statement. Williams told the court that, after his conviction in 1969, he predicted that other little girls and boys would be in danger from whoever really committed the crime against Pamela Powers. He went on to state that his prediction had turned out to be true. He claimed that in "July of 1969 Patricia Beech (phonetic) was smothered to death and sexually molested out on the east side of Des Moines."[32] Williams continued:

Someone's child is walking the streets in danger. I am not crazy. I am a Baptist minister, you know, and you all have lied for the past eight and half years and said that I have lied about being a minister and that I am an escaped nut and I am not. And the mere fact that I am alive and living in the penitentiary with this kind of crime shows that there is something wrong with the whole situation. And I don't appreciate having to go back to the penitentiary and fight all the way over again just because Mr. Blink prefabricated a case without having any interest in what I am saying as a human being who has not been declared insane. And I am telling this court and the people of the State of Iowa, the brother of this child and the family of this child that this case is not closed and the only reason I am going back to the penitentiary is because they do not want two cases against two little ten- and nine-year-old girls on the record as being unsolved.[33]

After the trial was over, the defense lawyers made public the extent to which public prejudices had been against Williams. They revealed that they had been the subject of numerous threats. John Owens said that he received threatening calls and notes at his office. Some of the calls were racist and called Owens "a nigger lover." He stated that some of the notes implied that, even if he lived through the trial, his children might not. One caller even referred to Owens's daughter by name. To protect his family, Owens took the precaution of sending them to Arizona during the trial. Gerald Crawford also stated that he was subject to regular threats throughout the process and that the threats were still continuing. Polk County District Attorney Dan Johnston told members of the Polk County Law Enforcement Association about the threats to the defense attorneys and said those threats were inappropriate, since all the lawyers in the case were fighting for the same thing—justice. He went on to say that Iowans "owe a debt of gratitude to all five lawyers in that courtroom because they were all serving the public interest."[34]

Just as Robert Williams's first trial had been impacted by decisions Judge Denato made about what the subjective facts were and how to apply the procedural law, so was his second trial. Once again Judge Denato had a variety of legal options to exercise, depending on which set of facts he accepted. Judge Denato's embrace of the prosecution's argument—that the body would have been discovered through legal methods shortly after it was actually discovered through the violation of Williams's Sixth Amendment right to counsel—allowed Judge Denato to then consider whether the body would have been found in the same condition. As part of his ruling, Judge Denato accepted the prosecution's argument advanced at the suppression hearing that the freezing temperatures the body would have been subjected to until the search was successful would have preserved its condition. Based on this view of the facts, he ruled that the exclusionary rule should not be enforced. Instead, the body and related evidence was allowed to be used because it would have been inevitably discovered through legal means.

In an interesting twist of strategy during the trial, the State argued against the subjective facts originally accepted in the ruling Judge Denato made at the suppression hearing concerning the inevitable discovery exception. At trial, the State reversed its position and sought to convince the jury that pieces of evidence, such as sperm, would indeed have been destroyed by the freezing temperatures and that a conviction could be justified even if this additional sign of guilt could not be presented at trial. The ability of the State to switch its position on this issue shows that legal arguments need not be based on principles. Instead, they are often based on the simple expediency of doing whatever is necessary to win a case. This change in the State's strategy demonstrates that the law is not as clearcut at resolving issues as we might like to believe. The effectiveness of Iowa's trial strategy cannot be questioned, since it resulted in a second conviction of Robert Williams for first-degree murder.

NOTES

1. Phillip E. Johnson, "The Return of the 'Christian Burial Speech' Case," *Emory Law Journal* 32 (1983): 381.
2. *Brewer v. Williams*, 430 U.S. 387 (1977).
3. *Des Moines Register*, 24 March 1977.
4. Ibid.
5. Ibid.
6. Ibid.
7. *Des Moines Register*, 25 March 1977.
8. *Des Moines Register*, 27 March 1977.
9. *Des Moines Register*, 1 April 1977.
10. *Williams v. Nix*, 700 F.2d 1164, 1168 (8th Cir. 1983).
11. Transcripts of Motions to Suppress, *Iowa v. Williams* (1977), p. 35.
12. Joint Appendix, *Nix v. Williams*, 467 U.S. 431 (1984), pp. 86–88.
13. Trial Transcript, Iowa v. Williams (1977), p. 7.
14. Ibid., p. 58.
15. Ibid., p. 192.
16. Ibid., pp. 344–345.
17. Ibid., p. 348.
18. Ibid., p. 349.
19. Ibid., p. 356.
20. Ibid., p. 387.
21. Ibid., pp. 389–90.
22. Ibid., pp. 392–93.
23. Ibid., p. 398.
24. Ibid., p. 401.
25. *Iowa v. Williams*, 285 N.W.2d 248, 269 (Iowa 1979).
26. *Des Moines Register*, 14 July 1977.
27. *Des Moines Register*, 16 July 1977.
28. Ibid.
29. Ibid.

30. Ibid.
31. Ibid.
32. Trial Transcript, *Iowa v. Williams* (1977), p. 417.
33. Ibid., pp. 418–419.
34. *Des Moines Register*, 19 July 1977.

Chapter 8

The Historical Development of the Exclusionary Rule of Justice

> To declare that in the administration of the criminal law the end justifies the means—to declare that the Government may commit crimes in order to secure the conviction of a private criminal—would bring terrible retribution. Against that pernicious doctrine this Court should resolutely set its face.
>
> —Justice Louis Brandeis[1]

CREATION OF A FEDERAL EXCLUSIONARY RULE

It came as no surprise that Judge Denato's use at trial of the inevitable discovery exception to the exclusionary rule led to a second round of appeals. The primary legal issue of the trial and appeals process in the second *Williams* case, *Nix v. Williams*,[2] was the exclusionary rule of justice which disallows the use of illegally gathered evidence at trial. As had *Brewer v. Williams*,[3] this case also questioned the desirability of protecting individual rights when they conflict with the ability of the judicial system to gather all the relevant evidence that could help determine the guilt or innocence of an accused person. Confrontations between these competing goals are common in criminal cases. What is unusual about *Nix v. Williams* is that the issue of whether evidence found as a result of the violation of the Sixth Amendment right to counsel should be excluded from trial was framed by Justice Stewart's majority opinion in *Brewer v. Williams*. This was done by Footnote 12, where Justice Stewart stated that while Williams's incriminating statements could not be submitted as evidence, "evidence of where the body was found and of its condition might well be admissible on the theory that the body would have been discovered in any event."[4]

The arguments that Iowa put forward throughout the appeals process to support the inevitable discovery exception to the exclusionary rule can be better understood once the history of the exclusionary rule itself has been reviewed. As with other areas of law, this history has developed based on the discretionary choices made by members of the judiciary. This chapter reviews the history of exclusionary rule. It also examines the application of the exclusionary rule to the actions of the national and state governments. In doing so, it probes the theoretical underpinnings of the exclusionary rule and why changes in the Burger Court's understanding of the purpose of the exclusionary rule allowed for the development of the inevitable discovery exception.

According to Jacob W. Landynski, the primary purpose of the exclusionary rule has been "to protect the vitality of the Fourth Amendment" by making unprofitable any benefit of evidence that might be gained through a violation of the Fourth Amendment.[5] The Constitution, however, fails to mention the exclusionary rule. Despite this, the values inherent in the rule are important for helping to protect rights that are specifically found in the Bill of Rights. Bradley Canon summarizes these values by stating, "Inherent in the rule are respect for privacy and individual autonomy, for the rule of the law, that is the law serving as a constraint on the governors as well as those being governed, and fair treatment in the relationship between government and citizen."[6]

Most of the exclusionary rule debate has been framed around the Fourth Amendment.[7] The Fourth Amendment states:

The right of the people to be secure in their persons, houses, papers, and effects, against unreasonable searches and seizures, shall not be violated, and no Warrants shall issue, but upon probable cause, supported by Oath or affirmation, and particularly describing the place to be searched, and the persons or things to be seized.

The debate concerning the origin and necessity of the exclusionary rule has not centered solely on the Fourth Amendment. Other provisions of the Constitution that have been involved in the exclusionary rule debate have been the Fifth Amendment's right against self-incrimination, the Sixth Amendment's right to counsel, and the Fourteenth Amendment's Due Process Clause.

The debate over the exclusionary rule results from the Constitution's inability to define what consequences the government would be subject to should it violate the provisions of the Bill of Rights. At no point does the Constitution state that evidence seized in violation of its provisions shall be excluded from submission in courts of law. Critics of the exclusionary rule have been quick to point out that exclusion should not therefore be considered a constitutional requirement. Judge Malcolm Wilkey of the Court of Appeals, D.C. Circuit, for example, has complained, "This rule of evidence did not come from on high. It's man-made. . . . It's not even in the Constitution."[8] Supporters of the exclusionary rule, on the other hand, have argued that the Constitution does not have an addendum stating that the government is free to benefit from constitutional violations. Yale Kamisar has written, "Because the Fourth Amendment has *nothing to say* about *any* consequences that might flow from its violation, reading it as *permitting* the use of evidence obtained by means of an unreasonable search and seizure . . . strikes me as no less 'creative' or 'judge-made' than" applying the exclusionary rule.[9] The lack of a specific amendment and concrete language creating an exclusionary rule, coupled with judicial confusion in opinions supporting the exclusionary rule, fueled the debate concerning the role that the exclusionary rule should play in the American system of justice.

Two important facets of American law delayed the development of the exclusionary rule. The first was the American judicial system's deep commitment to the provisions of British common law. For more than a century after the Revolution, American courts used the same common law rule of evidence as had English courts. It allowed evidence obtained through an illegal search and seizure to be admissible at trial.[10] Thus, as long as the rules of evidence were derived from common law, rather than constitutional interpretation, illegalities in obtaining evidence were overlooked.

The second reason behind the Supreme Court's delay in enunciating an exclusionary rule of evidence can be found by examining its appellate jurisdiction. Quite simply, Congress did not grant the Supreme Court appellate jurisdiction in all criminal cases until March 3, 1911.[11] In the absence of this jurisdiction, the Court did not, in most instances, have the ability to rule on the admissibility of evidence gained through a violation of constitutional rights. Without the leadership of the Supreme Court, lower courts continued to use the common law rule of evidence, allowing tainted evidence to be used at trial.

The most important case that made it to the Supreme Court concerning the use of evidence obtained in violation of the Constitution before the Court was granted general criminal appellate jurisdiction was *Boyd v. United States*[12] in 1886. The *Boyd* case, which was a civil case, involved a charge that George and Edward Boyd, New York City merchants, had committed fraud by importing 35 cases of glass into the United States without paying the required duty. In order to ascertain how much glass the Boyds had imported, the government subpoenaed an old invoice from the Boyds's import business. The Boyds then challenged the admissibility of the invoice, claiming that by being forced to produce the invoice they were being compelled to give evidence against themselves in violation of the Fifth Amendment.

After the district court allowed the invoice to be admitted into evidence, the case was appealed to the U.S. Supreme Court, which reversed the decision. The reason for the Court's reversal, as announced in Justice Joseph Bradley's opinion, was its belief that private papers were immune from search and seizure, since they were not contraband items. Furthermore, one of the purposes of the Fourth Amendment provision against unreasonable searches was to protect the broader Fifth Amendment right against self-incrimination. Therefore, the Court found that Fourth Amendment violations could be enforced through the Fifth Amendment. This made the use of the invoice gained from the Boyds's business inadmissible as evidence in court, since it violated the right against self-incrimination.

The *Boyd* case made it a matter of record that in civil cases evidence gained in violation of individual rights protected by the Constitution would not be admissible at trial. It did not address what would happen to similar evidence in criminal cases. The first criminal case in which the U.S. Supreme Court found evidence to be illegally admitted at trial was *Weeks v. United States*[13] decided in 1914. In that case, Weeks was sentenced to jail after his conviction for making illegal use of the U.S. Postal Service to distribute lottery tickets. The evidence obtained against Weeks was a result of the work of Kansas City, Missouri, police. The police entered Weeks's home without a search warrant, ransacked his home in a search for evidence, and then gave the evidence they found to U.S. marshals. Later that day, local police and the marshal returned to Weeks's home and gathered more evidence, again without a warrant. Prior to trial, Weeks filed a motion to regain possession of all the evidence that had been gathered from his home in violation of the Fourth Amendment. The district judge in charge of Weeks's trial ordered the return of all the seized articles that were not part of the prosecution's case against Weeks, but allowed the government to retain all the evidence it planned to use in the trial. After his conviction Weeks appealed, claiming that the evidence used against him was obtained in violation of the Fourth Amendment and should not have been admissible at trial.

In a unanimous decision, written by Justice William Day, the Supreme Court for the first time enunciated the rationale for an exclusionary rule under the Fourth Amendment. The Court first held that the search conducted at Weeks's home had indeed violated the Fourth Amendment. It went on to explain that when the trial court allowed illegally gathered evidence to be used, it had made a reversible error in the trial, forcing the case to be remanded for a new trial in which the evidence would have to be suppressed. The Court based its reasoning on several principles. The first was that the Fourth Amendment was meant to act as a restraint on both the police and the courts so both were obliged to enforce it. Second, Fourth Amendment rights continued to exist at trial, and use of illegally obtained evidence at this stage amounted to a continued governmental invasion of constitutionally protected privacy. Third, the integrity of justice in the federal system would be compromised if federal courts allowed illegally seized evidence to be admitted in court. These rationales were summarized in Justice Day's opinion as follows:

> If letters and private documents can thus be seized and held and used in evidence against a citizen accused of an offense, the protection of the Fourth Amendment, declaring his right to be secure against such searches and seizures is of no value, and, so far as those thus placed are concerned, might as well be stricken from the Constitution. The efforts of the courts and their officials to bring the guilty to punishment, praiseworthy as they are, are not to be aided by the sacrifice of those great principles established by years of endeavor and suffering which have resulted in their embodiment in the fundamental law of the land.[14]

Despite the Court's declaration in *Weeks* that evidence gathered in violation of the Fourth Amendment would not be admissible at trial, scholars have criticized the decision for not clearly articulating the principles on which the exclusionary rule has been founded. [15] This criticism, along with the exclusion of evidence based on Fifth Amendment grounds in *Boyd*, has led to a continuing debate about the true source and reasoning behind the exclusionary rule. Some scholars argue that the exclusionary rule is a direct constitutional requirement of the Fourth Amendment.[16] A second basis for the exclusionary rule could be that it is required as a Court-created remedy meant to further the protections of the Fourth Amendment as part of the Court's supervisory power over the federal courts. If it is a judicially created remedy, the Court could exercise two options. The first option would be to allow other methods of enforcing the provisions of the Constitution, which would not require the exclusion of all illegally obtained evidence, such as disciplining the officers involved. A second option would be to admit illegally obtained evidence when it would not help serve as a deterrent to future violators of constitutional provisions.

The opinion in *Weeks v. United States* also failed to discuss the scope of the exclusionary rule. The Court made no distinction between the two types of illegally obtained evidence—primary and derivative. Primary evidence is found as a direct result of illegal conduct. In the *Williams* case, the primary evidence was Williams's incriminating statements. Derivative evidence is obtained through information gathered as a consequence of the primary illegality of law enforcement officials, such as Pamela's body, which was found as a result of Williams's statements.

Clarification concerning the scope of the exclusionary rule came in 1920 in the case of *Silverthorne Lumber Co. v. United States*.[17] The factual situation of the *Silverthorne* case is as follows. The Silverthornes, a father and son, owned the Silverthorne Lumber Company when they were taken into custody after being indicted. While in custody, federal law enforcement officials, acting without a search warrant, entered the company's offices and seized all the books, papers, and documents they could find. These documents were then copied and studied for evidence of wrongdoing, which resulted in a new indictment. In the meantime, in reaction to a pretrial application by the defendants, the district court ordered all the documents that were seized in violation of the Fourth Amendment to be returned to the defendants. Based on the knowledge that the government gained from the copies it had made of the documents it was forced to return, it sought and received subpoenas ordering the defendants to produce the original documents before the grand jury. The Silverthornes refused to comply with the subpoenas, which resulted in the company being fined and the younger Silverthorne being jailed for contempt.

On appeal, the Supreme Court reversed the contempt judgment and helped to clarify the extent of the scope of the exclusionary rule. In an opinion written by Justice Oliver Wendell Holmes, the Court held that the exclusionary rule rejects not only the use of primary evidence that was illegally seized, but also the use of evidence derived from or found as a result of constitutional violations. This was clearly stated by Justice Holmes, who wrote, "The essence of a provision forbidding the acquisition of evidence in a certain way is that not merely evidence so acquired shall not be used before the Court, but that the facts thus obtained become sacred and inaccessible."[18] In this particular case the conviction was overturned because the subpoena didn't need to be honored, since the information that it was based on was too directly connected to the illegal search that had taken place earlier. Despite adding the derivative evidence rule, the Court went on and clarified that derivative evidence of this type could still be used under certain conditions. This, according to Holmes, was true "[I]f knowledge of them is gained from an independent source" as long as "the knowledge gained by the Government's own wrong cannot be used by it."[19]

Silverthorne thus contains two important constitutional doctrines. The first is the inadmissibility of derivative evidence gained through Fourth Amendment violations. The second is the *independent source exception* to the exclusionary rule, which allows derivative evidence to be used if law enforcement officials can show knowledge of it through a source independent of constitutional violation. The key to the independent source exception was that the evidence had to come from a source that was not associated with the police misconduct. An example of how the independent source exception works would be if the police had violated Williams's right to counsel and convinced him to tell police the location of the body, but he did not lead them to the body. In the meantime, if a separate group of police conducting a search for the body found it without communicating with the police involved with the violation, the body would be admissible because it was derivative evidence found through an independent source. The independent source exception rewards honest police work while taking away the incentive for police to violate the law.

Nineteen years later in *Nardone v. United States (Nardone II)*,[20] Justice

Felix Frankfurter coined the term "fruit of the poisonous tree" to describe the relationship between primary and derivative evidence in the application of the exclusionary rule.[21] The "tree" refers to primary evidence, obtained through constitutional violation and thus inadmissible, while the "fruit" refers to derivative evidence, also obtained through constitutional violation and also inadmissible in court. *Nardone* involved a tax fraud case that twice made it to the Supreme Court. In the first case, *Nardone I*[22] the Supreme Court reversed Nardone's tax fraud conviction because the prosecution had gained direct evidence through illegal wiretaps that were used to help convict Nardone.

In Nardone's second trial, the conversations from the wiretaps were not themselves admitted, but information gained from the conversations *was* admitted. Nardone was again convicted, again appealed, and the Supreme Court again reversed. In *Nardone II* the Court reaffirmed the holding in *Silverthorne* that derivative evidence could not be used unless it was also discovered from a source independent of the violation, since allowing such evidence would encourage law enforcement officers to continue to violate the law. The second *Nardone* case, then, added another exception to the blanket provision that all derivative evidence, originally discovered through a constitutional violation, was inadmissible at trial. This new exception was the *attenuation exception.* The attenuation exception to the exclusionary rule applies to derivative evidence. According to its provisions, such evidence can be admitted at trial if the prosecution can show that the connection between the initial constitutional violation and the derived evidence had become "so attenuated as to dissipate the taint."[23] Primary evidence, however, can never be attenuated. The derivative evidence in *Nardone II* was not found to be attenuated. In later cases, the attenuation exception has been used to allow evidence to be admitted when the connection between the illegal action and the discovery of the evidence is shown to be too remote to serve as a remedy to deter the actions of law enforcement officials from violating the law.

By 1946, the exclusionary rule was considered by the Supreme Court to be a settled enough rule of law within the federal court system that the Court could declare that illegally obtained "evidence is suppressed on the theory that the government may not profit from its own wrongdoing."[24] Despite this declaration from the Court, judges still lacked a clear explanation of the source of the exclusionary rule and why it was necessary in the federal courts. The Supreme Court had also failed to examine the issue of whether the exclusionary rule applied to violations of the Constitution that resulted from state—not federal—governmental action.

THE EXCLUSIONARY RULE IN THE STATES

The first time that the Court confronted the question of whether the Fourth Amendment and the exclusionary rule applied to actions of the states was in the 1949 case of *Wolf v. Colorado*.[25] The case entered the judicial system when the Denver, Colorado, district attorney heard that Julius Wolf, an obstetrician, was performing illegal abortions. The district attorney searched Dr. Wolf's office without a warrant and removed records covering 1943 and 1944. From the office records, the district attorney gained enough information to charge and convict Dr. Wolf of conspiracy to commit abortions. Wolf then appealed the conviction, claiming that the Fourteenth Amendment's Due Process Clause prohibited searches that were in violation of the Fourth Amendment and that the evidence gathered from such searches was inadmissible in state courts, just as it was in federal courts.

In resolving the issues presented in *Wolf*, Justice Felix Frankfurter's majority opinion did not hesitate to incorporate the Fourth Amendment through the Fourteenth Amendment since it was "implicit in the concept of ordered liberty."[26] In a gesture meant to convey respect for the principles of federalism, Justice Frankfurter did not, however, incorporate the exclusionary rule along with the Fourth Amendment. The Court's opinion distinguished between the federal rights protected under the Fourth Amendment and the federal remedy the Court had created to protect those rights. For the first time, the Court stated that the exclusionary rule as a remedy was "not derived from the explicit requirements of the Fourth Amendment" and not "an essential ingredient of the rights" contained in the Fourth Amendment.[27] Justice Frankfurter thereafter reasoned that exclusion was not required when states violated Fourth Amendment provisions because the states were free to develop other remedies that "would be equally effective."[28]

The opinion in *Wolf v. Colorado* created an interesting result, making the provisions against unreasonable search and seizure of the Fourth Amendment applicable to both the federal and state governments. But it only required exclusion of illegally gathered evidence in federal courts when it was obtained through the actions of federal government officials. This situation created a loophole in the application of the exclusionary rule known as the "silver platter" doctrine, which allowed evidence that was seized illegally by state and local officials to be used in federal courts.

THE WARREN COURT AND THE EXCLUSIONARY RULE

Eleven years after the Court decided *Wolf*, creating the silver platter loophole, the Court moved to close it in *Elkins v. United States*.[29] Movement in this direction was possible because of changes in personnel on the Supreme Court. Since *Wolf*, Earl Warren had taken over as Chief Justice and there were four new associate justices, including Justice Potter Stewart, who wrote the *Elkins* opinion. The other new justices were John Harlan II, William Brennan, and Charles Whittaker. In *Elkins*, the defendants in the case had been convicted after evidence gathered by state officials in violation of the Fourth Amendment was passed on to federal law enforcement officials and used in prosecution at federal district court. On *certiorari*, the defendants asked the Supreme Court to re-examine the silver platter doctrine. In a 5–4 decision, the Court closed the silver platter loophole as a source of admissible evidence. The opinion has been influential in later exclusionary rule cases because of the weight that Justice Stewart placed on the exclusionary rule not serving as a remedy for past violations of the Fourth Amendment, but instead as a deterrent for future violations. The emphasis on deterrence showed that the Court's primary concern in applying the exclusionary rule was "to prevent, not to repair" constitutional violations.[30] Furthermore, ending the silver platter loophole took away from state officials some of the incentive to disregard the Fourth Amendment. Justice Stewart also argued that ending the silver platter loophole advanced the principle of federalism by heading off conflicts between state and federal courts. He further noted that adherence to a strict policy of excluding illegally seized evidence in federal courts would further the goal of preserving judicial integrity by stopping judges from acting as accomplices to constitutional violations by rewarding law enforcement officials who disobeyed the Constitution.

While *Elkins* shows the unwillingness of the Warren Court to allow any evidence gained through Fourth Amendment violations into federal courts, the eagerness of the Warren Court to end the ability of state governments to submit similar evidence within their own courts can be seen in *Mapp v. Ohio*.[31] The record of *Mapp v. Ohio* shows that Dollree Mapp lived on the second floor of a two-family dwelling with her daughter. On May 23, 1957, three police officers knocked on Mapp's door and demanded to be admitted in order to search for a man who was a suspect in a recent bombing. Dollree Mapp called her attorney, who advised her not to let the officers in without a search warrant. After informing their headquarters of these events, the officers then established surveillance of the Mapp home. After three hours, four more officers were dispatched to Mapp's home. They then forcibly opened Mapp's door and entered the premises. When Mapp saw that the officers had broken into her house, she asked to see their warrant. When police waved a piece of paper that they claimed to be a warrant, Mapp grabbed the paper and placed it down the front of her blouse. The police then struggled with Mapp as they tried to retrieve the paper. Mapp was then handcuffed for becoming belligerent and the officers removed the paper from her blouse. At trial, no warrant was ever produced. In the meantime, Mapp's attorney had arrived on the scene, but was denied entry into the house or the ability to consult with his client. Mapp was then taken upstairs to her bedroom where police officers started their search. The search of the bedroom included an examination of a chest of drawers, a closet, and suitcases. The search then proceeded to include a look at her private papers and a photo album. The search moved on to the daughter's bedroom and the rest of the second floor. Finding neither the bomb suspect nor any other evidence, the searchers then moved to the basement where a trunk was located. Inside the trunk the officers found four obscene books and an obscene hand-drawn picture. As a result of the evidence found in the search, Mapp was tried and convicted under Ohio law for possession of obscene materials. Her conviction was upheld by the Supreme Court of Ohio and Mapp appealed to the U.S. Supreme Court.

The interesting thing about the Supreme Court's history of *Mapp v. Ohio* was that neither the Fourth Amendment nor the exclusionary rule were issues briefed or argued before the Court. Instead, it was appealed as a First Amendment case. Virtually all the legal briefs and oral arguments before the Court were directed at the issue of whether the Ohio obscenity law was vague and overbroad and, therefore, violated the First and Fourteenth Amendments. In fact, in the brief submitted by Mapp's counsel, there was no request that *Wolf v. Colorado* be overturned. Furthermore, when asked at oral argument whether he was seeking to have *Wolf* overruled and thus to exclude the evidence that had been seized in violation of the Fourth Amendment, Mapp's counsel answered that he had never heard of the *Wolf* case.[32] The only group to mention that this would be a good case to overrule *Wolf* was the American Civil Liberties Union in its *amicus curiae* brief. Even the American Civil Liberties Union did not dwell on overruling *Wolf*, covering the issue in a three-sentence paragraph in a twenty-page brief.

In the Court conference following the arguments for *Mapp v. Ohio*, a majority of the justices agreed that the conviction would be overturned because the Ohio obscenity statute violated the First and Fourteenth Amendment. The opinion was then assigned to Justice Tom Clark. For some reason, during the writing of the opinion, the reasoning for overturning the conviction of Mapp switched from First to Fourth Amendment grounds, including, for the first time, incorporation of the exclusionary rule to the states through the Fourteenth Amendment's Due Process Clause. The reason for this change in reasoning is not known. Justice Stewart, who objected to resolving the case on an issue that was not briefed or argued before the Court, speculated that the justices who made up the *Mapp* majority met in secret to discuss using the Fourth and Fourteenth Amendments as grounds for overturning the conviction.[33]

The *Mapp* decision was monumental because, in one fell swoop, it held that the exclusionary rule was constitutionally required in all criminal courts. It did not, however, build this monument on a firm foundation, since the decision still did not clarify the source of the exclusionary rule. As a result, debate has continued both on and off the Court as to where the justification for excluding evidence comes from and when it is appropriate.

The first theory of the exclusionary rule holds that the Constitution itself, either through the Fourth, Fifth, or some combination of those amendments, forbids the introduction of illegally seized evidence. Justice Clark's majority opinion emphasized a constitutional basis for the exclusionary rule, stating that "the exclusionary rule is an essential part of both the Fourth and Fourteenth Amendment."[34] Justice Clark believed that the lack of an exclusionary rule would reduce the Fourth Amendment to mere words. According to Justice Clark, *Wolf* had to be overruled and the exclusionary rule incorporated since "without that rule the freedom from state invasions of privacy would be so ephemeral and so nearly severed from its conceptual nexus with the freedom from all brutish means of coercing evidence as not to merit this Court's high regard as a freedom 'implicit in the concept of ordered liberty.'"[35] In his concurring opinion, Justice Hugo Black also asserted that the exclusionary rule was a constitutional requirement, but instead of grounding it solely in the Fourth Amendment, he also relied on the Fifth Amendment's right against self-incrimination.

A second theory expressed in Justice Clark's opinion finds the exclusionary rule necessary in order to preserve the integrity of the government and court system. This foundation of the exclusionary rule can be traced back to the majority opinion in *Weeks v. United States*. The application of the exclusionary rule was necessary to preserve judicial integrity because, in Justice Clark's words, "Nothing can destroy a government more quickly than its failure to observe its own laws, or worse, its disregard of the charter of its own existence."[36]

The third theory justifying the exclusionary rule that found its way into Justice Clark's opinion in *Mapp v. Ohio* was that the exclusionary rule was required as a remedy for constitutional violations. The primary purpose of the exclusionary rule as remedy was to prevent future constitutional violations by providing a deterrent to such abuses. The exclusionary rule as remedy also provided the majority in *Mapp* with one more piece of ammunition for overruling *Wolf v. Colorado*. In *Wolf* the Court had rejected applying the exclusionary rule to the states because it believed that the states could satisfy the requirements of the Fourth Amendment through other remedies. The states, however, had failed to develop other effective remedies to ensure that the Fourth Amendment would not be violated. This caused Justice Clark to call remedies other than the exclusionary rule "worthless and futile."[37] In fact, Justice Clark noted that since *Wolf* had been decided, a majority of the states had adopted the exclusionary rule. The exclusionary rule was, therefore, seen as the only effective remedy to deter Fourth Amendment violations by "removing the incentive to disregard it."[38]

In a dissent, written by Justice John Harlan and supported by Felix Frankfurter and Charles Whittaker, Harlan first criticized the way that the majority had used a First Amendment case to overrule *Wolf*. He then went on to express doubt that the exclusionary rule should be imposed on the states. Instead, he thought the imposition of the rule on the states would be destructive of the principles of federalism by denying to the states the ability to develop their own methods of dealing with unlawful searches.

Despite the lack of clarity over the source of the exclusionary rule in *Mapp v. Ohio*, the Warren Court continued to be firmly committed to the application of the rule at both the federal and state levels when governmental officials violated the Fourth Amendment. In later cases, the Supreme Court enlarged the scope of constitutional violations in which the exclusionary rule would be applied to include the Sixth Amendment right to counsel, and the Fifth Amendment right against self-incrimination.[39]

Researchers have called the mid-1960s the high-water mark for the exclusionary rule.[40] An example of the wide scope the Warren Court gave to the exclusionary rule can be found in *Wong Sun v. United States*,[41] which has been said to represent "the most comprehensive Supreme Court decision concerning the 'fruit of the poisonous tree.'"[42] *Wong Sun* expanded the application of the exclusionary rule to include the suppression of statements that were the product of an illegal arrest and any evidence found as a result.

THE BURGER COURT AND THE EXCLUSIONARY RULE

The decisions of the Warren Court, which extended the rights of the criminally accused, were immensely unpopular with both members of law enforcement and legal commentators.[43] The decisions were so unpopular that they became an issue in the election of 1968 when candidate Richard Nixon promised that if he were elected he would only appoint judges and justices who would advance the cause of "law and order" and narrow the scope of the decisions of the Warren Court. After winning the election, President Nixon quickly got his chance to start configuring the Supreme Court.

The Burger Court developed a fundamentally different approach to constitutional adjudication in the area of the rights of the criminally accused, especially concerning the exclusionary rule. The Warren Court had considered the exclusionary rule a tool that could be used to enforce the Fourth, Fifth, and Sixth amendments. The Burger Court did not adopt this view. Its difference in approach was summarized by Timothy Gammon as follows:

The Burger Court has shown the greatest interest in those rights that protect the innocent and thereby the trial process, such as the right to counsel and the prohibition against coerced confessions. It has shown less interest in those rights that may serve to protect the guilty, such as the exclusionary rule. A kind of "hierarchy of rights" has developed, based on the likelihood that denial of a particular right might result in the conviction of the innocent. Thus, where the guilt of an individual is obvious and a conviction appears reliable, but is challenged on the "technical grounds" of police misconduct or judicial error, the Court is inclined to limit rather than preserve or expand the individual's rights.[44]

The changes that were made by the Burger Court in cases involving the application of the exclusionary rule came through the leadership of Chief Justice Burger, who had a long history of skepticism of the rule.[45] During his tenure as a court of appeals judge, Burger had voted to support the application of the inevitable discovery exception to the exclusionary rule. The case, *Wayne v. United States*,[46] involved the admission of a body as evidence that had been located through an illegal entry of Lewis Wayne's apartment. Writing for the court, Judge Burger allowed the evidence to be used, stating, "[i]t was inevitable that, even had the police not entered the appellant's apartment at the time and in the manner they did, the coroner would sooner or later have been advised by the police of the information reported by the sister."[47]

In Chief Justice Burger's first term, the Court, in *Alderman v. United States*,[48] began the process of limiting the application of the exclusionary rule by emphasizing deterrence as the primary rationale for the rule. In *Alderman* the government had illegally wiretapped a phone line and thereby gathered incriminating evidence against a number of defendants. All the defendants objected to submission of the evidence resulting from the illegal wiretap. In *Alderman* the Court limited the application of the exclusionary rule by balancing its costs of possibly setting free criminals against its benefits of serving as a future police deterrent to constitutional violations. The Court held that, even though the deterrent value of the exclusionary rule was strong enough to justify its application in cases where the police have directly violated a person's rights, its costs of freeing the guilty was too great to allow it to be used in cases where the evidence had been illegally gained but not through a direct violation of a defendant's constitutional rights. Applying the ruling to this case, the Court stated that "suppression of the product of a Fourth Amendment violation can be successfully urged only by those whose rights were violated by the search itself, not by those aggrieved solely by the introduction of damaging evidence."[49] As a result, only the individual whose phone line was tapped had suffered the injury necessary to grant standing to object to the illegally seized phone conversations.

After *Alderman*, Chief Justice Burger continued to make his unhappiness with the exclusionary rule known. He again expressed his view of the rule by using the case of *Bivens v. Six Unknown Named Agents*[50] as his vehicle. In his dissenting opinion, Chief Justice Burger disclaimed the theories that had served to justify the exclusionary rule in past cases and declared that the exclusionary rule rested solely on the deterrence rationale. He also discussed the possibility of applying alternative remedies that could serve a deterrent function without the cost of letting criminals go free.

In 1974 Chief Justice Burger's approach to the exclusionary rule was accepted by the majority of the Court in *United States v. Calandra*.[51] *Calandra* came to the Court after a witness who had been summoned to appear before a grand jury refused to answer some questions on the grounds that the questions were based on the fruits of an unlawful search. In determining if such questions had to be excluded from grand jury inquiries, the Supreme Court, in an opinion written by Justice Lewis Powell, ruled that the exclusionary rule was inapplicable. The first thing that was made clear by the opinion was that the exclusionary rule was no longer considered by the Supreme Court to be required directly by the Constitution or to protect judicial integrity. Instead, Justice Powell wrote that the exclusionary rule was "a judicially created remedy designed to safeguard Fourth Amendment rights generally through a deterrent effect, rather than a personal constitutional right of the party aggrieved."[52] As a remedy, the sole purpose of the exclusionary rule was "to deter future unlawful police conduct and thereby effectuate the guarantee of the Fourth Amendment against unreasonable search and seizures."[53] As a deterrent, the rule would not automatically be applied in future cases. Instead, the rule should be "restricted to those areas where its remedial objectives are thought most efficiously served."[54]

A second thing that was made clear in the *Calandra* opinion was that the cost-benefit balancing approach used in *Alderman v. United States* would become the preferred method of determining whether the exclusionary rule should be applied. In reaching a balance in *Calandra*, the Court ruled that the extension of the exclusionary rule to grand juries would seriously impede their ability to perform their function, while the added deterrent effect it would serve would be "uncertain at best."[55] The Court also noted that the primary deterrent effect from the exclusionary rule came through the application of the rule to the prosecution's case-in-chief; therefore, little additional deterrence would come from denying the use of such material in grand jury proceedings.

While the Burger Court was not fond of the exclusionary rule, it did find circumstances in which it believed it was proper to exclude evidence to promote future deterrence. The first was in 1975 in *Brown v. Illinois*.[56] *Brown v. Illinois* came to the Court after Richard Brown had been convicted of murder in Chicago. His conviction followed an arrest without a warrant or probable cause. At the police station, Brown was given his *Miranda* warnings and interrogated about the murder. Brown cooperated with police and within two hours had made a number of statements implicating himself in the crime. The detectives who had been interrogating Brown then produced a written statement that he signed based on what he had told them. Later, after Brown unsuccessfully tried to help the police find the person who he said committed the crime, Brown was taken back to the police station where he was again given his *Miranda* warnings and repeated his story, in front of an assistant state's attorney and a court reporter. After the second rendition of the story, Brown refused to sign a second statement. Brown's admissions were allowed as evidence at trial and he was convicted. In his appeal to the Illinois Supreme Court, the court, relying on *Wong Sun*, ruled that Brown's statements were admissible because the presence of *Mir-*

anda warnings after an illegal arrest attenuated the connection between Brown's illegal arrest and his inculpatory statements.

The Supreme Court, through a majority opinion written by Justice Harry Blackmun, however, found that the confession in *Brown* was tainted fruit of the illegal arrest and overruled the decision of the Illinois Supreme Court. The fact that its decision was based on the deterrence principle as the foundation for the exclusionary rule can be seen in the opinion:

If *Miranda* warnings, by themselves, were held to attenuate the taint of an unconstitutional arrest, regardless of how wanton and purposeful the Fourth Amendment violation, the effect of the exclusionary rule would be substantially diluted. . . . Arrests made without warrant or probable cause, for questioning . . . could well be made admissible at trial by the simple expedient of giving *Miranda* warnings. Any incentive to avoid Fourth Amendment violations would be eviscerated by making the warnings, in effect, a "cure-all."[57]

Despite its finding that allowing confessions and statements that resulted from illegal arrests would not advance the goal of future deterrence, the Court in *Brown* did not close the door on the admission of all statements that were the product of such circumstances. The Court stated that a four-factor test should be applied to determine if confessions under these circumstances could be admitted as evidence. The first factor that the Court believed should be considered was whether the police did indeed give *Miranda* warnings prior to admissions after an illegal arrest. If no *Miranda* warnings were given to a suspect, any admissions would not be admissible. The second factor was the proximity in time between the illegality and any evidence obtained. The closer together the two were linked, the more suspect the evidence would be. The third factor was the presence of intervening circumstances between the illegal action and the point when the evidence was obtained. The fourth factor to be considered was the purpose behind the violation and the flagrancy involved. If the purpose was to avoid constitutional requirements or the illegality was flagrant rather than being akin to an honest mistake, the admissibility of the evidence would not be acceptable. In applying this test to *Brown*, the Court found that the connection between the illegal arrest and confession was not attenuated because, even though *Miranda* warnings had been given, Brown's statements were too close in time to the illegal arrest with no significant intervening circumstances between the two events. Furthermore, the Court believed that the police misconduct was a purposeful attempt to violate Brown's rights. Although in *Brown* the Court only considered the issue of confessions obtained through a violation of the Fourth Amendment, in 1978 in *United States v. Ceccolini*[58] it expanded the four-factor test to cases in which evidence was challenged that was a product of other types of police misconduct.

Even though the Court showed in *Brown v. Illinois* that it would exclude evidence under some conditions, in the ten years between when the Court decided *United States v. Calandra* and when it considered *Nix v. Williams,* the Court continued to insist that the sole purpose of the exclusionary rule was to serve as a deterrent remedy for future constitutional violations. In doing so, it applied the cost-benefit balancing approach to determine if the exclusionary rule would serve as a future deterrent. In a series of subsequent cases, the Court found that, under certain circumstances, the use of the exclusionary rule was inappropriate. In the 1974 case of *Michigan v. Tucker*[59] the Court held that even though the defendant's statements were inadmissible because of a violation of *Miranda,* evidence that was discovered as a result of the statements was admissible. In *Michigan v. DeFillippo*[60] the Court stated that when a search was conducted pursuant to a statute that was later found to be unconstitutional, any evidence gained through the search was admissible. In *United States v. Janis*[61] the Court held that evidence obtained illegally by state police was admissible in a federal civil tax proceeding since the police had acted in "good faith" when they obtained the evidence. In 1976 the Court ruled in *Stone v. Powell*[62] that in *habeas corpus* proceedings Fourth Amendment claims, including claims that the exclusionary rule was not properly applied, could no longer be reviewed. In 1980 the Court ruled in *United States v. Haven*[63] that evidence that was inadmissible in the prosecution's case-in-chief could be used to impeach the defendant at a criminal trial. In all the cases cited above, the Court found that the application of the exclusionary rule would contribute too little in the way of an added future deterrent in relation to its cost of freeing the guilty.

The Court's interest balancing between the costs associated with the exclusionary rule versus its benefits was not accepted by all legal scholars without criticism. Yale Kamisar, observing the vagueness of the basis of competition between the values at stake, asked the following questions of this approach to the exclusionary rule:

Does interest-balancing, at least when applying the exclusionary rule, turn largely, if not entirely, on *how* one identifies the competing interests and *how* one "weighs" them? How does one go about doing this: How for example, does one "quantify" the "privacy" or "individual liberty" the fourth amendment is supposed to protect and the exclusionary rule is supposed to effectuate? Is interest-balancing the "real" basis for judgement in the way to write an opinion once a judgement has already been reached on the basis of individual, subjective values?[64]

Criticisms of the Burger Court's interest balancing did not, however, change the Court's approach to the exclusionary rule. Recognizing that the Burger Court was rewriting the dimensions of the exclusionary rule may have emboldened some prosecutors and trial judges to keep testing the limits of what types of illegally gathered evidence would be admissible at trial.

During this sweeping transition—from the Warren Court's view that the exclusionary rule was a constitutionally protected right required both to serve as a deterrent to future violations and to protect judicial integrity, to the Burger Court's view that the rule was a judicial remedy that should only be enforced when it would deter future police misconduct—the second trial of Robert Williams for the murder of Pamela Powers was held in 1977. The trend on the Burger Court and Justice Stewart's footnote in *Brewer v. Williams* helped to prod Judge Denato in Williams's second trial to allow some evidence under the inevitable discovery exception to the exclusionary rule, even though the exception had been untested at the Supreme Court level and thus risked the possibility of another appeal and perhaps a third trial.

One other reason why Judge Denato probably had the confidence necessary to use the inevitable discovery exception to allow at trial evidence that was the fruit of a violation of Williams's Sixth Amendment rights was the acceptance of the exception by other courts in the United States. At the time of Williams's second trial, the inevitable discovery exception had been accepted by five of the circuits of the U.S. courts of appeal and the majority of the state supreme courts.[65] Adding to the momentum to legitimize the inevitable discovery exception to the exclusionary rule was the fact that in between the time of the second *Williams* trial and when the Supreme Court decided the issue in *Nix v. Williams*, every one of the circuits of the U.S. court of appeals had adopted the exception.[66]

Working against the sanctioning of the inevitable discovery exception by the Supreme Court was a longstanding tradition that illegally obtained evidence could not be used in the prosecution's case-in-chief. It had long been believed that use of illegally obtained evidence in the case-in-chief worked against the principle of providing future deterrence against constitutional violations. By the time that *Nix v. Williams* was argued before the Supreme Court, however, there was an indication by some of the justices that they might be willing to consider altering this tradition. Specifically, Chief Justice Burger and Justice Rehnquist had both advocated complete abolition of the rule[67] and Justices Powell and White had both indicated a willingness to adopt some form of "good-faith" exception to the exclusionary rule that would allow illegally obtained evidence to be admitted in the prosecution's case-in-chief if the officers had acted in good faith to accommodate constitutional requirements.[68]

When Judge Denato ruled in favor of admitting evidence under the inevitable discovery exception at Williams's second trial, no single understanding of what the exception included and how it should be applied had emerged from the lower courts. In general, it was thought that the exception's justification was linked to two earlier exceptions to the exclusionary rule. These were the independent source and attenuation exceptions.[69]

There is, however, one major difference between these two exceptions to the exclusionary rule and the inevitable discovery exception: Inevitable discovery deals with a hypothetical discovery of evidence, not an actual discovery. As it was generally being applied, the inevitable discovery exception required that, in order for illegally obtained evidence to be admitted, the prosecution had to show the judge that the evidence would have been discovered had there not been police misconduct. The judge's ruling in such a situation was based on a two-part test. The first question that a judge had to answer was, If there had been no violation, would the police have followed a determinable proper procedure and continued the investigation? The second issue that a judge had to confront was, If proper procedure had been followed, would the tainted evidence have, indeed, been inevitably discovered in usable condition?[70]

The application of this two-step test presented certain difficulties at both stages, resulting in inconsistencies of application at the lower-court level. The first difficulty in the application of the test was the determination of whether routine investigation would have led to the discovery of the tainted evidence had there not been a constitutional violation. In some instances, police have developed standard operating procedures, many of which are made mandatory in police manuals and guidelines, which treat all suspects the same at certain points in an investigation. Examples of police standard operating procedures include identification checks, investigation of abandoned vehicles, fingerprinting during booking, and the canvassing of pawn shops. In all these situations the likelihood of discovery of evidence through legal means would be enlarged. In other cases, however, the certainty of discovery through regular police procedures is less than positive. For example, are law enforcement officials to be trusted that had they not found the tainted evidence through a constitutional violation, they would have enlarged the investigation beyond the scope of traditional methods and found the evidence through other legal means?

The question of inevitability also raises a number of lingering concerns regarding the issue of when it is appropriate to apply the inevitable discovery exception. One issue of concern here is the time lapse that may have existed between the time in which the tainted evidence was unconstitutionally found and the time in which it would have been found without the violation. The question must be asked: Would it have been in usable condition if police had not discovered it at any early point in time due to the illegality? A second issue concerning the inevitability of later discovery is the location of discovery. The question is whether the evidence was discovered in a location where it would have been accessible to the police in a lawful investigation.

A third problem confronted by courts in applying the inevitable discovery exception concerns the burden of proof necessary to show that the evidence would indeed have been discovered through legal methods. This is an especially pertinent question since, unlike the independent source exception in which the prosecution has a legal source to which the evidence can be traced, the inevitable discovery exception traces the discovery of evidence to a *hypothetical* legal source that never was utilized.

A final question that was unanswered regarding the inevitable discovery exception was the scope of constitutional issues to which it would apply. Most often it had been applied to cases in which there was a violation of the Fourth Amendment's search and seizure provisions,[71] but it could also be applied to violations of the Fifth Amendment provision against self-incrimination and Sixth Amendment violations of the right to counsel.

The lack of a ruling precedent from the Supreme Court concerning the inevitable discovery exception left a number of questions open concerning whether the exception could find support in the Constitution and if so, how it should be applied. Indications from the Burger Court in how it had handled other exclusionary rule cases revealed a Court that had lost faith in the rule's blind application. Despite its uneasiness with the exclusionary rule, the overall Court precedents were broad enough for any number of legal options to be exercised as the *Williams* case moved though the appeals process. During the appeals process each judge or justice who heard the case would have the discretion to rely on a number of precedents, all resulting in different outcomes. For example, a judge could rely on a broad interpretation of *Mapp* and strictly enforce the exclusionary rule to disallow the evidence. Another option would be to apply the four-part test that came out of *Brown v. Illinois* and examine the circumstances under which Williams's rights were violated with an eye toward determining whether the purpose behind the violation was to circumvent the law. The possibility of accepting the inevitable discovery exception was yet another option. The variety of legal options available meant that in the second round of appeals the resolution of the case would again depend on the subjective facts and procedural law accepted by those making the final decisions.

NOTES

1. *Olmstead v. United States*, 277 U.S. 438, 485 (1928) (Brandeis, J., dissenting).

2. *Nix v. Williams*, 467 U.S. 431 (1984).

3. *Brewer v. Williams*, 430 U.S. 387 (1977).

4. Ibid., p. 406.

5. Jacob W. Landynski, *Search and Seizure and the Supreme Court: A Study in Constitutional Interpretation* (Baltimore: John Hopkins Press, 1966), p. 76.

6. Bradley C. Canon, "Ideology and Reality in the Debate Over the Exclusionary Rule: A Conservative Argument for Its Retention," *South Texas Law Review* 23 (1982): 579–580.

7. For a history of the Fourth Amendment, see Nelson Lasson, *The History and Development of the Fourth Amendment of the United States Constitution* (Baltimore: John Hopkins Press, 1937); and Landynski, *Search and Seizure.*

8. Cited in Charles McC. Mathias, Jr., "The Exclusionary Rule Revisited," *Loyola Law Review* 28 (1982): 7. For other criticisms, see also Bradford Wilson, "The Origin and Development of the Federal Rule of Exclusion," *Wake Forest Law Review* 18 (1982): 1073–1109.

9. Yale Kamisar, "Does (Did) (Should) the Exclusionary Rule Rest on a 'Principled Basis' Rather than an 'Empirical Proposition'?" *Creighton Law Review* 16 (1983): 585.

10. Wilson, "The Origin," p. 1074.

11. Brent D. Stratton, "The Attenuation Exception to the Exclusionary Rule: A Study in Attenuated Principle and Dissipated Logic," *Journal of Criminal Law and Criminology* 75 (1984): 139 n.1.

12. *Boyd v. United States*, 116 U.S. 616 (1886).

13. *Weeks v. United States*, 232 U.S. 383 (1914).

14. Ibid., p. 393.

15. Silas Wasserstrom and William J. Mertens, "The Exclusionary Rule on the Scaffold: But Was it a Fair Trial?" *American Criminal Law Review* 22 (1984): 85.

16. Thomas S. Schrock and Robert C. Welsh, "Up from Calandra: The Exclusionary Rule as a Constitutional Requirement," *Minnesota Law Review* 59 (1974).

17. *Silverthorne Lumber Co. v. United States*, 251 U.S. 385 (1920).

18. Ibid., p. 392.

19. Ibid., p. 392.

20. *Nardone v. United States*, 308 U.S. 338 (1939).

21. Ibid., p. 341.

22. *Nardone v. United States*, 302 U.S. 379 (1937).

23. Ibid., p. 341.

24. *Zap v. United States*, 328 U.S. 624, 630 (1946).

25. *Wolf v. Colorado*, 338 U.S. 25 (1949).

26. Ibid., p. 27.

27. Ibid., p. 28.

28. Ibid., p. 31.

29. *Elkins v. United States*, 364 U.S. 206 (1960).

30. Ibid., p. 217.

31. *Mapp v. Ohio*, 367 U.S. 643 (1961).

32. Potter Stewart, "The Road to *Mapp v. Ohio* and Beyond: The Origins, Development and Future of the Exclusionary Rule in Search-and-Seizure Cases," *Columbia Law Review* 83 (1983): 1367.

33. Ibid., p. 1368.

34. *Mapp v. Ohio*, 367 U.S. 643, 657 (1961).

35. Ibid., p. 655.

36. Ibid., p. 659.

37. Ibid., p. 652.

38. Ibid., p. 656.

39. The rule was applied to the Fifth Amendment right against self-incrimination in *Murphy v. Waterfront Commission*, 378 U.S. 52, 79 (1964), and the Sixth Amendment right to counsel in *United States v. Wade*, 388 U.S. 218, 239–240 (1967).

40. James Duke Cameron and Richard Lustiger, "The Exclusionary Rule: A Cost-Benefit Analysis," *Federal Rules Decisions* 101 (1984): 118.

41. *Wong Sun v. United States*, 371 U.S. 471 (1963).

42. Robert M. Pitler, " 'The Fruit of the Poisonous Tree' Revisited and Shepardized," *California Law Review* 56 (1968): 593.

43. Steven Cann and Bob Egbert point out that most of the law review articles written about the exclusionary rule have been critical of the rule, "The Exclusionary Rule: Its Necessity in Constitutional Democracy," *Howard Law Journal* 23 (1980): 300.

44. Timothy E. Gammon, "The Exclusionary Rule and the 1983–1984 Term," *Marquette Law Review* 68 (1984): 10.

45. For an extended example see Warren E. Burger, "Who Will Watch the Watchman?" *American University Law Review* 14 (1964): 1–23.

46. *Wayne v. United States*, 318 F.2d 205 (D.C. Cir., 1963).

47. Ibid., p. 219.

48. *Alderman v. United States*, 394 U.S. 165 (1969).

49. Ibid., pp. 171–172.

50. *Bivens v. Six Unknown Named Agents*, 403 U.S. 388 (1971).

51. *United States v. Calandra*, 414 U.S. 338 (1974).

52. Ibid., p. 348.

53. Ibid., p. 347.

54. Ibid., p. 348.

55. Ibid., p. 351.

56. *Brown v. Illinois*, 422 U.S. 590 (1975).

57. Ibid., p. 602.

58. *United States v. Ceccolini*, 435 U.S. 268 (1978).

59. *Michigan v. Tucker*, 417 U.S. 433 (1974).

60. *Michigan v. DeFillippo*, 443 U.S. 31 (1979).

61. *United States v. Janis*, 428 U.S. 433 (1976).

62. *Stone v. Powell*, 428 U.S. 465 (1976).

63. *United States v. Haven*, 446 U.S. 620 (1980).

64. Yale Kamisar, "Does (Did) (Should) the Exclusionary Rule Rest on a 'Principled Basis' Rather than an 'Empirical Proposition'?" *Creighton Law Review* 16 (1983): 642.

65. *State v. Williams*, 285 N.W.2d. 248, 255–57 (Iowa 1979).

66. Vincent A. Nagler, "*Nix v. Williams*: Conjecture Enters the Exclusionary Rule," *Pace Law Review* 5 (1985): 657.

67. *California v. Minjares*, 443 U.S. 916, 927 (1979).

68. *Stone v. Powell*, 428 U.S. 465, 538 (1976).

69. Leslie-Ann Marshall and Shelby Webb, Jr., "Constitutional Law—The Burger Court's Warm Embrace of an Impermissibly Designed Interference with the Sixth Amendment Right to the Assistance of Counsel—The Adoption of the Inevitable Discovery Exception to the Exclusionary Rule: *Nix v. Williams*," *Howard Law Journal* 28 (1985): 986.

70. Stephen H. LaCount and Anthony J. Girese, "The 'Inevitable Discovery' Rule, An Evolving Exception to the Constitutional Exclusionary Rule," *Albany Law Review* 40 (1976): 491.

71. Ibid., p. 508.

Chapter 9

The Second Appeals Process

Law is an art, not a science, and it often happens especially in cases complex and important enough to attract the Supreme Court's attention, that questions of great moment do not receive unanimous answers.

—Judge Richard Arnold[1]

THE STATE APPEALS PROCESS

Discretionary decisions that Judge Denato made, both prior to and during the second trial, based on his view of the subjective facts and applicable procedural law almost guaranteed that Robert Williams would appeal the case if convicted, and he did. During the appellate process, every court that would rule on the *Williams* case would have to review Judge Denato's decision. In the process, each court would have to determine if the inevitable discovery exception was supported by the Constitution and, if so, whether the subjective facts demonstrated that the body would have been discovered. Williams's appeal went to the Iowa Supreme Court and was settled by it on November 14, 1979. The attorneys who represented Williams were Gerald Crawford, who had been the trial attorney, and Robert Bartels, who had so capably assisted Williams in his first set of federal appeals. The State of Iowa was represented by a team of four attorneys—Thomas Miller, the Iowa attorney general; Dan Johnston, the Polk County prosecuting attorney; and Robert Blink and Rodney Ryan, who had acted as the prosecuting attorneys at the trial.

In *Iowa v. Williams*,[2] Williams's attorneys argued that several pretrial legal rulings by Judge Denato were inappropriate and provided the basis for reversal of the conviction. These included a refusal to appoint the attorney of Williams's choice to represent him, the admission of disputed evidence through the application of the inevitable discovery rule, the admission of evidence based on a challenged search warrant, denial of a motion to use public opinion polls to find a neutral venue, the refusal to allow the defendant to challenge a prospective juror for cause, and a failure to properly protect the jurors from publicity during the trial. Williams's attorneys also argued that Judge Denato had misapplied the law in several rulings during the trial. These included the denial of the defense motion for a directed verdict on the issues of premeditation and deliberation, and an error in the instructions that Judge Denato presented to the jury. A final argument made by the defense—which was ironic considering Gerald Crawford's participation in the appeal—was that Williams had ineffective counsel at trial. Despite the wide variety of rulings that provided grounds for appeal in this case, the most critical issue was whether the exclusionary rule included an inevitable discovery exception.

Williams argued that, due to the violation of his right to counsel, Pamela Powers's body and all other evidence found at its location had to be suppressed as "fruit of the poisonous tree." He therefore believed that the exclusionary rule should have been applied to the tainted evidence and that it should have been suppressed at trial.

The Iowa Supreme Court acknowledged that Williams's right to counsel had indeed been violated and that the violation led to the collection of additional evidence that would normally be considered as "fruit of the poisonous tree" and thus be inadmissible under the normal application of the exclusionary rule. It further pointed out that the Supreme Court had only recognized two exceptions to the exclusionary rule—the independent source and the attenuation exceptions. The court then went on and examined the extent to which other courts and scholars had embraced the inevitable discovery exception. It found that a large majority of all courts—federal and state—that had considered the issue had ruled in favor of application of the exception. Scholars, however, were more evenly split over their support for the exception.

After considering the sources they consulted, the justices reached the decision that Professor Wayne LaFave's approach to the inevitable discovery exception was the one that best conformed to the Constitution.[3] Professor LaFave would allow use of evidence gained by the inevitable discovery exception if the state could meet a two-part test. The first part was that law enforcement officials could not make use of the exception when they had acted in bad faith in order to speed up the process by which evidence was discovered. The second was that the state had to prove both that the evidence actually would have been found and how it would have been discovered prior to making use of the exception.

The justices believed that use of this particular test could overcome the two primary problems complained about by opponents of the exception: (1) the use of the exception by law enforcement officials as a shortcut method of gathering evidence and (2) nonuniform applications of the exception because of the ambiguity of the exception. The justices noted that the bad faith exception would continue to penalize police who would try to use the exception to hasten the gathering of evidence in violation of suspects' rights. The court also believed that the need by the State to prove that it would have discovered the evidence and by what legal means would help to ensure that the law would be applied in a consistent manner. Furthermore, review of the exceptions use by Iowa trial judges would rest in the hands of the Iowa Supreme Court, which would examine the question *de novo*, allowing it to ensure consistency in application.

The court then ruled that the inevitable discovery exception was a constitutionally sound exception to the exclusionary rule. It proceeded to explain the process to be followed when it was invoked:

After the defendant has shown unlawful conduct on the part of the police, the State has the burden to show by a preponderance of the evidence that (1) the police did not act in bad faith for the purpose of hastening discovery of the evidence in question, and (2) that the evidence in question would have been discovered by lawful means. This second element may require greater or lesser precision in showing the manner or time of discovery depending upon the circumstances of the case.[4]

After accepting the inevitable discovery exception, the court applied its rule to the particular facts of the *Williams* case. The court found that the police had not acted in bad faith when Captain Leaming violated Williams's right to counsel through the use of the Christian burial speech on the trip between Davenport and Des Moines. It explained that this finding was a reasonable conclusion, since in all of the courts that had reviewed the case there had been slim majorities as to whether there had been a constitutional violation.

The court then went on to determine whether a preponderance of the evidence indicated if the body of Pamela Powers would have been found by lawful means, had it not been located otherwise. To do this, the court considered the actions that the state took in trying to find the location of Pamela Powers prior to the violation of Williams's rights. It noted that this effort included the division of Poweshiek and Jasper counties into grid sections for the purpose of searching seven miles north and south of Interstate 80 to cover Williams's suspected escape route from Des Moines. Teams of four to six volunteers were then assigned to search particular sections of the counties. The teams were instructed to search all culverts and other places where a small child could be hidden. The search was cancelled at 3 P.M. when Captain Leaming told the officers in charge that there was a chance that Williams would lead the police to the body. Once the body was recovered, of course, it was unnecessary to resume the search. The officer in charge testified, however, that the search would have been resumed and would have continued into Polk County where the body was found. That location would have been reached in three to five hours. Furthermore, the State introduced evidence to show that, based on the freezing temperatures between December 1968 and April 1969, the body would have remained preserved in the same condition as that in which it was found. The court then ruled that a preponderance of the evidence did show that Pamela Powers's body would have lawfully been found in the culvert in basically the same condition that she was actually found. As a result, the body and related evidence had been properly admitted at trial under the inevitable discovery exception to the exclusionary rule. Not only did the Iowa Supreme Court find that the inevitable discovery exception was acceptable and properly applied at Williams's trial, but it denied all of Williams's other arguments that due process had been denied at trial.

HABEAS CORPUS AND THE FEDERAL COURTS PROCESS

District Court

After Williams's conviction was upheld by the Iowa Supreme Court, his appellate attorney, Robert Bartels, prepared a petition for a writ of *habeas corpus*, which was then filed in the U.S. District Court for the Southern District of Iowa. The petition was filed under 28 U.S.C., section 2254 and named David Scurr, the warden at the Iowa State Penitentiary where Williams was serving his life sentence, as the respondent.

As is normally true of the appellate process, the number of legal issues contested were narrowed as the appeal process went forward. The *habeas corpus* proceeding at the district court level involved the resolution of only six issues. Those issues were: (1) that the test applied by the Iowa Supreme Court for the admission of evidence under the inevitable discovery exception to the exclusionary rule was not constitutionally sound; (2) that even if the test for inevitable discovery was constitutional, the State of Iowa had failed to prove by a preponderance of the evidence that the victim's body would have been discovered if Williams's right to counsel had not been violated; (3) Williams had been denied a fair trial when his attorneys were denied their motion to challenge a juror for cause; (4) the evidence was too weak to allow a rational trier of fact to conclude beyond a reasonable doubt that deliberation and premeditation had been elements of the crime; (5) instructions to the jury that allowed them to consider concurrently both a felony-murder theory and a premeditated murder theory amounted to a denial of due process of law; and (6) the existence of both murder theories in the instructions allowed for the possibility that the jurors were not unanimous as to which murder theory they had in mind when they reached a verdict. Once again, the most critical issue was whether the inevitable discovery exception was supported by the Constitution.

When Crispus Nix replaced David Scurr as warden of the state penitentiary, the case title was changed to *Williams v. Nix.*[5] The *habeas corpus* proceeding was presided over by Judge Harold Vietor. Prior to making a ruling, Judge Vietor made his own independent review of the evidence by studying the record, including the transcripts of the trial proceedings, affidavits submitted by the parties, the legal briefs, and oral arguments by the attorneys to the case. He also held an evidentiary hearing on August 2, 1981, in which most of the arguments and evidence presented were repetitious of those made before the Iowa Supreme Court. There were, however, several new pieces of evidence that were considered by Judge Vietor.

Some of the new pieces of evidence were previously overlooked photographs that had been taken at the site when Pamela Powers's body was discovered. At the evidentiary hearing, Gerald Crawford was called to provide testimony that the defense team did not know of these photographs during the trial. Robert Bartels, Williams's attorney, argued that these photographs, and a recent deposition taken from Thomas Ruxlow, the investigative officer in charge of the search, cast doubt as to the inevitableness of the body's discovery had there not been a constitutional violation. This was because the only photographs of the body and scene of the crime presented at the suppression hearing prior to trial were revealed to have been taken after the crime scene had been altered by police. In particular, it was shown that only one photograph was taken of the body and crime scene prior to the police removing snow from the body and surrounding area in a search for evidence. Unlike the photos available at the suppression hearing, which showed the body almost completely exposed, this new photo demonstrated that the body was not easily detectable when it was first found. It was covered with snow and obscured by brush. Other photos taken from the road above the culvert, showed that the culvert where the body was placed was hidden from view at road level. The existence of these new photos led Bartels to question whether searchers would have ever gotten out of their cars where the body was hidden without Williams's guidance.

Robert Bartels also introduced into the record two Bureau of Criminal Investigation reports filed by Thomas Ruxlow and Daniel Mayer. These reports helped to demonstrate that at no point was there any discussion or order to include Polk County, where the body was actually found, in the parameters of the search. The defense hoped that knowledge of these reports would cast doubt on the inevitableness of the discovery of the body.

Robert Bartels also tried to use a deposition that was taken from Thomas Ruxlow to Williams's advantage. The deposition led to a few new pieces of information about the case. One was an admission on Ruxlow's part that, prior to his testimony at the 1977 suppression hearing, he had been told by the prosecutor, Robert Blink, that the purpose of the hearing was to determine whether the search would have resulted in the discovery of the body had it not previously been found. A second was an admission by Ruxlow that the photo he had identified at the suppression hearing in 1977 as showing the body as it was found, was actually a photo taken after snow had been brushed off the body.

Another new piece of evidence supporting Williams's position came in the form of a deposition taken from Richard Boucher, who had been a resident of the Y.M.C.A. on the day of the crime. Boucher testified that at about the same time as the crime, he had heard suspicious and belligerent noises coming from the room next to his and identified the voice as that of Albert Bowers, a Y.M.C.A. custodian. He then saw Bowers taking suitcases into his room and heard him packing. At the time Boucher informed the police about his concerns and he and a police officer then went to Bowers's room and asked him not to leave. He replied that he was not going anywhere. Shortly afterwards, however, Bowers left the building. Boucher said that he then found a towel in Bowers's room, which looked like it had bloodstains.[6]

Despite the new evidence and all the arguments made in the briefs and at oral argument, Judge Vietor's resolution of the issues closely followed the same line of argument as that of the Iowa Supreme Court. As a result, he ruled that there were no errors made by the trial court.

Court of Appeals

Williams's next step was to appeal the ruling of Judge Vietor of the District Court of Southern Iowa to the U.S. Court of Appeals for the Eighth Circuit. Robert Bartels again acted as his attorney. The State of Iowa was represented by Thomas Miller, Iowa's attorney general, and Tom McGrane, an assistant attorney general. The panel of judges who considered the appeal and heard oral argument consisted of Judges Gerald Heaney, Jess Henley, and Richard Arnold. Williams's appeal raised the same issues as had the original petition for *habeas corpus* with one additional point. The new issue was Williams's claim that Judge Denato should have excused himself from the case.

Despite all the grounds for reversal that Williams claimed existed, the court of appeals limited the scope of its inquiry to one issue. In so doing, the court of appeals decided that it was not necessary to determine whether the inevitable discovery exception to the exclusionary rule could withstand constitutional scrutiny. Instead, it assumed *arguendo* that the exception did exist and that the Iowa Supreme Court had correctly established the rules for its application. Under those rules, only two things were required for the exception to be applied: (1) that the police acted in good faith in their constitutional violation and (2) that the evidence would have been discovered had there not been a constitutional violation. This narrowing of the scope of the case by the court of appeals allowed it to avoid making a determination on all issues except the question of whether the police had lacked good faith. As a result, the court bypassed a determination as to whether the record supported the finding that the body would have been found by lawful means and whether the standard for such a discovery should have been a preponderance of the evidence, as used by the trial court, or clear and convincing proof, as Williams argued.

In the majority opinion written for the Eighth Circuit of the Court of Appeals by Judge Arnold, the court gave two reasons why it was inappropriate for the court of appeals to defer to the state courts in this case. The first was that Iowa Supreme Court's discussion of bad faith was not a finding of fact. Instead, it was a legal conclusion. A second reason why the Iowa Supreme Court's finding did not have to be accepted as fact was that it was without support in the record of the case. Judge Arnold argued that because the trial court had not considered the good faith issue at the suppression hearing, the record supported the court of appeals' view that the decision of the Iowa Supreme Court was not a matter of fact.

In its own attempt to try to determine if Detective Leaming had acted in good faith when he violated Williams's right to counsel, the court of appeals framed the issue in the following way:

The question is . . . what was in Detective Leaming's mind during that car ride back to Des Moines. If he honestly thought he was not violating Williams's rights, then the deterrent purpose of the exclusionary rule would arguably not be impaired by allowing proof of facts that would have come to light in any event. But if he had no such honest belief, and if the courts later hold his conduct unlawful, it matters not how close the division was among the judges. The relevant question—bad faith—is subjective. . . . If Leaming conversed with Williams in deliberate violation of the Sixth Amendment, the evidence must be excluded.[7]

The court of appeals then went on to state that Iowa had the burden of proof as to the factual question regarding Leaming's state of mind at the time of the constitutional violation. It then examined the record of the trial to determine if the State had met its burden.

The court of appeals found that the State had failed to meet the burden of proof necessary to show that the police had acted in good faith. Instead, several things in the record illustrated just the opposite. The first was that every court—state and federal—that had made a finding of fact on the issue had ruled that the police had broken an express promise they had made to attorney McKnight not to interrogate Williams on the trip between Davenport and Des Moines. The court also found that Detective Leaming broke his promise almost as soon as he arrived in Davenport by informing Williams that "We'll be visiting between here and Des Moines."[8] Furthermore, when attorney Kelly questioned this and asked to ride with his client back to Des Moines, Leaming denied his request and also denied that he had been instructed not to talk to Williams until they returned to Des Moines. The court of appeals was also leery of Leaming's honesty. It pointed out that, despite the fact that Leaming disputed the factual circumstances surrounding the right to counsel violation, the district court that had ruled on the issues in the very first *habeas corpus* proceedings ruled against Leaming's interpretation of events. The court found that another indicator of bad faith on Detective Leaming's part was his admission that the purpose behind his conversations with Williams was to get information that could be used against him prior to Williams being able to consult with his attorney. The court also noted that in *Brewer v. Williams* several of the concurring justices on the Supreme Court gave strong indications that they believed Detective Leaming had acted in bad faith.

Based on all the available information, the court of appeals then ruled that the police had not acted in good faith when they violated Williams's right to counsel so the inevitable discovery exception as formulated by the Iowa Supreme Court could not be applied to Williams's case. As a result, Pamela Powers's body and all the evidence gained at the scene should not have been admitted at trial. The court then reversed the case and remanded it with instructions to issue the writ of *habeas corpus* and release Williams unless the State of Iowa commenced proceedings against Williams within sixty days. The court order also noted that it would not be prejudiced against any attempt by the State of Iowa to begin civil commitment proceedings involving Williams.

The Eighth Circuit's ruling left the State of Iowa with several choices. One was to release Williams. A second was to retry Williams a third time. The third was to petition the U.S. Supreme Court for writ of *certiorari*. Iowa elected for the third option. If the Supreme Court would accept the case, the ability of the State of Iowa to keep Williams in prison without a third trial hinged on two related questions. The first was whether the inevitable discovery exception to the exclusionary rule was constitutionally sound. If it was, then what remained to be determined were the exception's parameters and whether the rule was applicable in this case. This left an unsettling situation for both the State of Iowa and Williams, since their hopes would rest on a legal theory that was untested at the Supreme Court level. As demonstrated by the lower court decisions, there were enough legal options for *Nix* to be decided in a variety of ways. As with *Brewer v. Williams*,[9] it seemed that once again a final resolution of *Nix v. Williams* would depend on the discretionary choices regarding what the subjective facts of the case were and how the applicable procedural laws would be applied.

NOTES

1. *Williams v. Nix*, 700 F.2d 1164, 1170 (8th Cir. 1983).
2. *Iowa v. Williams*, 285 N.W.2d 248 (Iowa 1979).
3. Ibid., p. 258.
4. Ibid., p. 260.
5. *Williams v. Nix*, 528 F.Supp 664 (S. Dist. Iowa 1981).
6. Respondent's Brief in Opposition, p. 27 n. 14, *Nix v. Williams*, 467 U.S. 431 (1984).
7. *Williams v. Nix*, 700 F.2d 1164, 1170–1171 (8th Cir. 1983).
8. Ibid., p. 1172, citing *Brewer v. Williams*, 430 U.S. 387, 391 (1977).
9. *Brewer v. Williams*, 430 U.S. 387 (1977).

_____

Chapter 10

Nix v. Williams

Nothing we write, no matter how well reasoned or forcefully expressed, can bring back the victim of this tragedy or undo the consequences of the official neglect which led to the respondent's escape from a state mental institution. The emotional aspects of the case make it difficult to decide dispassionately, but do not qualify our obligation to apply the law with an eye to the future in the particular case before us.

—Justice John Paul Stevens[1]

THE *CERTIORARI* DECISION

The State of Iowa decided to exercise the option of asking the Supreme Court to review the ruling of the Eighth Circuit of the Court of Appeals. Its petition for writ of *certiorari* was filed at the Supreme Court on April 7, 1983. In its petition the State of Iowa gave three reasons as to why the Supreme Court should grant review. The first of Iowa's concerns was that federal courts should be more respectful and deferential to the decisions of state courts. Iowa believed this was especially necessary in this case because the court of appeals had decided the case on an issue which had not been properly presented before the court. That issue was whether Williams's incriminating statements had resulted from a lack of good faith on the part of the police. Iowa believed that it was inappropriate for the court of appeals to overrule the Iowa Supreme Court on this issue, especially since there had been no evidentiary hearing on the issue. Iowa's petition also argued that it was necessary for the Supreme Court to grant review of this case to clarify a lack of uniformity in the application of the inevitable discovery exception that existed at the court of appeals level. In particular, Iowa believed it was necessary for the Court to determine if the exception included a good faith requirement, and if such a requirement was mandatory, whether it would be applied in a subjective or objective manner. The last request that Iowa made was to ask the Court to consider extending the ruling of *Stone v. Powell*[2] to Sixth Amendment cases. Iowa believed this would benefit the justice system by stopping federal review in *habeas corpus* proceedings where physical evidence that was highly probative and reliable had been granted a full and fair review in the state courts. Also favoring a grant of *certiorari* was an *amicus curiae* brief filed by the attorney general of Illinois and forty-two other state or territorial attorneys general.

Williams's brief in opposition, along with a motion to proceed *in forma pauperis*, which was granted, was filed with the Court on May 16, 1983. Robert Bartels responded as Williams's attorney. He presented six reasons why review should not be granted. The first was that, contrary to Iowa's claim, Iowa had ample notice prior to the court of appeals that the good faith issue was a point of appeal. The petition argued that the good faith issue had first been presented by the Iowa Supreme Court and had remained an issue of appeal. A second argument against granting *certiorari* was that Williams's incriminating statements and the resulting evidence had all directly resulted from a violation of his rights and should therefore have been excluded from trial. The brief went on to argue that if the Court were going to support the inevitable discovery exception to the exclusionary rule, it should include a good faith requirement. The point was made that a lack of uniformity at the court of appeals level over the inclusion of a good faith requirement in the exception did not necessarily exist. This was because not all circuits had been confronted with a case that involved a bad faith effort on the part of the police to gather evidence. It was pointed out that a good faith requirement would help to eliminate police incentive to violate the rights of future suspects and preserve judicial integrity. The brief went on to argue that the court of appeals was correct in its conclusion that there was a lack of good faith in this case regardless of whether Leaming's actions were judged by a subjective or objective standard. An argument was also made against granting review even if the Court supported the inevitable discovery exception without a good faith requirement, because in this case the new evidence introduced at the district court's *habeas corpus* evidentiary hearing showed that discovery of the body was not as inevitable as believed at the suppression hearing prior to trial. The last argument for why the Court should not grant review was that this was an inappropriate case for extension of *Stone v. Powell*.

Iowa's reply brief in support of granting *certiorari* made three main points. The first was that the respondent had misinterpreted *Stone v. Powell* as strictly applying only to Fourth Amendment cases, rather than being based on the character of the evidence involved. It was Iowa's belief that *Stone* was not limited to only evidence that was discovered through a violation of the Fourth Amendment. Instead, Iowa argued that the primary purpose of *Stone* was to allow the inclusion of highly probative and reliable evidence that had received fair treatment in the state courts. The second point was that it was unreasonable for the respondent to assert that the question of whether there was a lack of good faith had been properly litigated. The third was that, despite respondent's contention, a strong case could be made that the inevitable discovery exception could and should be applied in this case.

After studying these petitions, the Supreme Court granted review on May 31, 1983. According to the Court, it "granted *certiorari* to consider whether, at respondent Williams's second murder trial in state court, evidence pertaining to the discovery and condition of the victim's body was properly admitted on the ground that it would ultimately or inevitably have been discovered even if no violation of any constitutional or statutory provision had taken place."[3] After granting *certiorari*, the Court granted a motion from Williams for appointment of counsel and once again appointed Robert Bartels to that position.

THE DECISION PROCESS

Brief for the Petitioner

In Iowa's Brief for the Petitioner it argued that there were several grounds that supported reversal of the court of appeals order granting *habeas* relief to Williams. Its first argument was that, under certain conditions, the Court should be supportive of an inevitable discovery exception to the exclusionary rule. Those conditions, which Iowa argued existed in this case, were that the physical evidence gathered through illegal police activity needed to be highly probative and reliable. The evidence also had to have been discoverable through lawful independent investigative activity already in progress at the time of the original discovery. Iowa argued that both of these conditions had been met in this case.

To support its position, Iowa drew distinctions between the different types of factual scenarios in which the inevitable discovery exception could be applied. The first of these scenarios was referred to as "independent inevitable discovery."[4] The *Williams* case represented an example of independent inevitable discovery. In this scenario, which Iowa argued presented the strongest case for use of the inevitable discovery exception, law enforcement officials are aggressively pursuing lawful means of discovering the evidence at the simultaneous time it is found through illegal police conduct. Due to the competing methods of investigation, the courts do not have to speculate as to whether the lawful means would have actually led to discovery of the evidence. In effect, both methods would have been successful so the police should not be penalized for the illegal method when the legal method would have accomplished the same thing at a later point in time. In these cases, the inevitable discovery exception really represented a variation of the well-accepted independent source rule. Application of the exception in this manner, Iowa claimed, had not been controversial at the court of appeals level.

When application of the inevitable discovery exception had been controversial in the courts of appeals it was due to it being applied in different factual situations. Iowa referred to one of these situations as "hypothetical independent source."[5] In cases of this type, courts must engage in far-reaching speculation as to whether the questioned evidence would have been found through alternative legal methods. This was because, at the time when the evidence was discovered, no alternative legal method of discovering the evidence was being pursued. As a result, a court would be forced to guess as to how law enforcement officials would have behaved if the evidence were not found illegally. Often, as in cases involving standard operating procedures, such as checking a driver's license, the guess would not be too speculative. Other factual situations would result in much more speculation.

An even more controversial application of the inevitable discovery exception resulted in cases labeled "dependent inevitable discovery."[6] In such cases, there is no actual or hypothetical lawful means of discovery being pursued at the time of the legal violation. In these cases, application of the inevitable discovery exception is an effort to salvage unlawful conduct as an afterthought. One example provided in the brief was allowing evidence gathered through a warrantless search because the government had the probable cause necessary to obtain a warrant had it attempted to do so. Iowa did not support application of the inevitable discovery exception under these circumstances. Instead, it warned that if the exclusionary rule were ignored in such cases, the need to get warrants prior to searches would be virtually erased.

Because the facts of this particular case provided an example of "independent inevitable discovery," Iowa argued that the Court should overrule the court of appeals' grant of *habeas*. Iowa also argued that the exception should not include a good faith requirement. Even if the Court were to accept the inevitable discovery exception with a good faith requirement, Iowa believed that Detective Leaming's actions did not violate this principle. Iowa stated that the record supported its position that Detective Leaming had not acted in bad faith in trying to solicit information from Williams. On the contrary, Leaming not only warned Williams of his rights as required by *Miranda*, but he was also very careful not to ask Williams direct questions. Furthermore, Leaming's willingness to be frank in his testimony at the first trial's suppression hearing and again at the trial showed that Leaming had not been consciously trying to violate Williams's rights. Iowa then argued that if the Court was not convinced by the ability of the existent record to demonstrate that Detective Leaming had not acted in bad faith, the grant of *habeas* by the court of appeals should be reversed because of the absence of an evidentiary hearing to examine this particular issue in either the state or federal courts.

The final argument that Iowa presented was based on its interpretation of *Stone v. Powell.* According to Iowa, *Stone v. Powell* had as its primary purpose to help protect the truth-finding function of trials. It served this purpose by not allowing Fourth Amendment claims to be subject to *habeas corpus* proceedings when application of the exclusionary rule would take place so far from the infraction that it would not serve the exclusionary rule's deterrent function. Iowa argued that the decision should be enlarged to non–Fourth Amendment cases whenever the physical evidence in question was highly probative and reliable. This would not weaken the exclusionary rule in Sixth Amendment cases, such as this one, because the police would still have to fear that the state courts would find their behavior in violation of the law. It would have the added advantage of giving finality to cases without the necessity of waiting for the *habeas* process to unfold.

Brief for the Respondent

In the Brief for the Respondent, Robert Bartels advanced a number of reasons why the Supreme Court should either reject acceptance of the inevitable discovery exception to the exclusionary rule or, at a minimum, uphold the decision of the court of appeals. Central to the brief's argument was the distinction it made between the way that evidence gathered in violation of the Sixth Amendment should be treated versus Fourth Amendment evidence. Such a distinction had to be made because of the different purposes that the exclusionary rule served for each amendment. In Fourth Amendment cases, the exclusionary rule was meant to deter future police misconduct. In Sixth Amendment cases, however, the exclusionary rule was meant to protect the personal right of every defendant to a fair trial. This included the right to have counsel present during police interrogation. Interrogations that gained incriminating statements from defendants were just the first stage of the violation of the right to counsel. The second stage and the completion of the violation came when evidence gathered in this manner was presented at trial. The exclusionary rule for the Sixth Amendment was thus structured to stop all statements and resultant evidence from being admitted at trial in order to preserve the fairness and integrity of the trial. For that reason, application of the Sixth Amendment's exclusionary rule should not be subject to the same type of Fourth Amendment balancing in which the deterrent effect on future violations is contrasted with societal costs.

The Brief for the Respondent went on to explain that even if this were a Fourth Amendment case, the inevitable discovery exception to the exclu-

198   The Christian Burial Case

sionary rule could not be supported by the Constitution. This was because
it would create too many incentives for future police misconduct. It argued
that acceptance of an exception allowing police to prove that evidence would
have been found legally had there not been a violation would result in all
sorts of rationalizations to justify the hypothetical legal means of discovery.
In those situations when the state could not demonstrate that lawful actions
would have resulted in discovery of evidence, the police will not have lost
anything in their attempt to get the evidence admitted despite the presence
of a constitutional violation.

After discussing the inherent problems concerning future deterrence of
legal violations that would result from the inevitable discovery exception,
the Brief for the Respondent then examined the particular form of the exception supported by Iowa. Iowa's application of the independent inevitable
discovery exception was also problematic because the facts of this case required more speculation than Iowa was willing to admit. The brief argued
that the discovery of the body was far from inevitable in light of the facts
that had come out at the evidentiary hearing during the district court's
habeas proceedings. These facts cast doubt on the state's contention that
the search for the body would have been extended into Polk County. There
were also questions raised about whether the culvert would have been seen
from the road. This brought into focus whether anyone would have actually
examined the culvert where the body was found. Agent Ruxlow's testimony
concerning which photos accurately portrayed the original condition of the
body when it was found also raised further doubt.

After first arguing that the Court should not give its support to the inevitable discovery exception, the Brief for the Respondent went on to state
that if it did, it should uphold the decision of the court of appeals and
include a good faith requirement. It argued that an examination of how the
Court had resolved exclusionary rule cases involving the attenuation exception demonstrated that a good faith requirement was necessary.[7] Such an
examination showed that, prior to evidence being suppressed, three factors
had to be considered. Those factors were (1) the proximity in time between
the illegality and discovery of the evidence; (2) the presence of any intervening circumstances; and (3) the purpose and flagrancy of the legal violation. The last factor, the brief argued, created the necessity of a good faith
requirement. The brief also encouraged the Court to reach the same conclusion as the court of appeals had in finding that Detective Leaming's actions were undertaken in bad faith and, in consequence, uphold the grant
of *habeas.* Bad faith had been demonstrated by Detective Leaming in two
instances—by violating the agreement made with McKnight not to interrogate Williams on the trip from Davenport to Des Moines and by his
purposeful attempt to gather information from Williams in the absence of
his attorney.

The Brief for the Respondent then argued that if the Court did not accept any of its arguments and adopted the inevitable discovery exception in any of its forms, it would not affect this particular case since the State had not met its burden in showing that the disputed evidence would have been discovered. This was because at the district court's *habeas* proceeding the evidentiary hearing had demonstrated that the state courts had applied the exception based on false testimony and information. The newly available evidence showed that the body probably would not have been discovered had it not been for the violation of Williams's rights.

The final argument in the Brief for the Respondent addressed whether the reasoning of *Stone v. Powell* should be expanded beyond Fourth Amendment exclusionary rule cases. It pointed out that there was a fundamental difference between the purpose of the exclusionary rule in Fourth and Sixth Amendment cases. It also argued that expansion of *Stone* to Sixth Amendment cases would give greater incentives for future police misconduct. Furthermore, because the Iowa Supreme Court had decided this case by applying the inevitable discovery exception, a doctrine that had been constitutionally untested at the U.S. Supreme Court level, *Stone* should not be used to disallow federal review of such a far-reaching change in the law.

Reply Brief for the Petitioner

After receiving the Brief for the Respondent, Iowa presented the Court with a Reply Brief for the Petitioner in hopes of clarifying its position. The first point it made was that the respondent's brief was incorrect in claiming that acceptance of the inevitable discovery exception would give police additional incentive to violate the legal rights of citizens. Iowa also emphasized that the position of the Court in cases involving a state's violation of legal rights had consistently been that the state should be in the same position it would have been in had there been no violation. The inevitable discovery exception simply reinforced this position. Iowa also denied the respondent's position that the Sixth Amendment protected special rights that would be offended by the application of the inevitable discovery exception. Iowa noted again that it was not the nature of the right that was important, but the nature of the evidence. Furthermore, since the evidence in question was highly probative and reliable, it should be admissible, especially since the defense had the opportunity to cross-examine witnesses who testified about the evidence. Iowa went on to argue that there were adequate facts in the record to support the position of both the state and federal district courts to rule that the body of Pamela Powers would have been legally discovered by the proper standard, that of a preponderance of the evidence. This was especially true since there was also adequate evidence in the record to support a finding that Detective Leaming had acted in good faith. Iowa also made one last plea that the issue of expanding *Stone v. Powell* to Sixth Amendment cases, such as this one, was properly before the Court.

Amicus Curiae Briefs

Iowa's brief was supported by three separate *amicus curiae* briefs. The first of the *amicus* briefs was written by the attorney general for the State of Illinois. It was supported by an additional forty-two state or territorial attorney generals. The major premise advanced in this brief was that the ruling of *Stone v. Powell* should be expanded to stop federal review on *habeas* of Sixth Amendment claims when the fundamental fairness of the state trial and proceedings have not been challenged. The brief argued that if state courts could adequately adjudicate on Fourth Amendment issues, they were just as capable of doing so in Fifth and Sixth Amendment cases. The central concern in such cases, the brief argued, should be that the admission of statements taken when counsel was not present does not harm the fundamental fairness of the truth-finding process at trial. Therefore, it made perfect sense to expand the reasoning in *Stone* to Sixth Amendment cases. This argument was enhanced when the societal costs of collateral review were weighed against the constitutional interests involved. This was because delay in criminal punishment undermined the deterrent effect of the criminal law. Delay also undercut public confidence in the criminal justice system while wasting the limited resources available for criminal prosecution and defense. Furthermore, delay ignored the interest of the victims of crime to see an individual quickly punished for the crimes inflicted upon them. In conclusion, the brief argued that the grant of *habeas* should be reversed and in future cases the Court should respect the principles of federalism by limiting the ability of state prisoners to attack their convictions on grounds that their Sixth Amendment rights had been violated.

The Legal Foundation of America (LFA) and Americans for Effective Law Enforcement (AELE) also submitted a *joint amicus* brief. This brief also argued that this case should be disposed of by *Stone v. Powell.* The majority of its argument, however, focused on its desire for the Court to adopt the inevitable discovery exception to the exclusionary rule. The first point that the brief made regarding the inevitable discovery exception was that the court of appeals had erred in requiring good faith. This was because the exception was so closely related to the independent source exception that its major concern was with the causation of why the questioned evidence was or would have been discovered. Because legal alternative police methods would have been the cause behind the discovery of Pamela's body, bad faith was not a proper concern in inevitable discovery cases. In effect, regardless of how egregiously the police may violate an individual's rights, the violation is not related to how the evidence would have been inevitably discovered, so police behavior should not be an issue.

The brief for the LFA and the AELE went on to argue that even if the Court did adopt the inevitable discovery exception with a good faith requirement, the court of appeals had erred in finding that bad faith existed in this case. This was because the court of appeals had applied a standard of law to Detective Leaming's actions that he could not realistically have been expected to have knowledge of at the time. In addition, Leaming had not acted with actual malice. The brief ended by arguing that if the Court included a good faith requirement, then, rather than upholding the grant of *habeas*, the case should be remanded for a hearing on that issue alone.

The last *amicus* brief supporting the State of Iowa was filed for the United States by the Solicitor General, Rex Lee. The United States filed its brief in the belief that because "the proper application of the exclusionary rule is central to the fair and efficient administration of criminal justice, the United States has a substantial interest in the outcome of this case."[8] In its brief the United States argued that the inevitable discovery exception should be adopted by the Court as a logical extension of both the independent source and attenuation exceptions to the exclusionary rule. This brief held that there was a common theory of causation between illegal police conduct and the discovery of evidence. In both independent source and attenuation cases, the evidence is not excluded from trial because the official misbehavior was not the cause necessary for discovery of the evidence. The link between inevitably discovered evidence and official misconduct was also broken so that the misconduct could not been seen as the cause behind the discovery of the evidence. This was especially true, the United States suggested, because the nature of the inevitable discovery exception went beyond evidence that might have been discovered to only allow admission of evidence that would have been discovered. This could be ensured by applying the preponderance of evidence standard prior to a finding that inevitably discovered evidence was admissible.

Despite its stated desire to limit judicial speculation regarding whether evidence would be admissible, the United States' position would allow considerably more latitude for evidence to be admitted under the exception than Iowa's. The reason was that Iowa argued only for admission of evidence when the factual record could demonstrate that police already had in place a line of lawful investigation that would have led to discovery of the questioned evidence. The United States' position, on the other hand, would allow admission of evidence under that circumstance, plus whenever predictable investigative practices would have led to discovery, even when the police had not initiated it at the time of the violation. It would also allow admission when a private individual would have provided the information necessary to lead police to the evidence. The United States went on to argue that, just as there was no linkage been good faith and admission of evidence in the independent source or attenuation exceptions, there should also be none in the inevitable discovery exception.

The United States also stated that the lack of a good faith requirement would not threaten the deterrent effect of the exclusionary rule. Furthermore, the societal cost of possibly letting criminals go free outweighed any future incentive that adoption of the exception might give police to violate the rights of suspects. The brief went on to argue that because it would almost always be easier to prove that a piece of evidence *was* actually legally discovered than to prove that it *would have been* legally discovered, police were not likely to take legal shortcuts in gathering evidence. There were also, the brief pointed out, other alternative methods, such as civil actions and departmental disciplinary actions, which could act as deterrents on police from relying on the inevitable discovery exception.

Even though the United States did not desire to see a good faith requirement added to the inevitable discovery exception, it argued that if one were, it should be based on the offending police officer's objective understanding of the law rather than his or her subjective intent. Application of such a standard would be devoid of awkward attempts at suppression hearings to try to determine the reasoning behind the offending officer's misbehavior. The United States ended its argument by declaring that if this standard were applied, there would be no basis for ruling that Detective Leaming knew or should have known that he was violating Williams's constitutional rights.

The last *amicus curiae* brief was filed by the National Legal Aid and Defender Association. It supported Williams's position. Its primary argument was that the doctrine of *Stone v. Powell* should not be expanded to eliminate *habeas* review of claimed Sixth Amendment violations. This was because the exclusionary rule was not applied in Sixth Amendment cases for purposes of deterring police from future misbehavior. Instead, it was to ensure that evidence gathered in violation of the right to counsel did not corrupt trial fairness. The reliability of evidence gathered in violation of the Sixth Amendment should not be relevant to its admissibility because the introduction of such evidence at trial undermined the function of the defense counsel and allowed such misbehavior to infect the trial. Allowing the continued exclusion of evidence gathered in violation of the Sixth Amendment and the continual review of such decisions through *habeas* thus helped to safeguard the fairness of the trial process.

Oral Argument

Oral argument for *Nix v. Williams* was held on Wednesday, January 18, 1984. The case was the first argued in the afternoon session, with argument beginning at 1:11 P.M. Brent Appel argued on behalf of Iowa; Kathryn Oberly was granted permission to argue on behalf of the United States as *amicus curiae* supporting the petitioner, and Robert Bartels again argued on behalf of Williams. Brent Appel began with a short history of the case. He then moved on to argue in favor of acceptance of inevitable discovery which was described as an "independent source case with a twist."[9] He was quickly questioned as to whether it was Iowa's position that the scope of the search to find the body was to stop at the county line. He answered that the record demonstrated that the search would have continued into Polk County had Williams not led police to the body. At a later point, Appel discussed all the various parts of the record that demonstrated that the body would indeed have been found. The Court then asked if the only issue really before the Court was whether the questioned evidence was admissible due to the bad faith of Detective Leaming's actions, which resulted in Williams leading the police to the body. Appel answered in the affirmative, adding that it was inappropriate to tack on a good faith requirement to the inevitable discovery exception. This was especially true if the Court adopted the limited version of the inevitable discovery exception supported by Iowa of only allowing illegally gained evidence when the state could demonstrate that a lawful alternative means of discovery was already being pursued. Formulation of the exception in this manner would not give incentive for police to violate rights in the future. Appel also added that, even though the Respondent's Brief argued that the exception should not be applied in Sixth Amendment cases, that was an inappropriate reading of precedents because the exception still allowed the defense to cross-examine all witnesses at trial concerning the questioned evidence, thus preserving a fair trial. Appel emphasized to the Court:

All the Petitioner asks here is to put law enforcement back in the status quo before the unconstitutional violation occurred. This Court has never applied the exclusionary rule, to the best of my knowledge, in a context that in fact puts law enforcement in a position that's worse.[10]

When the justices had no further questions, Appel requested that he be allowed to reserve the remainder of his time for rebuttal.

Speaking for the United States, Kathryn Oberly argued in favor of the inevitable discovery exception because it followed the tradition that the Court had established with the independent source exception by not allowing the police to be placed in a better position due to legal violations, while at the same time not placing society in a worse position by keeping reliable, untainted evidence from the jury. She also argued that the two major objections to the inevitable discovery exception—that it undermines the deterrent function of the exclusionary rule and that it forces courts to engage in speculation—were unfounded if the exception were properly applied. In replying to a question by the Court, Oberly also clarified that even though the United States had not taken a position in its brief on expanding the reasoning of *Stone v. Powell* to Sixth Amendment cases such as this one, it fully supported the State's position.

Based on how the oral argument went, Robert Bartels may have had a premonition that the justices were not predisposed to Williams's position. Bartels was only allowed to finish his first sentence before the justices began interrupting him with questions. In fact, Bartels was interrupted a total of sixty-seven times, compared to twenty-three interruptions for the State of Iowa and seventeen for the United States. Bartels was pressed hard to explain why he believed that Sixth Amendment exclusionary cases should not be resolved in the same way as Fourth Amendment exclusionary cases. After explaining that the exclusionary rule protected different interests depending on which constitutional amendment was violated, Bartels went on to try to convince the Court that the questioned evidence would not have been inevitably discovered. As a result, Bartels suggested that either the Supreme Court or the Eighth Circuit of the Court of Appeals, which had not ruled on inevitability due to its finding that there was a lack of good faith, should review the issue. He then explained the various reasons why he believed the issue should be revisited. One of the lighter moments during Bartels's presentation occurred when he was being pressed by the Court to admit that there were real societal costs incurred by excluding evidence that may have the effect of allowing a guilty person to go free. After arguing that Williams's guilt was in question, the Court again asked him about the societal costs. His answer—"Your honor, there is always a social cost, and believe me, I know about it. Fifteen years I have been on the same case"—drew laughter from the Court.[11]

THE DECISION AND OPINIONS

After oral argument, the Court retired from public view on the case until it announced its decision on June 11, 1984. In that decision the Court in a 7–2 decision reversed the grant of *habeas corpus*. The majority opinion, written by Chief Justice Warren Burger and joined by Justices Byron White, Harry Blackmun, Lewis Powell, William Rehnquist, and Sandra Day O'Connor, started with a review of the facts in the case and its history. Chief Justice Burger then moved on to discuss the heart of the case, the role of the exclusionary rule in the American legal system. The opinion pointed out that Williams's arguments in favor of upholding the grant of *habeas corpus* because the body and the related physical evidence should not have been admitted at trial were based on two things. The first was that the body and all resulting evidence should have been considered "fruit of the poisonous tree" since it was directly found through the violation of Williams's right to counsel. The second was that if the inevitable discovery exception to the exclusionary rule were constitutionally permissible, it had to include the element of police good faith, which Williams claimed had not existed.

After an examination of the history of the exclusionary rule, the Court found the inevitable discovery exception to be compatible with the Constitution. The Court reached this decision by reading the history of the exclusionary rule to ensure that its only function was to deter future police violations of constitutionally protected rights. While this interpretation of the reasons behind the exclusionary rule demonstrates a selective reading of its entire history, it was consistent with how the Burger Court had interpreted the rule. In the opinion's reading of *Silverthorne Lumber Co. v. United States*[12] the lesson to be learned was *not* that derivative evidence would also be excluded from trial when its discovery was the result of illegal behavior. Instead, the point that the Court emphasized from *Silverthorne* was that such information did not become sacred and inaccessible due to the independent source exception to the exclusionary rule. *Wong Sun v. United States*[13] provided a similar lesson about the attenuation exception, which explained that illegally seized evidence did not have to be suppressed if it "has [also] been come at by . . . means sufficiently distinguishable to be purged of the primary taint."[14] The existence of these two exceptions to the exclusionary rule, neither of which required good faith on the part of the police, allowed the Court to conclude that the court of appeals had erred in insisting that police act in good faith in order for the inevitable discovery exception to be applicable.

The central point in the majority opinion's reading of the history of the exclusionary rule was that our judicial system has accepted the exclusionary rule because of its deterrent effect despite its high social cost of, at times, letting the guilty go free. This has been acceptable since the "prosecution is not to be put in a better position than it would have been in if no illegality had transpired."[15] In cases where there was police misconduct, the Court believed that a balance had to be reached between the competing interests of deterring police abuses and allowing juries all probative evidence. The Court then pointed out that in past cases involving the independent source doctrine it had been understood "that the interest of society in deterring unlawful police conduct and the public interest in having juries receive all probative evidence of a crime are properly balanced by putting the police in the same, not a *worse*, position that they would have been in if no police error or misconduct had occurred."[16] As a result of this past history, even though there was a difference between the independent source and inevitable discovery exceptions to the exclusionary rule, the Court believed there was "a functional similarity between these two doctrines in that exclusion of evidence that would inevitably have been discovered would also put the government in a worse position, because the police would have obtained that evidence if no misconduct had taken place."[17]

Having accepted the inevitable discovery exception to the exclusionary rule into our body of law, the Court had to set some standards for its application. In doing so, the Court stated that tainted evidence would be admissible if the prosecution could prove by a preponderance of the evidence that the information would have been found inevitably by lawful means. When such a situation exists, "then the deterrence rationale has so little basis that the evidence should be received."[18]

The Court also held that in meeting its burden the prosecution did not have to show that the police acted in good faith. This was because such a showing would place courts in the position of withholding truthful evidence from juries that would place the "police in a *worse* position than they would have been if no unlawful conduct had transpired."[19] This, the Court believed, would have placed too high a societal cost on our system of justice and its search for truth. Furthermore, the Court believed that a showing of good faith on the part of police wouldn't effect future deterrence because "when an officer is aware that the evidence will inevitably be discovered, he will try to avoid engaging in any questionable practice" to ensure the evidence's admissibility.[20]

Overall, the Court believed that integrity and fairness required that evidence that would inevitably have been discovered should be admitted at trial, even in the case of Sixth Amendment right to counsel violations. The Court noted that the purpose of the right to counsel was to promote fairness through the adversary process by allowing cross-examination to test the reliability of evidence. Furthermore, the presence of counsel during the trip from Davenport to Des Moines would have had no "bearing on the reliability of the body as evidence."[21] Fairness is assured only when the State and the accused stand in the same position that they would be in had there been no illegalities, and "when, as here, the evidence in question would inevitably have been discovered without reference to the police error or misconduct, there is no nexus sufficient to provide a taint and the evidence is admissible."[22]

In *Nix* the Court was persuaded that the discovery of the body of Pamela Powers and related physical evidence was inevitable. This was largely due to the testimony at the suppression hearing of Agent Ruxlow of the Iowa Bureau of Criminal Investigation. Agent Ruxlow had testified that he had organized a search party of around 200 volunteers. These searchers had divided the area consisting of Poweshiek and Jasper counties in grid fashion and then split into teams responsible for specific areas where they were instructed to "check all the roads, the ditches, any culverts . . . or any other places where a small child could be secreted."[23] There was additional testimony that had Williams not led the police to the body, the search would have been resumed and the body discovered in an additional three to five hours. The Court therefore believed that it was clear that the body and additional evidence would have inevitably been discovered by lawful means and overruled the judgment of the court of appeals. Due to its ruling that the inevitable discovery exception was constitutionally permissible, the Court did not decide the question as to whether *Stone v. Powell* should be extended to stop *habeas corpus* review of Sixth Amendment claims.

Justice Byron White wrote a short concurring opinion in which he took pains to point out that in his opinion Detective Leaming had not acted improperly on the trip between Davenport and Des Moines. Instead, Detective Leaming "was no doubt acting as many competent police officers would have acted under similar circumstances and in light of the then-existing law. That five Justices later thought he was mistaken does not call for making him out to be a villain or for a lecture on deliberate police misconduct and its resulting costs to society."[24]

Justice John Paul Stevens also wrote a concurring opinion in which he explained that he could not join in the majority opinion because of its failure to adequately discuss the importance of several key features of the case. Those features included the unusually tragic facts of the case, the clarity of the constitutional violation on the part of the police, and the societal costs incurred when the police avoid following constitutional requirements.

Justice Stevens's first point was that, despite the emotional pull of the issues presented by the facts of this case, the Court in *Brewer v. Williams* made a reasoned decision based on the law. This was despite the fact that none of the justices wished to see a child murderer escape justice. Justice Stevens went on to state that the Court in *Nix v. Williams* had again reached its decision based on reasoned principles rather than the emotional pull of the case.

The second section of Justice Stevens's opinion focused on the constitutional violation that had taken place. Justice Stevens explained that Detective Leaming had clearly violated Williams's Sixth Amendment right to counsel which, according to the ruling in *Massiah v. United States*,[25] began at the start of judicial proceedings.

After emphasizing the callous manner in which Detective Leaming had violated Williams's right to counsel, Justice Stevens went on to state that the inevitable discovery exception was constitutionally permissible and that the preponderance of evidence burden was correct. This was because, despite the denial of counsel during the trip, the admission "of the victim's body, if it would have been discovered anyway, means that the trial in this case was not the product of an inquisitorial process; the process was untainted by illegality."[26] He disagreed, however, with the majority who viewed the societal costs of the exclusionary rule as the exclusion of probative evidence. He believed, instead, that society's cost was the delay in justice that resulted when police officers did not comply with the law. He then ended his opinion by asking and answering questions concerning these societal costs:

What is the consequence of the shortcuts that Detective Leaming took when he decided to question Williams in this case and not to wait an hour or so until he arrived in Des Moines? The answer is years and years of unnecessary but costly litigation. Instead of having a 1969 conviction affirmed in routine fashion, the case is still alive 15 years later. Thanks to Detective Leaming, the State of Iowa has expended vast sums of money and countless hours of professional labor in his defense. That expenditure surely provides an adequate deterrent to similar violations; the responsibility for that expenditure lies not with the Constitution, but rather with the constable.[27]

Justice William Brennan filed a dissenting opinion, which was joined by Justice Thurgood Marshall. The opinion agreed that the inevitable discovery exception was constitutionally permissible due to the similarities between it and the independent source exception to the exclusionary rule. Despite this similarity, however, Justice Brennan believed that the majority's opinion showed a disrespect for the exclusionary rule, which caused the majority to be overly zealous in its desire to undermine the rule. This resulted in the majority's failure to identify a basic difference between the two exceptions. That difference was that, in cases involving the independent source exception, the evidence is actually found through lawful means. The inevitable discovery exception, on the other hand, involves evidence that only hypothetically would have been discovered through some alternative legal means. Due to this basic difference, Justice Brennan reasoned, "to ensure that this hypothetical finding is narrowly confined to circumstances that are functionally equivalent to an independent source, and to protect fully the fundamental rights served by the exclusionary rule, I would require clear and convincing evidence before concluding that the government had met its burden of proof on this issue."[28] Justice Brennan went on to state that he would have remanded the case, instructing the lower courts to apply this standard of proof.

As it had done in *Brewer v. Williams*, the Court exercised one of the many legal options open to it. While the inevitable discovery exception was innovative in the sense that this was the first time that the Supreme Court had supported its use, the majority opinion relied on a well-established line of precedents to provide the foundation. Its decision continued the Burger Court trend of narrowing the situations in which the exclusionary rule would be applied. It also allowed the Court to continue its practice of permitting the use of reliable probative evidence when the Court believed its admission would not impact police deterrence in future cases. The Court could just as easily have found support in past decisions if it would have decided to refuse to accept the inevitable discovery exception or determined that it should include a good faith requirement.

NOTES

1. *Brewer v. Williams*, 430 U.S. 387, 415 (1977), (Stevens, J., concurring).
2. *Stone v. Powell*, 428 U.S. 465 (1977).
3. *Nix v. Williams*, 467 U.S. 431, 434 (1984).
4. Brief for Petitioner, p. 11, *Nix v. Williams*, 467 U.S. 431 (1984).
5. Ibid., p. 13.
6. Ibid., p. 15.
7. *Brown v. Illinois*, 422 U.S. 690 (1975), and *Dunaway v. New York*, 442 U.S. 200 (1979).
8. U.S. Amicus Brief, p. 1, *Nix v. Williams*, 467 U.S. 431 (1984).

9. Oral Argument, p. 4, *Nix v. Williams*, 467 U.S. 431 (1984).

10. Ibid., p. 13.

11. Ibid., p. 52.

12. *Silverthorne Lumber Co. v. United States*, 251 U.S. 285 (1920).

13. *Wong Sun v. United States*, 371 U.S. 471 (1963).

14. *Nix v. Williams*, 467 U.S. 431, 442 (1984), *citing Wong Sun v. United States*, 371 U.S. 471, 407.

15. Ibid., p. 443.

16. Ibid.

17. Ibid., p. 444.

18. Ibid.

19. Ibid., p. 445.

20. Ibid., pp. 445–446.

21. Ibid., p. 447.

22. Ibid., p. 448.

23. Ibid., pp. 448–449.

24. Ibid., p. 451 (White, J., concurring).

25. *Massiah v. United States*, 377 U.S. 201 (1964).

26. *Nix v. Williams*, 467 U.S. 431, 456 (1984), (White, J., concurring).

27. Ibid., pp. 457–458.

28. Ibid., p. 459 (Brennan, J., dissenting).

Chapter 11

Aftermath

The restraints which any society must impose upon its police if it wishes to preserve private rights and safeguard the innocent operate inevitably, in some measure, to impair public safety and to afford protection for the guilty. Every society is obliged, therefore, to seek a rational balance between public safety and private rights—to choose between the exigencies of law and order on the one hand and the imperatives of freedom on the other.

—Alan Barth[1]

As Robert Williams has remained in prison to serve his life term, the procedural laws important to the final resolution of the *Williams* case have continued to change. The changes have resulted from the continued exercise of judicial discretion in determining both the facts and law in new cases. The changes in the law have been mixed. Some have helped to clarify what procedures must be followed in order for evidence to be admissible at trial. Other new decisions have made law enforcement officials and lower court judges less sure of what procedures are acceptable. This chapter summarizes the changes in the procedural laws that were central to the *Williams* case.

CHANGES IN *MIRANDA*

In the years after *Brewer v. Williams*[2] the Court has tried to clarify when and how to apply the procedural guidelines created in *Miranda v. Arizona*[3] that were designed to protect Fifth and Sixth Amendment rights. One of the legal issues that had separated many of the judges who had an opportunity to rule on the *Williams* case was whether the "Christian burial speech" had indeed constituted an interrogation. The lack of direct questioning led some of the judges who heard the case to believe that there had been no interrogation, while others concentrated on Detective Leaming's comment that he was trying to get as much information out of Williams as possible during the trip and found that there was an interrogation. In *Rhode Island v. Innis*,[4] decided by the Supreme Court in 1980, the Court addressed the issue of what constitutes interrogation in cases involving possible police abuses of *Miranda*. The Court's opinion, written by Justice Potter Stewart, held that an interrogation under *Miranda* includes not only direct questioning, but also any actions or words that are the functional equivalent of interrogation. Under this definition, *Miranda* has been violated when police have not secured a proper waiver from a suspect held in custody and they can reasonably foresee that their words or actions would be likely to result in the suspect giving incriminating statements. The Court noted that the focus in determining whether police actions would cause suspects to incriminate themselves should be on the suspects' perceptions of the situation, not the intent of the police. The Court's decision to define interrogation broadly to include not just direct questioning but also functional equivalents gives judges better guidance in factual circumstances such as those presented in the *Williams* case. However, it still gives them considerable discretion in determining whether police actions were reasonably likely to result in the suspect giving incriminating statements.

Another issue concerning *Miranda* warnings that the Court has had to consider involves what constitutes custody. One answer as to what constitutes custody for the purposes of *Miranda* came in *Berkemer v. McCarty*.[5] The case involved the question as to whether *Miranda* applied to routine traffic stops. The Court ruled that, because routine traffic stops are usually brief and the motorist is then allowed to continue down the road, *Miranda* was not applicable. If, however, a person is stopped for a traffic violation and then taken into custody as a result, *Miranda* is applicable. The Court believed that when people were taken into custody, they had an equal right to the procedural safeguards of *Miranda* regardless of the severity of the offense for which they were arrested. Furthermore, creating different procedures depending on the severity of the charge would only serve to undermine the clarity and purpose of *Miranda*.

The Court's movement to firm up the definition of interrogation and the meaning of custody can be seen as an attempt to clarify what types of police actions constitute violations of *Miranda*. In the 1981 case of *Edwards v. Arizona*[6] the Supreme Court attempted to re-establish a blanket rule that would provide clear guidelines that police and lower court judges could apply in all cases when a person was in custody. This case came to the Court after Robert Edwards was arrested on charges of robbery, burglary, and first-degree murder. After arrest, Edwards was given his *Miranda* warnings and after answering some questions he requested an attorney. The police respected his request and the interrogation was cut off because no attorney was present. The next morning, the police initiated another round of interrogation, even though Edwards told the jailer that he did not want to speak with anyone. Edwards was told that he had to speak with the officers and was again advised of his rights. During the second interrogation, the police drew incriminating statements from Edwards that were used at the trial, which ended with a conviction. The Supreme Court reversed the conviction, ruling that once an individual asserted his rights, a valid waiver could not be demonstrated simply by the fact that he cooperated when the police initiated a later interrogation session. The Court went on to clarify that once rights have been asserted, suspects may not be subject to further attempts at interrogation without the presence of counsel. The only exception was to be if the suspect initiated further conversations with the police.

The desire of the Court for *Edwards v. Arizona* to serve as a blanket rule can be illustrated by the 1990 case of *Minnick v. Mississippi*.[7] In this case, the Court clarified that the *Edwards* rule did not allow the State to fulfill its obligations by giving individuals who had asserted their rights an initial consultation with an attorney, but then making repeated attempts to get those suspects to waive their rights and agree to be interrogated. Instead, the Court again emphasized that *Edwards* required suspects to initiate all conversations with the police after they have asserted their rights, even after an initial consultation with an attorney.

A line of cases that moved away from the clarity of *Edwards* and risked confusing police and the lower courts in their efforts to adhere to *Miranda* included *California v. Prysock*[8] and *Duckworth v. Eagan*.[9] In both of these cases the Court ruled that police do not have to be precise in their recitation of the *Miranda* warnings. In these cases the police gave versions of the warnings that differed from those the Court had announced in *Miranda*. In *Prysock* the police did not mention that the suspect had a right to appointed counsel until after he was told that he had the right to consult with an attorney before and during any police questioning. In *Duckworth* the suspect was informed that he had a right to appointed counsel if and when he went to court. In both cases the suspect proceeded to give self-incriminating statements that were used at trial to gain a conviction. On review the Supreme Court ruled that both of the faulty warnings were acceptable and that police did not have to be precise in using the language of *Miranda*. The Court reasoned that police warnings simply had to convey to suspects the rights to which they were entitled and that both of these versions adequately explained all of the basic protections of *Miranda*.

CHANGES IN THE EXCLUSIONARY RULE

In 1984, the same year that *Nix v. Williams*[10] was decided, the Court made two other decisions that had a dramatic effect on the exclusionary rule. These were *New York v. Quarles*[11] and *United States v. Leon*.[12] *New York v. Quarles* also had an influence on *Miranda*. In *Quarles* a rape suspect, Benjamin Quarles, whom police were told had a gun, was sighted. When police caught up to him in a supermarket, Quarles was frisked and hand-cuffed. When the officer noticed that Quarles's holster was empty, he asked where the gun was and Quarles told the officer. Quarles was then read his rights and continued to cooperate with the police. At trial, Quarles successfully tried to have the gun and original statements suppressed for being tainted due to the lack of *Miranda* warnings. The State appealed and the Supreme Court granted *certiorari*. Rather than applying the exclusionary rule and suppressing the use of the gun as evidence found in violation of *Miranda*, the Court created a "public safety" exception to the exclusionary rule. The Court's decision applied a cost-benefit balancing approach to the competing interests and found that public safety was more important than the protection of the right against self-incrimination in this circumstance. Justice William Rehnquist's majority opinion explained that, in the course of their duties, police have to make snap decisions based on the information available to them. Under these conditions, if an officer believes the public safety to be at risk, the courts should not try to second-guess the situation with *post hoc* reasoning. The opinion went on to reason that because this exception did not give police incentive to engage in future violations, courts should allow officers to follow their best instincts to protect their own and the public's safety.

United States v. Leon established the "good faith" exception to the exclusionary rule. In *Leon* police had information from a confidential informant whose reliability was unproven. Due to the tip, police established surveillance over Leon and others suspected of drug trafficking. Based on what the police learned, they, with the help of the district attorney's office, prepared an application for a search warrant. The warrant was signed by a magistrate and then served by the police, resulting in a variety of evidence. At trial the defendants moved to have the evidence suppressed and the judge found that the affidavit supporting the warrant was inadequate, and the warrant should not have been granted. As a result, the evidence was suppressed. The government then sought review of the decision. The Supreme Court again applied a cost-benefit balancing approach and ruled that since the police had followed the letter of the law there was not enough deterrent effect in suppressing the evidence to outweigh the high social costs of allowing the guilty to go free, so it was unnecessary to suppress the evidence. This was because the purpose of the exclusionary rule was to deter police misconduct, not punish the errors of members of the judicial branch. The Court noted, however, that the key to future applications of the exception was that police had to have acted in good faith. It warned that if an officer knowingly made false remarks or was reckless with the truth in an affidavit, the exception could not be applied. Nor could it be applied if a magistrate abandoned the judicial duty of fairly judging the merits of each application for a warrant.

The Application of the Inevitable Discovery Exception

The most interesting change in law to come out of the entire *Williams* case was the Court's acceptance of the inevitable discovery exception to the exclusionary rule. Even though the Court clearly embraced the exception in *Nix v. Williams*, it did not do much to clarify the scope of the exception. As Iowa's brief in *Nix* had pointed out, there were a wide variety of factual situations in which the exception could possibly be applied. The Supreme Court, however, did not explain under which circumstances the exception would be applicable. In fact, there were only two areas in which the Supreme Court provided clear guidelines. The first was its instruction in the burden of proof required to invoke the exception. The Court clearly announced that the burden to be used in these cases is a preponderance of the evidence. The second guideline the Court established in *Nix* was that the good faith requirement had no place in determining whether evidence should be suppressed under the inevitable discovery exception. The unwillingness of the Supreme Court to establish other guidelines for the exception has given the lower courts the ability to exercise their own discretion in determining when the exception should be applied.

Because of the factual situation in *Nix*, there was never any question that all the lower federal courts would accept the application of the inevitable discovery exception in cases that met the requirements that Iowa's Brief for the Petitioner categorized as "independent inevitable discovery." In these cases the police are simultaneously carrying out two lines of investigation that would eventually lead to discovery of the evidence, but an illegal method bears fruit before the legal alternative. All the lower federal courts have demanded that the lawful means that police claim would have led to the inevitable discovery of evidence have to be totally independent of the legal violation they are hoping to overcome.[13] The lower courts have also been uniform in applying the exception to a wider range of legal violations beyond the right to counsel.[14]

A more difficult question that has been confronted by the lower federal courts since *Nix v. Williams* is whether the exception can be used when the police were not engaged in an ongoing lawful investigation at the time that the constitutional violation occurred. This was the factual circumstance that Iowa's Brief for the Petitioner referred to as "hypothetical independent source." If one reads *Nix* narrowly, it can be interpreted to require an ongoing alternative legal investigation, such as the grid search that was being conducted in that case. The Court, however, failed to specify whether such an ongoing investigation was a requirement in applying the inevitable discovery exception.

Due to the Supreme Court's silence concerning the need for an ongoing, parallel investigation, the possibility for a variety of applications of the exception by the lower federal courts had existed. At first glance it would seem that such variations have developed in the courts of appeals. A minority of the courts of appeal have stated that evidence can only be inevitably discovered when police have an ongoing investigation in place at the time of illegality.[15] These courts describe the inevitable discovery exception as being quite narrow in its scope. Despite the claims of these courts, it would be wrong to conclude that there is a lack of uniformity regarding the need for an ongoing, concurrent, legal investigation. This is because, with the exception of the Second Circuit of the Court of Appeals, the few courts that have said there is a need for an ongoing investigation have gone on to rule that inevitable discovery may exist in a wider variety of circumstances.[16]

The vast majority of lower federal courts have allowed admission of tainted evidence under a wider variety of circumstances. These courts may be said to have adopted the "hypothetical independent source" model of the exception. These circuits have been direct in asserting that there is no need for an ongoing independent investigation at the time of a legal violation to apply the inevitable discovery exception.[17] This group of courts has ruled that if routine police procedure would have resulted in discovery of the tainted evidence at a later point in time, it is admissible.[18] The routine police procedures that have satisfied a finding of inevitable discovery, even though a constitutional violation took place first, have included stop and frisks,[19] standard operating procedures for establishing sales of firearms,[20] searches incident to a lawful arrest,[21] development of probable cause through drug-sniffing dogs,[22] and identifications leading to alien status.[23] One of the more common routine procedures used to overcome legal violations in which evidence is discovered involves inventory searches. An inventory search does not have to meet the probable cause requirements of the Fourth Amendment because inventory searches are not conducted for purposes of investigation. Instead, the purpose is to protect a person's possessions while the police have control of them. The existence of support for discovery coming out of standardized procedures demonstrates that the rulings of the lower federal courts have been close to uniform in their support of the "hypothetical independent source" standard for the exception.

The last category of inevitable discovery cases described by Iowa's Brief for the Petitioner was that of "dependent inevitable discovery." In this scenario, police claims of discovery are seen as highly speculative because of the lack of a lawful ongoing investigation or standardized police procedure that would have led to discovery. The exception is relied on as a last-ditch attempt to salvage use of evidence that was found through constitutional violations. The largest variations in how the inevitable discovery exception is applied by the lower federal courts involve this category of cases.

In "dependent inevitable discovery" cases, one question the lower federal courts have had to answer is whether the exception should be applied in Fourth Amendment cases when there was an illegal search due to the lack of a warrant. The lower federal courts have developed three different answers as to whether the police can claim inevitable discovery after a warrant violation. The first answer has been that if the police gained a legal warrant after the original violation, the tainted evidence can avoid suppression.[24] The second answer has provided police with even more leeway in avoiding the warrant requirement of the Fourth Amendment. These courts have used inevitable discovery to allow tainted evidence if police can show that they had probable cause for a search warrant, regardless of the fact that one was never secured.[25] A third answer has been provided by a number of courts that have been stubborn and consistently held that the warrant requirement must be followed or all evidence has to be suppressed due to the exclusionary rule.[26]

Another indication that the government may be trying to salvage the admissibility of illegally gathered evidence can be found when the government argues that it would have been led to evidence by the efforts of private individuals. The courts who have examined this question have interpreted the exception to mean that the police do not have to be the ones initiating the alternative means of discovery; instead, it could be a private party.[27]

The Supreme Court also failed to provide specific guidance as to whether the exception applies to both primary and derivative evidence. In *Nix*, the Court only had to decide whether the exception applied to derivative evidence. The lower federal courts have been uniform in ruling that the exception applies to both derivative and primary evidence.[28]

Despite the possibility for variations in how the inevitable discovery exception has been applied, there are not wide discrepancies in the lower courts. In fact, in cases in which the factual scenario is comparable to either the "independent hypothetical discovery" or "hypothetical independent source," the lower federal courts have been uniform in their willingness to apply the exception. The lower federal courts have also been amazingly uniform in using the exception to allow both derivative and primary evidence. The only scenario in which there has been a lack of uniformity in the lower federal courts has been in "dependent inevitable discovery" cases.

CONCLUSION

Despite its acceptance by the public, mechanical jurisprudence oversimplifies the process by which decisions are made in court, as does the myth that judges play little role in deciding the meaning of the law. The *Williams* case illustrates the fallacies of these myths. The *Williams* case demonstrates that the courts that heard the case were not capable of mechanically arriving at a single solution. The existence of procedural laws complicated the process by giving the judges who heard the case a plethora of legal options that they could use their discretion to select among. The complex and lengthy legal histories that exist for most procedural laws have created a number of precedents that allow judges to consider a variety of legal options when resolving a legal issue. This means that the decision as to which procedural law a judge will rely on frustrates the myth that we are ruled by laws rather than by the decisions of judges. On top of this problem, mechanical jurisprudence suffers further inadequacies because judges are also in a position to pick and choose from the competing versions of the facts that have been presented at trial. Thus, judges have the judicial freedom to be able to rely on a set of subjective facts and procedural laws that neatly advance the decision that they make. This freedom of action means that, on any given case, no two judges may agree on the decision reached, let alone the reasoning behind their decisions. It also give individuals who are convicted incentive to appeal their case. These appeals have the capacity to create substantial delays in the legal system. The delay in bringing a final resolution to the *Williams* case and other criminal cases are aggravating when people desire a system of quick and sure justice. Before concluding that the delays resulting from the appeals process are intolerable, some of the goals that we want the legal system to achieve should be considered. These goals include the ability to predict the law, the consistent application of the law, the ability to pragmatically advance justice in individual cases, and the ability to ensure that only the guilty are punished.

If the ability to predict the outcome of how a court will decide a case is an essential goal, the *Williams* case shows that present practice falls short. The inability to determine which subjective facts a judge will find convincing adds to the difficulty of being able to reason with any assurance as to how the procedural law will be interpreted and applied. There are, however, ways to improve predictability in the law.

One way prediction could be enhanced would be if changes were made in the *habeas corpus* process. By narrowing the types of cases that could be brought up for *habeas corpus* review, as was done in *Stone v. Powell*,[29] the Supreme Court or Congress could give greater authority to the courts of original jurisdiction. In *Stone v. Powell* the Court denied state prisoners review of exclusion claims in Fourth Amendment cases if their search and seizure claims had received a full and fair review in state courts. Expanding the scope of *Stone v. Powell* would increase the capacity for predicting decisions within state jurisdictions. Unfortunately, limiting *habeas corpus* review would not only improve predictability at the state level, but it would also have a negative impact on the desire to have consistent application of the law. By removing cases from federal review, the interpretation given to constitutional provisions would primarily be left to the state courts. This could result in a multiplicity of interpretations at the state level. An example may be found in the period in which *Betts v. Brady*[30] was the ruling precedent in right to counsel cases and states differed in their decisions as to what circumstances required appointment of counsel for indigents.

In *Nix v. Williams* Iowa asked the Supreme Court to broaden *Stone* to also include cases involving *Miranda* violations. In 1993 in the case of *Winthrow v. Williams*[31] the Court declined another opportunity to limit the ability of federal courts to review claims of *Miranda* violations in *habeas corpus* proceedings. Justice David Souter's majority opinion explained that there was a substantial difference in the interests protected by the exclusionary rule and *Miranda*. The differences he expressed reflected the views of the Brief of the Respondent filed by Williams in *Nix v. Williams*. This was because Justice Souter stated that the purpose behind exclusion of Fourth Amendment claims was to deter future police violations against unreasonable search and seizures and any correction to police procedures in *habeas* proceedings came so late as to not serve that function. In addition, because the evidence found in Fourth Amendment violations was reliable, it frustrated the truth-finding function of the courts. *Miranda*, on the other hand, protected a fundamental trial right by ensuring that unreliable statements that came from custodial interrogation could not be used at trial. Due to the differences in the kinds of protections offered by the Fourth Amendment and *Miranda*, the Court decided to continue to review state court decisions that *Miranda* had not been violated.

Prediction of outcome could also be gained and delays halted at the expense of discretion. Better prediction would result if the Supreme Court developed blanket rules regarding procedural violations of the Constitution. For example, in the first round of appeals Judge Hanson of the district court believed that the Sixth Amendment created a blanket rule when there was an agreement between police and the suspect's attorney not to interrogate the suspect. In such a situation, according to Judge Hanson, no interrogation could proceed unless the attorney was informed first. Blanket rules such as this clearly distinguish proper procedure from improper. However, in the years leading up to *Brewer v. Williams*, the Court shied away from blanket rules and instead emphasized a decision-making process that concentrated on the hazy world of case-by-case reasoning. Since the *Williams* case was decided, some steps have been taken toward creating blanket rule requirements, such as the decision in *Edwards v. Arizona*, but there is still considerable opportunity for judges to make unpredictable decisions.

Removal of discretion to allow for better prediction by the creation of blanket rules would affect the goal of pragmatically ensuring the imposition of individualized justice based on the particular circumstances of each case. The ability to adjust the application of procedural laws on a case-by-case basis preserves the flexibility that allows judges to find legal rules to attempt to ensure that people will be treated fairly by the legal system in light of their actions. In some cases judges may find legal rules that further the desire that dangerous individuals whose guilt is not in question will not avoid punishment. In essence, flexibility in some cases helps to create a legal safety net to ensure that people who commit heinous crimes will not go free. The evolution of the inevitable discovery exception demonstrates this phenomenon. After Williams's conviction was overturned in *Brewer v. Williams*, the majority of opinions written expressed concerns that Williams may win his freedom. It was in light of this worry that Justice Stewart suggested that there might be an inevitable discovery exception to the exclusionary rule. Then, when inevitable discovery was first announced by the Supreme Court in *Nix v. Williams*, it seemed to be a narrow exception to the exclusionary rule, which was to be applied to derivative evidence when police were already involved in an ongoing investigation that would have led police to the evidence that was illegally discovered. Because the exception neatly fit the factual scenario of Williams's case, his conviction was upheld. In application by the lower federal courts, the exception has expanded to allow police to use inevitable discovery in much broader circumstances. The exception is now broad enough so that it can be applied to both primary and derivative evidence. The exception also allows admission of evidence gathered by methods that are clearly outside those accepted by the Constitution, even when there was no ongoing alternative investigation in place at the time of the legal violation. The broadness of the exception has allowed the conviction of individuals who otherwise may have avoided this fate.

The unfortunate part of flexibility is that it allows judges so much discretion that it takes away from the ability to provide consistency in the law and to predict the outcome of cases. This produces an environment similar to that described by Frank Horack when he wrote, "When a judicial decision is pegged on one rule of interpretation and in a succeeding case the contrary result is dictated by a conflicting but equally authoritarian rule, it is time to recognize that we are dealing neither with 'rules' nor with 'interpretation,' but with 'explanations' of decisions independently determined."[32] Indeed, a casual observation of the ability of each court in the *Williams* case to rely on different subjective facts and procedural laws could easily cause observers to believe that the law only means what the last court to review it says it means.

If the right to appeal a conviction were withdrawn, it would end delays in justice but it would also have an impact on the ability of the legal system to be able to ensure that only the guilty are punished. To many people it may seem that appeals are nothing more than a process used by the guilty to avoid the punishment that comes with conviction. Historically, however, the appeals process has and continues to play a much larger role in our legal system. This includes the function of protecting the innocent from unjustifiably being convicted and punished. In *Brown v. Mississippi*,[33] for example, there is little doubt that had it not been for Supreme Court review, the conviction of an innocent person would have led to a severe injustice. The delay brought about in the appeals process allows a higher court to review a lower court's decision and may result in upholding legal rights by requiring a new and fairer second trial in which the government may not be able to meet its burden of proof and gain a conviction due to the innocence of the accused. The appeals process has also helped to ensure that there will be a limitation on the ability of the governments to arbitrarily interfere in the lives of their citizens. If it were not for cases such as *Mapp v. Ohio*,[34] it is unlikely that police would have stopped the use of intrusive police procedures that most Americans consider objectionable. Therefore, another benefit that continues to be gained from the appeals process is the increased professionalization of law enforcement.

While we may wish that our legal system worked as smoothly as mechanical jurisprudence suggests, the complexities of the legal system reveal no easy answers for developing a functional system that has the capacity for attaining all of the goals that we hope a system of criminal justice will accomplish. The dilemma apparent in satisfying all the goals we have for the legal system is not surprising, since the system attempts to balance two competing factors that often run at cross-currents with each other. These are the desire for the government to itself obey the law and be fair when interfering in the lives of citizens, while also ensuring that the guilty be caught and punished. Because of the difficulty involved in realizing both these values, it will remain imperative for members of the judiciary to continue to try to maintain a judicious balance. As in the cases of *Brewer v. Williams* and *Nix v. Williams*, the decisions that will be made by judges to balance these values will continue to be a source of outrage to some and admiration to others.

NOTES

1. Cited in Jacob W. Landynski, *Search and Seizure and the Supreme Court: A Study in Constitutional Interpretation* (Baltimore: The John Hopkins Press, 1966), p. 124.
2. *Brewer v. Williams*, 430 U.S. 387 (1977).
3. *Miranda v. Arizona*, 384 U.S. 436 (1966).
4. *Rhode Island v. Innis*, 446 U.S. 291 (1980).
5. *Berkemer v. McCarty*, 468 U.S. 420 (1984).
6. *Edwards v. Arizona*, 451 U.S. 477 (1981).
7. *Minnick v. Mississippi*, 498 U.S. 146 (1990).
8. *California v. Prysock*, 453 U.S. 355 (1981).
9. *Duckworth v. Eagan*, 492 U.S. 195 (1989).
10. *Nix v. Williams*, 467 U.S. 431 (1984).
11. *New York v. Quarles*, 467 U.S. 649 (1984).
12. *United States v. Leon*, 468 U.S. 897 (1984).
13. See *United States v. Salgado*, 807 F.2d 603, 608 (7th Cir. 1986); *United*

States v. Pimentel, 810 F.2d 366, 369 (2nd Cir. 1987); *United States v. Zapata*, 18 F.3d 971, 978 (1st Cir. 1994); *United States v. Eng*, 971 F.2d 854, 861 (2nd Cir. 1992); *United States v. Martinez-Gallegos*, 807 F.2d 868, 870 (9th Cir. 1987); and *United States v. Vasquez de Reyes*, No. 97-7328, 1998 U.S. App. LEXIS 15119, at *9–10 (3rd Cir. July 8, 1998).

14. The inevitable discovery exception was held applicable to Fifth Amendment violations in *United States v. Martinez-Gallegos*, 807 F.2d 868, 870 (9th Cir. 1987); and the Fourth Amendment in *United States v. Cherry*, 759 F.2d. 1196, 1206–07 (5th Cir. 1985). It has also been held to apply to civil cases in *Center Art Galleries-Hawaii, Inc. v. United States*, 875 F.2d 747 (9th Cir. 1989).

15. See *United States v. Satterfield*, 743 F.2d 827, 846 (11th Cir. 1985); *United States v. Terzado-Madruga*, 897 F.2d 1099 (11th Cir. 1990); *United States v. Eng*, 971 F.2d 854, 861 (2nd Cir. 1992); *United States v. Wilson*, 36 F.3d 1298, 1304 (5th Cir. 1994); and *United States v. Conner*, 127 F.3d 663, 667 (8th Cir. 1997).

16. See *United States v. Gonzalez*, No. 96-3148, 1997 U.S. App. LEXIS 6126 at *5 (8th Cir. April 1, 1997); *United States v. Hernandez-Cano* 808 F.2d 779, 783–84 (11th Cir. 1987); and *Wicker v. McCotter*, 783 F.2d 487, 498 (5th Cir. 1986).

17. See *United States v. Silvestri*, 787 F.2d 736, 744–46 (1st Cir. 1986); *United States v. Zapata*, 18 F.3d 971, 978 (1st Cir. 1994); *United States v. Larsen*, 127 F.3d 984, 986 (10th Cir. 1997); *United States v. Thomas*, 955 F.2d 207, 210 (4th Cir. 1992); *United States v. Kennedy*, 61 F.3d 494, 499–500 (6th Cir. 1995); *United States v. Jones*, 72 F.3d 1324, 1329–34 (7th Cir. 1995); *Wicker v. McCotter*, 783 F.2d 487, 498 (5th Cir. 1986); *United States v. Boatwright*, 822 F.2d 862, 864 (9th Cir. 1987); and *United States v. Merriweather*, 777 F.2d 503 (9th Cir. 1985).

18. See *United States v. Boatwright*, 822 F.2d 862, 864–65 (9th Cir. 1987) (This case does, however, express concerns that the lack of an ongoing independent lawful investigation may be a disincentive for deterrence); *United States v. Thomas*, 955 F.2d 207, 210–11 (4th Cir. 1992); *United States v. Ramirez-Sandoval*, 872 F.2d 1392, 1399 (9th Cir. 1987); and *United States v. Vasquez de Reyes*, No. 97-7328m 1998 U.S. App. LEXIS 15119 at *9–10 (3rd Cir. July 8, 1998).

19. *United States v. Eyclicio-Montoya*, 70 F.3d 1158, 1167–68 (10th Cir. 1995).

20. *United States v. Gravens*, No. 96-3704, U.S. App. LEXIS 33284, at *19 (7th Cir. April 17, 1997).

21. *United States v. Glen*, No. 98-1361MN, U.S. App. LEXIS 20858, at *8–9 (8th Cir. June 9, 1998); and *United States v. Jones*, No. 96-10464, U.S. App. LEXIS 16446 (9th Cir. July 21, 1998) at *26–27.

22. *United States v. Toledo*, No. 97-3065, U.S. App. LEXIS 1954, at *12–13 (10th Cir. Feb. 12, 1998); and *United States v. Hammons*, No. 98-1101, U.S. App. LEXIS 20786, at 15–16 (8th Cir. May 12, 1998).

23. *United States v. Meglar*, No. 96-4582, U.S. App. Lexis 6864, at *32 (4th Cir. Oct. 27, 1997); and *United States v. Ramirez-Martinez*, No. 96-4360 U.S. App. LEXIS 8796 at *2–3 (4th Cir. April, 1997) (per curiam).

24. See *United States v. Merriweather*, 777 F.2d 503, 505 (9th Cir. 1985); *United States v. Fitzharris*, 633 F.2d 416, 421 (5th Cir. 1980); *United States v. Salgado*, 807 F.2d 603, 608–09 (7th Cir. 1986); *United States v. Moscatiello*, 771 F.2d 589, 603–04 (1st Cir. 1985); and *United States v. Whitehorn*, 813 F.2d 646, 650 (4th Cir. 1987).

25. *United States v. Silvestri*, 787 F.2d 736, 746 (1st Cir. 1986). See also *United*

States v. Lamas, 930 F.2d 1099, 1103 (5th Cir. 1991); *United States v. Raborn*, 872 F.2d 589, 595 (5th Cir. 1989); *United States v. Medina*, 887 F.2d 528, 533 n. 7 (5th Cir. 1989); and *Calamia v. New York*, 879 F.2d 1025, 1032 (2nd Cir. 1989).

26. *United States v. Johnson*, 22 F.3d 674, 684 (6th Cir. 1994); *United States v. Cherry*, 759 F.2d 1196, 1206 (5th Cir. 1985); and *United States v. Allen*, No. 97-4100, 1998 U.S. App. LEXIS 24124, at *27–28 (4th Cir. Sept. 28, 1998); *United States v. Brown*, 64 F.3d 1083, 1085 (7th Cir. 1995); *United States v. Madrid*, No. 97–3959, 1998 U.S. App. LEXIS 20785, at *24 (8th Cir. August 26, 1998); *United States v. Satterfield*, 743 F.2d 827, 846–47 (11th Cir. 1984); *United States v. Mejia*, 69 F.3d 309, 319–20 (9th Cir. 1995); *United States v. Cherry*, 759 F.2d 1196, 1206 (5th Cir. 1985); *United States v. Echegoyen*, 799 F.2d 1271, 1280 (9th Cir. 1986); and *United States v. Buchanan*, 904 F.2d 349, 357 (6th Cir. 1990).

27. *United States v. Hernandez-Cano* 808 F.2d 779, 783–84 (11th Cir. 1987).

28. See *United States v. Pimentel*, 810 F.2d 366, 368–70 (2nd Cir. 1987); *United States v. McConnell*, 903 F.2d 566, 570 (8th Cir. 1990); *United States v. Vasquez de Reyes*, No. 97-7328m 1998 U.S. App. LEXIS 15119 at *9–10 (3rd Cir. July 8, 1998); *United States v. Andrade*, 784 F.2d 1431, 1433 (9th Cir. 1986); *United States v. Silvestri*, 787 F.2d 293, 307 (8th Cir. 1983); *United States v. Eyclicio-Montoya*, 70 F.3d 1158, 1167–68 (10th Cir. 1995); *United States v. Silvestri*, 787 F.2d 736, 746 (1st Cir. 1986); *United States v. Zapata*, 18 F.3d 971, 979 (1st Cir. 1994); *United States v. Whitehorn*, 813 F.2d 646, 650 (4th Cir. 1987); *United States v. Moscatiello*, 771 F.2d 589, 604 (1st Cir. 1985); *United States v. Arango*, 879 F.2d 1501, 1506–07 n.2 (7th Cir. 1989); *United States v. Mancera-Londono*, 912 F.2d 373 (9th Cir. 1990); *United States v. Gale*, 952 F.2d 1412, 1416 (D.C. Cir. 1992); *United States v. Merriweather*, 777 F.2d 503, 506 (9th Cir. 1985); and *United States v. Hernandez-Cano*, 808 F.2d 779, 784 (11th Cir. 1987).

29. *Stone v. Powell*, 428 U.S. 465 (1976).

30. *Betts v. Brady*, 316 U.S. 455 (1942).

31. *Winthrow v. Williams*, 507 U.S. 680 (1993).

32. Frank E. Horack, "The Disintegration of Statutory Construction," *Indiana Law Journal* 24 (1949): 335.

33. *Brown v. Mississippi*, 297 U.S. 278 (1936).

34. *Mapp v. Ohio*, 367 U.S. 643 (1961).

Bibliography

Abadinsky, Howard. *Law and Justice: An Introduction to the American Legal System.* 2nd ed. Chicago: Nelson-Hall Publishers, 1991.

Appel, Brent R. "The Inevitable Discovery Exception to the Exclusionary Rule." *Criminal Law Bulletin* 21 (1985): 101–124.

Arenella, Peter. "Rethinking the Functions of Criminal Procedure: The Warren and Burger Courts' Competing Ideologies." *The Georgetown Law Journal* 72 (1983): 185–248.

Bain, Jeffrey M., and Michael K. Kelly. " 'Fruit of the Poisonous Tree': Recent Developments as Viewed Through its Exceptions." *University of Miami Law Review* 31 (1977): 615–650.

Barak, Aaharon. *Judicial Discretion.* New Haven, Conn.: Yale University Press, 1989.

Baum, Lawrence. *American Courts.* Boston: Houghton Mifflin Co., 1994.

Berger, Mark. *Taking the Fifth: The Supreme Court and the Privilege Against Self-Incrimination.* Lexington, KY: Lexington Books, 1980.

Bergman, Paul. *Trial Advocacy.* St. Paul, Minn.: West Publishing Co., 1979.

Bloom, Robert M. "Inevitable Discovery: An Exception Beyond the Fruits." *American Journal of Criminal Law* 20 (1992): 79–103.

Boeckman, Richard A. "Habeas Corpus: A New Look at Fourth Amendment Claims." *Washburn Law Journal* 16 (1976): 528–534.

Boggins, John V. " 'Inevitable Discovery' or Inevitable Demise of the Exclusionary Rule? *Nix v. Williams* 104 S. Ct. 2501 (1984)." *Akron Law Review* 18 (1984): 309–324.

Bradley, Craig M. *The Failure of the Criminal Procedure Revolution.* Philadelphia: University of Pennsylvania Press, 1993.

Braswell, Mark K., and John M. Sheb II. "Conservative Pragmatism Versus Liberal

Principles: Warren E. Burger on the Suppression of Evidence, 1956–86." *Creighton Law Review* 20 (1987): 789–831.

Brennan, William J., Jr. "State Court Decisions and the Supreme Court." *Pennsylvania Bar Association Quarterly* 31 (1960): 393–407.

Brewer, Saundra T. "*Brewer v. Williams*: The End of Post-Charging Interrogation?" *Southwestern University Law Review* 10 (1978): 331–353.

Buethe, Linda S. "The Right to Counsel and the Strict Waiver Standard *Brewer v. Williams*, 430 U.S. 387 (1977)." *Nebraska Law Review* 57 (1978): 543–554.

Burger, Warren E. "Who Will Watch the Watchman?" *American University Law Review* 14 (1964): 1–23.

Calderia, Gregory A., and John R. Wright. "The Discuss List: Agenda Building in the Supreme Court." *Law and Society Review* 24 (1990): 807–836.

Calvi, James V., and Susan Coleman. *American Law and Legal Systems*. 2nd ed. Englewood Cliffs, NJ: Prentice-Hall, Inc., 1992.

Cameron, James Duke, and Richard Lustiger. "The Exclusionary Rule: A Cost-Benefit Analysis." *Federal Rules Decisions* 101 (1984): 109–159.

Cann, Steven, and Bob Egbert. "The Exclusionary Rule: Its Necessity in Constitutional Democracy." *Howard Law Journal* 23 (1980): 299–323.

Canon, Bradley C. "Ideology and Reality in the Debate Over the Exclusionary Rule: A Conservative Argument for Its Retention." *South Texas Law Journal* 23 (1982): 559–582.

Cardozo, Benjamin. *The Nature of the Judicial Process*. New Haven, Conn.: Yale University Press, 1921.

Carp, Robert A., and Ronald Stidham. *Judicial Process in America*. Washington, D.C.: Congressional Quarterly Inc., 1993.

Carpenter, William Seal. *Foundations of Modern Jurisprudence*. New York: Appleton-Century-Crofts, 1958.

Coffin, Frank M. *On Appeal Courts, Lawyering, and Judging*. New York: W. W. Norton, 1994.

Cole, George D. "The Decision to Prosecute." *Law and Society Review* 4 (1970): 331–343.

Cord, Robert L. "Neo-Incorporation: The Burger Court and the Due Process Clause of the Fourteenth Amendment." *Fordham Law Review* 44 (1975): 215–248.

Cotterrell, Roger. *The Politics of Jurisprudence*. London: Butterworths, 1989.

Danelski, David. "Explorations of Some Causes and Consequences of Conflict and Its Resolution in the Supreme Court." In *Judicial Conflict and Consensus*, pp. 21–49. Edited by Sheldon Goldman and Charles M. Lamb. Lexington: University Press of Kentucky, 1986.

"Developments in the Law: Confessions." *Harvard Law Review* 79 (1966): 938–1119.

Duker, William F. *A Constitutional History of Habeas Corpus*. Westport, Conn.: Greenwood Press, 1980.

Engstrom, Richard, and Michael Giles. "Expectations and Images: A Note on Diffuse Support for Legal Institutions." *Law and Society Review* 6 (1972): 631–636.

Enker, Arnold N., and Sheldon H. Elsen. "Counsel for the Suspect: *Massiah v. United States* and *Escobedo v. Illinois*." *Minnesota Law Review* 49 (1964): 47–91.

Epstein, Lee, and Jack Knight. *The Choices Justices Make.* Washington, DC: Congressional Quarterly Inc., 1998.

Fennelly, John E. "Refinement of the Inevitable Discovery Exception: The Need for a Good Faith Requirement." *William Mitchell Law Review* 17 (1991): 1085–1109.

Fishkin, James Andrew. *"Nix v. Williams:* An Analysis of the Preponderance Standard for the Inevitable Discovery Exception." *Iowa Law Review* 70 (1985): 1369–1383.

Forbes, Jessica. "The Inevitable Discovery Exception, Primary Evidence, and the Emasculation of the Fourth Amendment." *Fordham Law Review* 55 (1987): 1221–1238.

Foshee, David J. "Limitations Placed on Federal Habeas Corpus Jurisdiction in Fourth Amendment Cases—A Further Erosion of the Exclusionary Rule." *Loyola Law Review* 22 (1976): 856–862.

Frank, Jerome. *Courts on Trial.* Princeton, NJ: Princeton University Press, 1950.

Friedman, Wolfgang. "Judicial Philosophy and Judicial Lawmaking." *Columbia Law Review* 61 (1961): 820–845.

Galloway, John, ed. *Criminal Justice and the Burger Court.* New York: Facts on File, 1978.

Gammon, Timothy E. "The Exclusionary Rule and the 1983–1984 Term." *Marquette Law Review* 68 (1984): 1–25.

Gibson, James L. "From Simplicity to Complexity: The Development of Theory in the Study of Judicial Behavior." *Political Behavior* 5 (1983): 7–50.

———. "Understandings of Justice: Institutional Legitimacy, Procedural Justice, and Political Tolerance." *Law and Society Review* 23 (1989): 469–496.

Goldman, Sheldon, and Thomas P. Jahnige. *The Federal Courts as a Political System.* 3rd ed. New York: Harper & Row, 1985.

Goldman, Sheldon, and Austin Sarat. *American Court Systems.* 2nd ed. New York: Longman, 1989.

Goodman, James E. *Stories of Scottsboro.* New York: Vintage Books, 1995.

Grossman, Joel, and Richard Wells. *Constitutional Law and Judicial Policymaking.* 3rd ed. New York: Longman, 1988.

Grossman, Steven P. "The Doctrine of Inevitable Discovery: A Plea for Reasonable Limitations." *Dickinson Law Review* 92 (1988): 313–361.

Handberg, Roger, and William S. Maddox. "Public Support for the Supreme Court in the 1970's." *American Politics Quarterly* 10 (1982): 333–346.

Hans, Valerie P., and Neil Vidmar. *Judging the Jury.* New York: Plenum Press, 1986.

Harvard Law Review. "The Supreme Court, 1975 Term." *Harvard Law Review* 90 (1976): 56–282.

Horack, Frank E. "The Disintegration of Statutory Construction." *Indiana Law Journal* 24 (1949): 335–352.

Howard, J. Woodford. *Courts of Appeals in the Federal Judicial System: A Study of the Second, Fifth, and District of Columbia Circuits.* Princeton, NJ: Princeton University Press, 1981.

"Interrogation of Criminal Suspects." *Northwestern University Law Review* 59 (1964): 661–667.

Israel, Jerold H. "Criminal Procedure, the Burger Court, and the Legacy of the Warren Court." *Michigan Law Review* 75 (1977): 1319–1425.

Jaros, Dean, and Robert Roper. "The U.S. Supreme Court: Myth, Diffuse Support, Specific Support, and Legitimacy." *American Politics Quarterly* 8 (1980): 85–105.

Johnson, Phillip E. "The Return of the 'Christian Burial Speech' Case." *Emory Law Journal* 32 (1983): 349–381.

Kamisar, Yale. "Does (Did) (Should) the Exclusionary Rule Rest on a 'Principled Basis' Rather than an 'Empirical Proposition'?" *Creighton Law Review* 16 (1983): 565–667.

———. "Foreword: *Brewer v. Williams*—A Hard Look at a Discomforting Record." *Georgetown Law Review* 66 (1977): 209–243.

———. "How We Got the Fourth Amendment Exclusionary Rule and Why We Need It." *Criminal Justice Ethics* 1 (1982): 4–14.

Keedy, Edwin R. "The Third Degree and Legal Interrogation of Suspects." *University of Pennsylvania Law Review* 85 (June 1937): 761–777.

LaCount, Stephen H., and Anthony J. Girese. "The 'Inevitable Discovery' Rule, An Evolving Exception to the Constitutional Exclusionary Rule." *Albany Law Review* 40 (1976): 483–512.

Lamb, Charles M. "The Making of a Chief Justice: Warren Burger on Criminal Procedure, 1956–1969." *Cornell Law Review* 60 (1975): 743–788.

Lamberth, R. Bradley. "The Inevitable Discovery Doctrine: Procedural Safeguards to Ensure Inevitability." *Baylor Law Review* 40 (1988): 129–149.

Landynski, Jacob W. *Search and Seizure and the Supreme Court: A Study in Constitutional Interpretation.* Baltimore: The John Hopkins Press, 1966.

Lasson, Nelson. *The History and Development of the Fourth Amendment of the United States Constitution.* Baltimore: John Hopkins Press, 1937.

Lavine, Emanuel H. *The "Third Degree," A Detailed and Appalling Exposé of Police Brutality.* New York: Vanguard Press, 1930.

Lester, William H., Jr. "Constitutional Law—Criminal Procedure—A Confession Alone Does Not Effectively Waive the Right to Counsel if it Follows an Interrogation, *Brewer v. Williams*, 97 S. Ct. 1232 (1977)." *Texas Tech Law Review* 9 (1977–1978): 312–322.

Levine, James P. *Juries and Politics.* Pacific Grove, Calif.: Brooks/Cole Publishing Company, 1992.

Lewis, Anthony. *Gideon's Trumpet.* New York: Vintage Books, 1989.

Maguire, Kathleen, and Ann L. Patore, eds. *Sourcebook of Criminal Justice Statistics 1995.* Washington, D.C.: U.S. Government Printing Office, 1996.

Marshall, Leslie-Ann, and Shelby Webb, Jr. "Constitutional Law—The Burger Court's Warm Embrace of an Impermissibly Designed Interference with the Sixth Amendment Right to the Assistance of Counsel—The Adoption of the Inevitable Discovery Exception to the Exclusionary Rule: *Nix v. Williams.*" *Howard Law Journal* 28 (1985): 945–1003.

Mason, Alpheus Thomas. "Myth and Reality in Supreme Court Decisions." *Virginia Law Review* 48 (1962): 1383–1406.

Mathias, Charles McC., Jr. "The Exclusionary Rule Revisited." *Loyola Law Review* 28 (1982): 1–12.

Nagler, Vincent A. "*Nix v. Williams*: Conjecture Enters the Exclusionary Rule." *Pace Law Review* 5 (1985): 657–692.

Nardulli, Peter. "The Social Cost of the Exclusionary Rule: An Empirical Assessment." *American Bar Foundation Research Journal* (1983): 585–689.

Neubauer, David W. *America's Courts and the Criminal Justice System.* 2nd ed. Monterey, Calif.: Brooks/Cole Publishing Company, 1984.

———. *Judicial Process: Law, Courts, & Politics in the United States.* Pacific Grove, Calif.: Brooks/Cole Publishing Company, 1991.

Novikoff, Harold S. "The Inevitable Discovery Exception to the Constitutional Exclusionary Rules." *Columbia Law Review* 74 (1974): 88–103.

O'Brien, David M. "The Fifth Amendment: Fox Hunters, Old Women, Hermits, and the Burger Court." *Notre Dame Lawyer* 54 (1978): 26–74.

———. *Storm Center.* 3rd ed. New York: W. W. Norton and Co., 1993.

Pellicciotti, Joseph M. *Handbook of Basic Trial Evidence: A College Introduction.* Bristol, Ind.: Wyndham Hall Press, 1992.

Phillips, Emily M. 1977. "The Right to Counsel: An Alternative to *Miranda.*" *Louisiana Law Review* 38 (1977): 239–249.

Picou, Cynthia. "Miranda and Escobedo: Warren v. Burger Court Decisions on 5th Amendment Rights." *Southern University Law Review* 4 (1978): 175–197.

Pitler, Robert M. " 'The Fruit of the Poisonous Tree' Revisited and Shepardized." *California Law Review* 56 (1968): 579–651.

Pohren, Edward F. "Constitutional Law—Criminal Procedure—Where Suspect Has Not Waived his Right to an Attorney's Assistance, Confession Prompted by Detective's Statements When Counsel was Absent is Inadmissible—*Brewer v. Williams,* 430 U.S. 387 (1977)." *Creighton Law Review* 11 (1978): 997–1030.

Pound, Roscoe. *Jurisprudence.* 5 vols. St. Paul, Minn.: West Publishing Co., 1959.

Raz, Joseph. *The Concept of a Legal System.* 2nd ed. Oxford, UK: Clarendon Press, 1980.

Ritchie, Larry J. "Compulsion That Violates the Fifth Amendment: The Burger Court's Definition." *Minnesota Law Review* 61 (1977): 383–431.

Rothstein, Paul F. *Evidence in a Nutshell: State and Federal Rules.* 2nd ed. St. Paul, Minn.: West Publishing Co., 1981.

Saltzburg, Stephen A. "Foreword: The Flow and Ebb of Constitutional Criminal Procedure in the Warren and Burger Courts." *Georgetown Law Journal* 68 (1980): 151–209.

Schiller, Marvin. "On the Jurisprudence of the Fifth Amendment Right to Silence." *American Criminal Law Review* 16 (1979): 197–231.

Schrock, Thomas S., and Robert C. Welsh. "Up from Calandra: The Exclusionary Rule as a Constitutional Requirement." *Minnesota Law Review* 59 (1974): 251–383.

Schubert, Glendon. *The Judicial Mind: The Attitudes and Ideologies of Supreme Court Justices, 1946–1963.* Evanston, Ill. Northwestern University Press, 1965.

Schulhofer, Stephen J. "Confessions and the Court." *Michigan Law Review* 79 (1981): 865–893.

Segal, Jeffrey A., and Harold J. Spaeth. *The Supreme Court and the Attitudinal Model.* New York: Cambridge University Press, 1993.

Skogan, Wesley. "Judicial Myth and Judicial Reality." *Washington University Law Quarterly* (1971): 309–334.

Smith, Christopher E. *Courts, Politics, and the Judicial Process.* Chicago: Nelson-Hall Publishers, 1993.

Songsten, John O., Roger Haydock, and James J. Boyd. *The Trialbook.* St. Paul, Minn.: West Publishing Company, 1984.

Spiegel, Frederick C., and Dee Wampler. "Inevitable Discovery: An Exception to the Exclusionary Rule." *Journal of Missouri Bar* (October–November 1982): 495–500.

Stephens, Otis H. The Assistance of Counsel and the Warren Court: Post-Gideon Developments in Perspective." *Dickinson Law Review* 74 (1970): 193–217.

———. "The Burger Court: New Dimensions in Criminal Justice." *Georgetown Law Journal* 60 (1971): 249–278.

———. *The Supreme Court and Confessions of Guilt.* Knoxville: University of Tennessee Press, 1973.

Stewart, Jim. "Criminal Law—Right to Counsel—Incriminating Statements Obtained During In-Custody Interrogation Not Admissible Without Proof of Waiver of Defendant's Right to Counsel." *North Dakota Law Review* 54 (1977–1978): 307–317.

Stewart, Potter. "The Road to *Mapp v. Ohio* and Beyond: The Origins, Development and Future of the Exclusionary Rule in Search-and-Seizure Cases." *Columbia Law Review* 83 (1983): 1365–1404.

Stocker, David E. "*Brewer v. Williams*: Express Waiver Extended to the Sixth Amendment Right to Counsel." *Ohio Northern University Law Review* 4 (1977): 833–840.

Stone, Geoffrey R. "The Miranda Doctrine in the Burger Court." In *The Supreme Court Review: 1977*, pp. 99–169. Edited by Philip B. Kurland and Gerhard Casper. Chicago: University of Chicago Press, 1978.

Stratton, Brent D. "The Attenuation Exception to the Exclusionary Rule: A Study in Attenuated Principle and Dissipated Logic." *Journal of Criminal Law and Criminology* 75 (1984): 139–165.

Tarr, G. Alan. *Judicial Process and Judicial Policymaking.* St. Paul, Minn.: West Publishing Co., 1994.

Thompson, David M. "Of Trumpeters, Pipers, and Swingmen: What Tune is the Burger Court Playing in Right to Representation Cases?" *Vanderbilt Law Review* 29 (1976): 776–806.

Van Dervort, Thomas R. *Equal Justice Under the Law.* Eagan, Minn.: West Publishing Co., 1994.

Walker, Thomas G., and Lee Epstein. 1993. *The Supreme Court of the United States: An Introduction.* New York: St. Martin's Press, Inc., 1993.

Warden, Karl P. "Miranda—Some History, Some Observations, and Some Questions." *Vanderbilt Law Review* 20 (1966): 39–60.

Wasby, Stephen. *The Supreme Court in the Federal Judicial System.* 3rd ed. Chicago: Nelson-Hall, 1988.

Wasserstrom, Silas, and William J. Mertens. "The Exclusionary Rule on the Scaffold: But Was it a Fair Trial?" *American Criminal Law Review* 22 (1984): 85–179.

Wilson, Bradford. "The Origin and Development of the Federal Rule of Exclusion." *Wake Forest Law Review* 18 (1982): 1073–1109.

Zabak, Richard. "Constitutional Law: No Clear Standard for the Waiver of an As-

serted Right to Counsel." *University of Florida Law Review* 29 (1977): 778–
787.
Zimmerman, H. Fredrick. "Constitutional Law—Sixth Amendment Right to Counsel—Waiver." Tennessee Law Review 45 (1977): 111–127.

Index

About the Author

THOMAS N. McINNIS is an Associate Professor at the University of Central Arkansas where he teaches courses in judicial systems, constitutional law, civil liberties, and American government. He has published numerous articles.